Romanov

Roman Zakharin-Koshkin

Anastasia Romanovna = Ivan IV

Evdokia 1) = Peter = 2) Catherine I
Lopukhina   the Great

Tsarevich Alexei   Anna   Elizabeth

Peter II   Peter III = Catherine II
          Duke of Holstein

ELIZABETH
EMPRESS OF RUSSIA

ELIZABETH
Empress of Russia

TAMARA TALBOT RICE

PRAEGER PUBLISHERS
New York · Washington

BOOKS THAT MATTER

Published in the United States of America in 1970
by Praeger Publishers, Inc., 111 Fourth Avenue,
New York, N.Y. 10003

© 1970 in London, England, by Tamara Talbot Rice

Library of Congress Catalog Card Number: 73–100926

Printed in Great Britain

Contents

Illustrations

ILLUSTRATIONS

Facing page

Acknowledgements

I am deeply indebted to Dr E. Nekrassova of Moscow and to Dr Marvin Ross, Curator of the Hillwood Collection, Washington, D.C., for most of the photographs used in this book, as well as to Mrs Merriweather Post for permission to publish those from Hillwood. I should also like to thank Their Graces the Duke and Duchess of Buccleugh and Queensbury for permission to use that of the Meissen figurine of the Empress Elizabeth.

I have likewise received assistance in one form or another from Mr W. J. Adams of the Foreign Service; the Hon. Baron Dimsdale for permission to quote from the diary of Catherine, wife of the first Baron; Lady Erskine Hill; Mr Ian Finlay, Director of the Royal Scottish Museum, Edinburgh; Dr Militza Greene of Edinburgh University; Mr R. A. Leys of Trinity College, Cambridge; Mr Michael Maclagan of Trinity College, Oxford; Mr C. L. Robertson of the Foreign Office Library; Mr and Mrs Wheeler-Carmichael, Mrs F. Middleton, and the staffs of Edinburgh's National, University and Public Libraries, to all of whom I am most grateful.

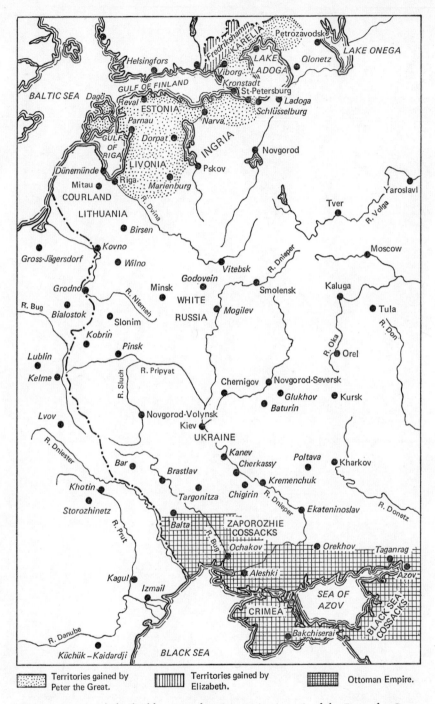

Territories gained by Peter the Great.

Territories gained by Elizabeth.

Ottoman Empire.

Western Russia in Elizabeth's reign, showing territories gained by Peter the Great and Elizabeth

Summary of Events
(1672-1761)

1672 Birth of Peter the Great
1682 Death of Peter's half brother Tsar Feodor. Peter and his half-brother Ivan appointed his successors, with their sister Sophia assuming control
1683 Birth of Catherine I
1689 Peter marries Evdokia Lopukhina
1697/8 Peter's first visit to western Europe
1703 Founding of St Petersburg
c. 1704 Meeting of Peter and Catherine
1708 Birth of Anna Petrovna
1709 Russian victory at Poltava
      Birth of Elizaveta Petrovna
1710 Marriage of Anna Ivanovna to Duke of Courland
1711 Peter the Great marries Catherine
1716 Ekaterina Ivanovna marries the Duke of Mecklenburg
1717 Peter visits France and raises question of a French marriage for Elizabeth
1719 Charles Frederick, Duke of Holstein Gottorp, arrives in St Petersburg
1721 Louis xv becomes engaged to the Infanta of Spain
1722 Peter alters the law regarding the succession to the Russian throne. The Regent of France agrees in principle to the marriage of the Duke of Chartres to Elizaveta Petrovna, but in the following year the young man becomes engaged to the Princess of Baden
1723 Peter the Great proclaims Catherine his consort
1724 Catherine crowned the tsar's consort
1725 Death of Peter the Great
      Louis xv annuls his engagement to the Infanta of Spain

Anna Petrovna marries Charles Frederick of Holstein Gottorp
Louis xv becomes engaged to Marie Leszinska
Austro-Russian alliance
Diplomatic relations with France broken off, and remain so till
1739

1726 Arrival of Charles Augustus, Duke of Holstein, in St Petersburg and
his engagement to Elizaveta Petrovna

1727 Death of Catherine I
Accession of Peter II
Death of Charles Augustus of Holstein
Fall of Prince Menshikov

1728 Coronation of Peter II
Birth of Peter Ulrich, Duke of Holstein, later Tsar Peter III
Death of Anna Petrovna
Death of Prince and Princess Menshikov and their daughter Marie

1729 Peter II becomes engaged to Catherine Dolgorukaya
Ekaterina Ivanovna, Duchess of Mecklenburg, returns to Russia to
live with her mother, bringing her three-year-old daughter with
her

1730 Death of Peter II
Coronation of Anna Ivanovna

1731 Death of Peter the Great's first wife, Evdokia

1732 The Court returns to St Petersburg

? Elizabeth and Alexei Razumovsky meet and fall in love

1734 General Münnich commands army in successful war with Poland

1737 Death of Augustus II, Elector of Saxony, King of Poland; he is
succeeded by his son, Augustus III
Russia and Austria at war with Turkey

1738 Anna Leopoldovna marries Prince Anton Ulrich of Braunschweig

1739 End of Turko-Russian war
Death of Charles Frederick of Holstein Gottorp, father of Peter III

1740 Birth of Tsar Ivan
Death of Anna Ivanovna and of Charles VI of Austria
Anna Leopoldovna seizes the regency

1741 The Nymphenburg Convention unites Prussia, France, Bavaria,
Saxony and Spain against Austria
24/5 November, Elizabeth seizes the throne
Alexei Bestuzhev appointed Vice-Chancellor of Russia
The Braunschweig family detained in Riga

1742 The court moves to Moscow for Elizabeth's coronation
The Austrians inform Elizabeth of the contents of an intercepted
French despatch compromising Monsieur de la Chétardie
Peter, Duke of Holstein, is brought to Russia and proclaimed the
empress's heir
The truce with Sweden breaks down and hostilities resume
A British alliance is agreed to in principle

1743 The heavily defeated Swedes sue for peace
The Botta affair
Elizabeth enters into a treaty of friendship with Frederick II of
Prussia and agrees to consider Sophie of Anhalt Zerbst as a bride for
the Grand Duke Peter

1744 The Braunschweig family is sent to prison in Siberia
The Princess of Zerbst and her daughter come to Russia
The state visit to the Ukraine
The Grand Duke Peter contracts smallpox

1745 The marriage of the Grand Duke Peter to the Grand Duchess
Catherine

1746 Austro-Russian Alliance
Death of Anna Leopoldovna
The Choglokovs appointed to spy on the grand ducal household

1748 End of the War of the Austrian Succession
Lestocq's arrest

1749 The empress's first serious illness

1750 The British attempt to renew Russian alliance

1752 The Grand Duchess Catherine's liaison with Saltykov and her
rapprochement with Alexei Bestuzhev

1754 The birth of the Tsarevich Paul

1755 Founding of Moscow University

1756 Anglo-Russian treaty signed
Treaty of Westminster signed by Prussia and Britain
Treaty of Versailles between France and Austria, later extended to
include Russia and Sweden
Tsar Ivan transferred to Fortress of Schlüsselburg
Start of Seven Years' War

1757 Count Apraxin appointed to command Russian troops involved in
the war
Elizabeth has a stroke
Russian victory of Gross Jägersdorf

1758 Disgrace of Count Apraxin and the Grand Duchess Catherine; arrest of Alexei Bestuzhev

Academy of Fine Arts founded

Russian victories at Königsberg and Zorndorf

1759 Russian victory of Künersdorf; banishment of Alexei Bestuzhev

1760 Esterhazy agreement entitles Russia to territorial gains in eastern Prussia

The Prussians raid and penetrate to Berlin

Chernyshev's advance enables Totleben to occupy Berlin

1761 Buturlin's successes at Schweidnitz and Kolberg spells disaster for Frederick of Prussia

Death of the Empress Elizabeth on 25 December

BRITISH REPRESENTATIVES IN RUSSIA DURING ELIZABETH'S REIGN

1740 Mr Edward Finch, Envoy Extraordinary and Minister Plenipotentiary

1742 Sir Cyril Wich, Bart, Envoy Extraordinary and Minister Plenipotentiary

1743 Lord Tyrawley, Ambassador Extraordinary and Plenipotentiary

1744 Earl of Hyndford, Minister Plenipotentiary

1749 Colonel Guy Dickens, Envoy Extraordinary

1755 Sir Charles Hanbury Williams, Ambassador in ordinary

1757 Robert Keith, later The Right Honourable Sir Robert, Envoy Extraordinary

I

A Difficult Start

On 18 December 1709,* Peter I, soon to be proclaimed Great, was in Moscow. He was there to attend the official celebrations arranged in honour of the victory he had won over Charles XII of Sweden at Poltava on 26 June. Although the Swedes were never wholly to recover from their defeat, the battle had not brought the Great Northern War to an end. Hostilities had continued during the remainder of the summer. By 9 November the Russian army had reached the walls of Riga. Five days later, at five o'clock in the morning, Tsar Bombardier Peter personally launched the attack on the town by firing the three opening shots of the siege. The tsar then entrusted the further conduct of the battle to Prince Repnin and left for St Petersburg. A month later, on 6 December, he laid the keel of a new battleship there, proudly naming the vessel *Poltava*. His childhood loathing of Moscow had not diminished and he set out reluctantly for the older capital, to conform with the tradition of reporting to it on the course of the year's fighting. The welcome accorded to him by Moscow surpassed all his expectations. None of his earlier successes had been acclaimed with such delight. The festivities planned in his honour culminated in a banquet in the great vaulted hall of the Kremlin's Granovitaya Palata and a display of fireworks.

As the tsar entered the Kremlin to attend a service of thanksgiving a messenger informed him that a daughter had been born to him some hours earlier in the Palace of Kolomenskoe, the oldest of Muscovy's royal country residences. Peter kept the news to himself, but as soon as the *Te Deum* of Thanksgiving had been sung he slipped away and hurried to Kolomenskoe. His daughter's birth could not form the subject of a public announcement, nor could it be officially celebrated, for the child was illegitimate.

* Throughout, dates are based on the Russian calendar.

At the age of seventeen Peter had been hurried into a marriage by his mother, the widowed Tsaritsa Natalia. Peter scarcely knew the girl selected – Evdokia Lopukhina – and made no attempt to understand her after the marriage. They were so ill-suited that the indifference which Peter had at first felt for her speedily turned to active dislike. Peter considered her too ignorant and superstitious to meet the foreign diplomats at court and, in 1698, on returning to Moscow from his first foreign tour he tried to persuade her to become a nun. This he at first failed to do and so banished her to the Pokrovsky Convent near Suzdal, where she was eventually obliged to take her vows.*

It was some years before he met the woman he was to love above all others. There have been suggestions that she was illegitimate, but there is no reason to doubt that she was the daughter of a poor Livonian yeoman called Samuel Skavronsky, or to question the legality of her birth. When fortune smiled on her she sought out all her Skavronsky relations, brought them to St Petersburg and established them at court. She was born into the Skavronskys' Roman Catholic household in about the year 1683 and christened Marfa. Her parents were living at the time in the village of Ringen in the Livonian district of Dorpat, but within a year of her birth her father contracted the plague and died. Her mother outlived him by barely two years and at her death the family broke up. Marfa was fortunate for she was adopted by the Reverend Glück, protestant pastor of Marienburg. He was to end his days as a teacher at Peter the Great's School of Mathematical Sciences and Navigation in St Petersburg. Glück ensured the young orphan learnt to read and write a little. She was already an exceptionally lovely child, and her beauty increased with each passing year. In 1702 Johan Kruse, a young trumpeter in the Swedish Dragoons sent to defend Marienburg from the Russians, saw her and fell so deeply in love that he asked the pastor for her hand. Mrs Glück, possibly resentful of Marfa's charm and beauty, readily fell in with Johan's wish for an immediate marriage. Their wedding was celebrated three days later: within another eight the Russians had besieged Marienburg.

Johan was probably killed in the bitter fight for the town for he could not be found after its capture by the Russians. There are two stories of what happened to Marfa when the town was overrun. One assents that the Swedish officer commanding the garrison warned the Glücks of his

* At the time of Tsarevich Alexei's trial the ex-empress was transferred at the tsar's orders to the Fortress of Schlüsselburg and treated as a prisoner. Pardoned and brought to Moscow by her grandson Peter II, she ended her days in the Novodevichy convent.

intention to blow up the citadel before surrendering it and that the Glücks* crossed the enemy lines accompanied by Marfa and a young theological student called Gottfried Wurms, and threw themselves on the mercy of the Russian Commander in Chief, Field Marshal Sheremetiev. According to the other and more generally accepted story, Marfa was captured by the Russians in the course of the fighting. When the battle was over and her captors had taken stock of their prisoner's remarkable beauty they thought it wise to hand her over to the Field Marshal. They brought her to him naked but for the military cloak which they had wrapped round her.

Sheremetiev was struck by Marfa's beauty. Her dark hair, sparkling eyes, splendid colouring and skin, good figure and excellent carriage delighted him. He installed her as his housekeeper. Six months later Alexander Menshikov, Peter's closest friend and collaborator, chanced to see her and persuaded Sheremetiev to sell or cede her to him, ostensibly to become his wife's maid.† She probably became his mistress before Menshikov introduced her to the tsar with the same purpose in mind. No records survive to disclose when she first met Peter or when they became lovers, but by 1705 Peter and Marfa had already had two sons; both were to die in infancy. In 1708 a daughter was born to them; she was called Anna. The new baby was their fourth child; they named her Elizabeth.

When she became the tsar's mistress Marfa lived in great seclusion in a small though luxuriously furnished house which Peter provided for her on the outskirts of Moscow. At Anna's birth the child's parents abandoned their efforts to conceal their relationship and Marfa overcame her reluctance to live in one of the tsar's palaces, perhaps because she was at last convinced that Peter wanted to make her his life's companion. Peter had by then discovered that she alone, merely by holding his head in her hands, could still the convulsions which afflicted him; she alone could calm his outbursts of rage, make him laugh, and share in his worries and griefs. She was also always ready to leave her children in order to accompany him on one of his campaigns or long expeditions, yet she never showed any signs of fatigue and could always charm those whom they met by her beauty, tact, gay good nature and kindliness.

---

* He died in 1705, but his widow was granted a pension and his children prospered.

† Prince Alexander Danilovich Menshikov (c. 1670–1729) was of peasant birth. At a very young age he became a playmate of the young tsar, who, in 1693, gave him the title of bombardier in his Preobrazhensky regiment. Menshikov remained the tsar's closest friend and adviser, and rose to be his chief minister.

Peter probably wanted to marry her before the birth of their children but this presented many difficulties. The fact that Peter's wife was still alive and regarded as his wife by the nation was an almost insurmountable obstacle. Furthermore, Marfa was a Catholic and, in the eyes of eighteenth-century Russians, that was still tantamount to being a heretic. Nevertheless, when Peter's mind was made up no one could make him alter it. A year after Elizabeth's birth Marfa was received into the Orthodox Church under the name of Catherine. The Tsarevich Alexei, Peter's heir and only surviving son, was twenty-three years old. At Peter's wish he acted as her sponsor, his name serving as her patronymic, so that from then on she was addressed as Ekaterina Alexeevna.* A year later Peter forced the church to dissolve his first marriage. The formalities were completed in the following year, leaving him free to marry Catherine. Their wedding took place at seven o'clock in the morning in the private chapel in Menshikov's Petersburgian palace. The Dowager Empress Prascovia, the widow of Peter's half brother, the late Tsar Ivan, and the wife of the senior vice-admiral in Peter's navy, acted as the bride's two sponsors. Peter wore the uniform of a rear-admiral for the occasion and none but naval men were invited to attend the ceremony. Peter and Catherine's two little daughters, Anna aged almost four and Elizabeth not yet three, ranked as bridesmaids, but as they were too young to be able to stand throughout the whole of the long religious service their duties were carried out for them by two of the tsar's nieces. After the ceremony Peter conferred the title of Gossudary-nia – a lower one than tsaritsa – on his wife, and that evening he gave a banquet in her honour. The entire diplomatic corps was present and also attended the magnificent ball followed by a firework display which marked the end of the celebrations.

In 1722 Peter issued an edict which must surely have been intended to pave the way for Catherine's elevation to the supreme rank of tsaritsa. In it he stated that succession to the throne should become dependent on the sovereign's personal choice, not on heredity. A year later an order dated 15 November announced Catherine's forthcoming coronation as the tsar's consort. The edict was fiercely opposed by the nation, but its unpopularity had no effect on the tsar. Disregarding all protests, Peter ordered Moscow to prepare for the event.

Catherine's coronation took place on 7 May 1724 in the Cathedral of the Assumption, in the heart of the Kremlin. It was conducted with

* The entry of Menshikov in the 1967 *Encyclopaedia Britannica* refers to Marfa as 'Peter's wife since 1707'. In fact they were not legally married till 1712.

unprecedented pomp and magnificence. As dawn broke on the morning of
7 May the cannons Peter was so proud of started to fire a salute which
lasted till ten o'clock. Escorted by his entire court, his Senate and his
general staff Peter made his way to the cathedral. The cathedral's interior
had been hung with cloth of gold for the occasion. A platform covered in
velvet, reached by twelve carpeted steps, occupied the centre of the nave.
Two antique, jewel-encrusted thrones stood on it beneath a velvet canopy.
The coronation service was conducted by Theodosius, Archbishop of
Novgorod, and Theophanes, Archbishop of Pskov, but it was the tsar who
personally placed the crown on his wife's head. As he did so to the sound
of the Mnogolithic Hymn tears of gratitude streamed down Catherine's
cheeks.

No one realized that Peter was already mortally ill. The long service
exhausted him. When it ended he returned to the palace to rest while the
tsaritsa presented herself to the assembled people. She looked magnificent in
full imperial regalia. Peter had had her crown specially made for her in Paris
on Byzantine lines. It had cost him more than any Russian sovereign had
ever paid for his own crown, and was studded with 2,564 jewels. Though
each pearl had cost 200 roubles* Peter had not been satisfied and had given
orders for the largest diamond in his own crown to be removed and set on
his wife's together with a ruby the size of a pigeon's egg. The latter had been
bought in Peking by the merchant Spafiry who, at Menshikov's insistence,
disposed of it to the tsar for the sum of 60,000 roubles. The final touch
was added to the crown by the addition of a cross made of fine-quality
diamonds.

Catherine's robe rivalled her crown in splendour. It was of purple
velvet studded with gold eagles. Despite its enormous weight of 150 pounds,
she walked with a dignified gait at the head of a long procession, scattering
gold and silver coins among the assembled crowds. On reaching the
Granovitaya Palata, where the official banquet was to be held, she was
welcomed on the tsar's behalf by her future son-in-law, the Duke of
Holstein-Gottorp. While the emperor's guests celebrated within the
banqueting hall, the people feasted outside it. They devoured great oxen,
stuffed with game and poultry, and roasted on huge spits before their eyes;
they quenched their thirst from fountains specially constructed to dispense
red and white wine. Not the least impressed by this magnificent spectacle
were the tsar's two young daughters.

* In 1698 Peter created the silver rouble to correspond in value to the thaler and, from
1704, began minting it annually.

Many historians assert that Anna was Peter's favourite; others that he preferred Elizabeth. He was in the habit of calling her his 'little chicken'. When she reached the age of seven he often sent for her to appear before his guests in a Spanish dress slashed with gold and silver, to entertain them by her graceful performance of the quadrille and minuet. He also had her portrait painted by the foreign artists whom he employed; when she was seven years old Caravaque painted her in the guise of a little Venus. Even so Peter was seldom able to spend more than a few days on end with his daughters. Weeks would slip by without their seeing him. Their infancy had been particularly lonely. They had grown up in the immense, only partially inhabited palace of Kolomenskoe. Despite its murals and beautifully carved doors and fittings, the palace's 247 rooms, though lit by a thousand windows, must always have seemed mysterious, and often even rather frightening. To begin with the children were looked after by two nurses, a Russian woman called Ilin'ichnaya and Elizaveta Andreevna, a Karelian Finn who taught them a little Swedish. Though their mother was often absent, the description given later by the empress Catherine II[1] of their lives at this period cannot, however, be wholly correct for she stated that, at any rate to begin with, 'they had been much neglected. Their father treated them at first as bastards. The two little girls had no one during their earliest childhood other than Finnish maid-servants, and after them such singular Germans that the children served them as playthings.' It is easy to contest such statements and it looks as though Catherine, on this occasion, obtained her information from biased courtiers.

Peter and his wife quickly realized that their daughters needed something more than what was available at Kolomenskoe. Soon after their wedding they put the children in the care of the Dowager Tsaritsa Prascovia, and although she liked living at Ismailovo, the royal estate three miles to the east of Moscow, Peter insisted that she spent part of the year in the house he had built for her in St Petersburg.* Prascovia was both a dour and a deeply religious woman. She was a strict observer of the Church's every rule and was highly superstitious. Though harsh, she was extremely charitable. Her house was a haven for the sick and needy; it overflowed with pilgrims and vagrants whom she delighted in providing with food and

---

* It was not until 1720 that Peter began to build a palace for Prascovia Feodorovna in St Petersburg. He chose a site adjoining that of his Kunstkamera, but the building was unfinished at the tsar's death in 1725. Two years later it was decided to use it to house the Academy of Sciences, and the architects Mattarnovi, Quarenghi and Zemtsov did the necessary alterations. Today the Zoological Institute and the Academy of Sciences' Geological Museum occupy the site.

shelter. Peter detested her way of life, the people who took advantage of her compassion and stupidity, and the atmosphere she created. They typified all that he hated most in the Muscovite outlook and he made no attempt to conceal the annoyance he felt at the sight of them. Whenever he visited Prascovia they fled from him in terror.

Though Peter placed his daughters in the Tsaritsa Prascovia's care it was at his wish that a French tutor, Monsieur de la Tour, was chosen to take charge of their education. His wife, who later called herself the Countess La Tour Annois, became their French teacher, but Monsieur de la Tour also engaged an Italian, the Countess Marianni Marigi, and a German called Glück. A Frenchman, Stephen Rambour, gave them dancing lessons and, in 1716, a Greek, Laura Palikali, joined their staff. It was the first time in Russia's history that foreigners were entrusted with the education of the sovereign's children, but although Anna could write a good letter in both Russian and German by the time she was eight and both children learnt to speak French fluently and Italian and German adequately, and acquired a smattering of English, they remained poorly educated. Elizabeth's fine mind remained untrained and the lessons never went beyond the elementary stages. Peter was determined to make higher education compulsory for the nobility and bring it within reach of the majority of his subjects but he took no steps to ensure that his daughters received even the schooling which tradition prescribed for Russia's princes, let alone the more advanced instruction which he considered essential for his noblemen, and which many of them were to provide for their own children.*

Peter had been fond of his half-brother, Tsar Ivan. At Ivan's death he swore to care for his thirty-two-year-old widow, the Tsaritsa Prascovia, and their three baby daughters. According to his own lights he faithfully did so. Even so it was primarily for political considerations that he decided in 1710 that the eldest girl, the seventeen-year-old Anna Ivanovna, was to marry Frederick William, reigning Duke of Courland. He personally arranged for the wedding feast to be held in Menshikov's palace of Oranienbaum, still the largest and finest residence in St Petersburg. The celebrations lasted for a month. Peter was responsible for its more boisterous features. One took the form of a procession of seventy-two dwarfs walking in pairs, another consisted of a gargantuan banquet which was made

---

* Alexander Vorontzov, when envoy in Berlin, engaged a Mademoiselle Ruisseau to act as governess to his brother's children in Russia. Her pupils included his niece, the future Princess Dashkova; under her guidance the children had read and understood the works of Corneille, Racine, Boileau and Rousseau before reaching the age of twelve.

memorable by the inclusion of a huge pie; it formed the table's centre piece and when its crust was cut two elegantly dressed dwarfs stepped out of it and proceeded to dance a minuet on the table. The feasting proved too much for Anna Ivanovna's husband. He had a cold when they set out for Courland. On reaching the village of Dudenhof, thirty miles from St Petersburg, he was seized by a fatal colic. His death was ascribed to a surfeit of food and drink. The unfortunate young widow returned to St Petersburg and begged to be permitted to stay there, but the tsar insisted that she should go to Courland in order to settle in Mittau (now Jelgava) and to create there a pro-Russian party able to counteract the pro-Polish policy of the new Duke. At the latter's expulsion from Courland in 1717 Anna Ivanovna became the duchy's virtual ruler. She had as her chief adviser Michael Bestuzhev, an uncle of Alexei, Russia's future Grand Chancellor, but she remained wholly dependent on Russia for funds.

Soon after the death of Louis XIV of France the political alliances which had been built up in Europe over the years started to lose their significance. This was largely due to the growing influence Russia was able to exercise as a result of her victory over the Swedes at Poltava. In the time of Louis XIV France could still discount Russia and continue to base her foreign policy on her traditional friendship with Turkey, Poland and Sweden, but early in the reign of Louis XV Turkey, while retaining the appearance of an unconquerable military power, was in fact made vulnerable by the terms which Austria had imposed on her at the peace of Pasarewitz. By that time Poland had also lost much of its former importance and had to submit to being ruled from Dresden by Augustus II, Elector of Saxony, a man who carried little weight in international politics. By 1715 Peter had become so conscious of the shift in power which had taken place in Europe that he assumed that the French were also aware of the change. He had never visited France nor entered into direct contact with that country. It therefore never occurred to him that the French might not want to take advantage of what Saint Simon had perspicaciously recognized as 'Russia's intense passion to unite in friendship with France'.[2] He was startled when, in 1716, the request submitted at his orders by his ambassador to Holland, Prince Kurakin, to the French Ambassador, for a meeting to discuss the possibility of an alliance, met with silence. It was to some extent in order to secure such an alliance, partly too because of his desire to see Paris and the Palace of Versailles, that the tsar left for France in the spring of 1717.

Two days after his arrival in Paris Peter was received in audience by the boy king of France in the Tuileries Palace. To the horrified consternation of the assembled French courtiers the gaunt, immensely tall tsar bent down and, raising the young ruler in his arms, proceeded warmly to kiss him.

Peter was cordially welcomed at Versailles and encouraged to discuss the alliance with the regent of France, Philip, Duke of Orleans. During one of their meetings he broached the possibility of a marriage between his daughter, the Grand Duchess Elizabeth, and a French prince of the blood royal, indeed even with the young king of France. He stated that if Elizabeth were to marry a French prince he would favour her husband's nomination to the Polish throne at the death of Augustus II, reigning king of Poland and Elector of Saxony. The regent was anxious to avoid offending the tsar. Though he liked neither suggestion he temporized about the marital proposals while encouraging those for the alliance. In August they signed a treaty of commerce and agreed to establish diplomatic relations.

Even if Peter sensed that there was little likelihood that Elizabeth would marry the King of France while Versailles continued to refuse to address him by his full imperial title, he cannot have supposed that his daughter would be considered an unsuitable wife for a French prince of the royal blood. But in fact the French had decided that it would not be fitting for a member of their royal house to marry a bride born out of wedlock and only partly of royal descent. So they marked time, alternately stalling, then resuming the talks. Not until the engagement of Louis XV to the Infanta of Spain had been announced did Peter abandon hope that Elizabeth would marry the king. At that point the name of the regent's son, the young Duke of Chartres, was suggested to him as that of a likely groom. M. de Campredon, France's ambassador to Russia, had from the start wished to link both countries closer together; now he entreated Versailles carefully to consider the tsar's request, more especially since Peter would uphold a French son-in-law's candidature to the Polish throne. As an alternative suitor the ambassador suggested the profligate and hot-tempered Charles, Comte de Charolais, a son of the Duke of Bourbon. The name of Prince Louis de Conti was also mentioned. The regent was sufficiently attracted by the thought of his own son becoming king of Poland that he expressed himself favourable in principle to the marriage, provided it did not take place before his son's elevation to the Polish throne. When Peter refused to delay the wedding till the death of Augustus II, the thought of what Elizabeth's tarnished birth and the fear of the political repercussions which such a marriage might cause in England led the regent to hesitate for a further six months. Although French dislike of Britain was as strong as in the past, the interests of both countries happened for once to coincide in requiring a peaceful Europe, and it was therefore not until the autumn of 1722 that the regent definitely agreed in principle to the marriage, though he persisted in his wish to defer it until his son's elevation to the Polish throne. By the time the French courtier entrusted with his letter reached St Petersburg Peter was in the east, immersed in conducting the war against Persia. The letter did not reach him till his return to his capital at the start of the winter. On reading it he joyfully summoned the French ambassador.

Receiving him in private audience, with Catherine seated at his side, Peter told M. de Campredon how honoured he felt by the regent's decision to consent to the Duke of Chartres's marriage to Elizaveta Petrovna. Since he could not agree to the postponement of the wedding till such time as the Polish throne might fall vacant, he wished to send an envoy to Versailles to discuss arrangements for the ceremony to take place in the near future.

The ambassador urged his government to send a quick and warm acceptance of Peter's terms. Thus, after five years had been spent in disheartening discussions, Elizabeth's future at last seemed settled. On 18 December her birthday was celebrated with particular pomp, the firework display ending with a set piece in the form of her monogram. However, it soon became obvious that the regent had reverted to his delaying tactics. Indeed, his earlier doubts had revived partly because his son stood second in succession to the French throne, partly too because the young man was falling in love with the young German princess whom he was soon to marry. No answer to the tsar's letter had reached St Petersburg by the end of the year. The French ambassador was so bitterly ashamed of his government's silence that he feigned ill health in order to avoid appearing at court. The regent's sudden death on Christmas Day 1723 seemed finally to rule out all possibility of a French marriage for Elizabeth, but when rumours started reaching the Russian court that Louis was not attracted by the little Infanta Peter's hopes revived and he refused to consider the names of eligible suitors of other than French blood for Elizabeth's hand.

Peter the Great died on 25 January 1725 without naming his successor. His eldest daughter Anna Petrovna stood next in succession to the throne, but she had recently become engaged to the Duke of Holstein Gottorp and this was thought to have deprived her of her right to it. Others in the direct line included her sister Elizabeth and the late tsar's grandson, the ten-year-old Grand Duke Peter, the boy's father, the unfortunate Tsarevich Alexei, having died under torture when tried by his father for conspiring to overthrow him. There were also the daughters of Peter's half-brother Tsar Ivan to consider. The eldest, the widowed Duchess of Courland, was living at Mittau, the capital of her duchy; the second, Catherine, was married to the reigning Duke of Mecklenburg, and the third was considered temperamentally unsuitable and therefore ineligible. Although it was assumed that Peter had intended his grandson to succeed him, the boy's youth was against him. Few wished to see the country governed by a regent, and only those courtiers who hankered after the old, indolent yet cosy Muscovite way of life supported the idea. Others who believed in the late tsar's westernizing reforms and who wanted Russia to evolve along the lines he had laid down wondered whether Catherine, the tsar's widow, might not make a better ruler. At the time Menshikov was the most powerful man in Russia. His affection for Catherine had never faltered and was now to dictate his conduct. Acting at any rate to some extent in good faith, if also out of self-interest, he set himself to persuade the Guards Regiments that it would be both right and desirable for Catherine to succeed to the throne. He proved so persuasive and convincing that Catherine found herself empress of Russia. She was the first woman to rule the country.

Elizabeth's future was a matter of great concern to Catherine. In 1722 the little Spanish Infanta whom Louis xv was to marry had arrived in France to complete her education and fit herself for her future role as queen of France. She was only seven years old at the time; Louis was almost fourteen. By 1724 French public opinion was in favour of their king marrying a girl nearer in age to his own, but it was not until Louis' severe illness in the following year that his ministers became seriously concerned and decided to break off his engagement. In April 1725 the young Infanta was sent back to Spain dishonoured, her reputation tarnished for no reason other than her extreme youth. Even though the name of the Margrave Charles of Brandenburg, a Prussian prince of the blood, was being coupled with Elizabeth's, Catherine's hopes rose when she heard from a Dutch source of the Infanta's disgrace. With no loss of time she asked for her daughter's name to be added to the list of eligible brides to be submitted to the king. To make doubly sure of a French marriage she also secretly put forward the Duke of Bourbon's name.[3] To strengthen Elizabeth's chance of success Catherine suggested that the Duke of Chartres, who had now succeeded his father as Duke of Orleans, should marry Marie Leczinska, daughter of the deposed king of Poland, and thereby acquire a claim to the Polish throne, for she did not know that he was about to marry the Princess of Baden. Once again de Campredon, the French ambassador, warmly pressed Elizabeth's name, adding as a reason in her favour that 'she must possess great personal merit to have done so well in her studies of French and German, both of which she speaks and writes really well, and also to have acquired such delightful manners both in conversation and in her mode of conduct . . . bearing in mind the lack of ability in those persons to whom her education has been entrusted.'⁴ His courtier took a month to reach Versailles, but even after reading his memorandum the authorities proceeded to delay taking action upon it, and omitted to reply. The tsaritsa was so deeply offended by their silence that she began seriously to doubt the possibility of establishing friendly relations with France.

In May 1725, at a time when the tsaritsa was carefully considering Russia's relationship with France, a certain Captain Hay arrived in St Petersburg. He was one more in the seemingly endless stream of adventurers and exiles who, under one pretext or another, poured into Russia to seek fame and fortune there. Captain Hay, though a Scot and a Jacobite, was no lover of France or the French. On finding himself barred from his native land he had sought employment with a group of anti-French politicians headed by a Baron de Ripperda, who was in his turn dependent on and encouraged by the king of Spain. Philip v had felt profoundly affronted by the way in which his daughter, the Infanta, had been treated at the French court. He longed for revenge. Scarcely a month before the affront de Ripperda had been of use to Philip, by helping to persuade Austria, Spain's traditional enemy, to agree to a Spanish alliance. Now Philip turned to the baron again in the hope that de Ripperda would on this occasion help him effectually to vent the bitter anger and resentment he felt against the French. De Ripperda was a gay and unprincipled adventurer, and was always ready to serve a powerful patron; indeed, in the course of his life he was to feel no scruples at changing his nationality and religion a total of three times, with the result that he was able to end his days as Pasha of Morocco. To further Philip's wishes de Ripperda picked on Captain Hay as a likely person to send to Russia for the purpose of pitting the inexperienced Catherine against both France and Britain.

The empress received Hay graciously and did not seem averse to his suggestion that she should break off diplomatic relations with France, but she refused to abandon Peter the Great's policy until the question of Elizabeth's French marriage had been settled. The French ambassador sensed the existence of an intrigue and urgently pressed his government to decide in favour of a Russian marriage. He waited anxiously for a reply to his despatches and it came as no less of a surprise to him than it did to the rest of Europe when, on 27 May, the French court announced the engage-ment of Louis xv to none other than Marie Leszinska. France was appalled by the news, de Campredon profoundly disturbed by it, and Catherine deeply resentful that the daughter of the deposed king of Poland should have been preferred to that of Peter the Great of Russia.

The Russians interpreted France's discourtesy in failing to notify the empress in advance as an intentional insult, especially since it was not until 30 June that the official letter containing Versailles' reasons for refusing Elizabeth's hand reached St Petersburg. By then the French ambassador, who had asked for his passport on the day on which he learnt of his sovereign's engagement, was no longer there to transmit the document. He had left St Petersburg by sea on 31 May. The letter con-tained little that was likely to soothe Russian feelings.[5] It was addressed to de Campredon and read,

Je réponds par cette lettre, Monsieur, à celle par laquelle vous rendez compte de la proposition qui vous a été faite par le prince Menshikoff pour le marriage du Roi avec la princesse Elizabeth. Vous jugerez aisèment que, lorsqu'il a été question du choix d'une princesse épouse de sa Majesté, l'on n'a pas fait peu d'attention à l'avantage que l'on aurait pu trouver dans l'alliance d'une princesse fille du Tsar et de la Tsarina, et que d'un côté les grandes qualitées qui ont portées la Tsarina au degré d'èlèvation ou elle est, et de l'autre les agréments personnels dont on savait que la princesse Elizabeth était douée, n'aurait pour ainsi dire pas permis á sa Majesté de fixer son choix ailleurs, si l'on avait pu espérer que la religion que la Tsarina et as famille professent n'eut pas été un obstacle au succés des voeux de sa Majesté.

No documents survive to divulge what Elizabeth herself felt on hearing the news of Louis' engagement and on having the suggestion that she should marry either the Duke de Charolais or Prince Louis-François de Bourbon Conti passed over in silence. Madame de Prie, the interfering mistress of the Duke of Bourbon, Prime Minister of France, had been so vexed by Catherine's plan that her lover should marry the tsarevna that she persuaded him to oppose both proposals. She probably was also partly responsible for his decision to choose Marie Leszinska as the young king's bride. In the face of these insults the tsaritsa and her daughter con-ducted themselves with dignity. Elizabeth gave no sign of knowing, let alone of caring, and seemed to think of nothing but amusing herself. Though Catherine longed to break off diplomatic relations with France she was too proud to do so until she had a political excuse for justifying such an action. She did not consider France's refusal to renew the Russian alliance on the grounds of her traditional friendship with Sweden as a sufficient reason, but at the same time she recalled the desire felt by Peter during the closing months of his life to improve relations with Britain and remembered that his unfinished draft for a treaty of friendship with England lay on his desk at the time of his death. She therefore instructed her Council of State to outline new proposals for a British alliance. Such a change in policy disturbed certain politicians, especially Menshikov, Apraxin, Tolstoy, Galitzine and other close friends of Peter the Great: under the late tsar's guidance they had become staunch lovers of France and formed the core of the court's pro-French party.

The affairs of Catherine's son-in-law, Charles Frederick, Duke of Holstein Schleswig Gottorp and a candidate for the Swedish throne, were to furnish the Empress with the excuse she desired for quarrelling with France. The ownership of the Duchy of Schleswig – an issue which had already bedevilled political life in northern Europe for thirty years and which was to do so for another thirty-five – became the bone of contention. Although the matter directly concerned only the Scandinavian countries, France, Britain, Holland, Prussia and Russia were all to become involved in it. The Duchy had belonged to Holstein for many years. During most of them Sweden's interests had coincided with those of Holstein and the latter had been able to rely on Sweden's protection. But in the early seventeenth century, at the very time when Denmark had begun to covet Schleswig, Sweden's attitude began to change so that the reign of Christian Albert of Holstein was fraught with difficulties. He was twice deposed and Denmark took advantage of his weakness to seize Schleswig. Christian Albert eventually succeeded in regaining his territory largely through the help he received from Brandenburg. It enabled his son, Frederick IV of Holstein Schleswig Gottorp, to retain his inheritance and to rule over his Duchy. His marriage to Hedwig-Sophia, the eldest daughter of Charles XII of Sweden, had made him an heir to the Swedish throne. In order to strengthen his hand Frederick had entered into alliances not only with Sweden, but also with Holland and Britain, moves which were counteracted by Frederick IV of Denmark's decision to obtain similar treaties from Peter the Great and from Augustus, Elector of Saxony and king of Poland. Having done so he declared war on Holstein in 1699 and quickly captured Schleswig. The timely appearance there of an Anglo-Dutch fleet alone deterred him from pressing his advance. In 1700 the peace treaty of Travendal accorded him possession of Schleswig, its retention being guaranteed to him by both Britain and France. Frederick, Duke of Holstein, died in 1702 leaving as heir both to his own duchy and to the Swedish throne his four-year-old son, Charles Frederick. The little boy was sent to live at the court of his uncle, King Charles XII of Sweden. The crushing defeat inflicted upon the Swedes at Poltava, and the Duke of Holstein's extreme youth, encouraged the Danes to attempt to annex Holstein. They invaded Gottorp in 1714 and occupied Schleswig. Their hold here was to prove permanent. Within two years of the death of Charles XII, Charles Frederick learnt that the great powers had decided to confer the Swedish throne on Ulrica Elenore's husband; by doing so they had deprived him of the Swedish crown and made it necessary for him to seek a new refuge.

Charles Frederick's claim to the throne of Sweden and to Schleswig was so well founded that he had every reason to press it. It also served to make him a useful pawn in the hands of politicians. He recognized the danger he was in and his need for a strong protector. His eyes rested on Russia and Peter did not rebuff him. In 1721 the young duke was invited to visit St Petersburg. Courtiers there were almost unanimous in considering him a sickly youth lacking in charm and ability. But though he was physically unattractive and boring in conversation the Russians misjudged him. He was to prove efficient and reasonable – and sufficiently astute to realize that he could hardly do better than marry one of Peter's daughters. Of the two he preferred the younger, but the idea did not appeal to the tsar. Reiterating that 'he loved both his girls like his own soul'[6] he refused to consider the proposal for either. Catherine, on the other hand, liked the young man and determined to persuade Peter to accept him as a son-in-law. Peter continued to assert that Elizabeth was too young to marry, but shortly before his death he agreed to Anna doing so. The Duke of Liria, Spain's ambassador to Russia, described Anna as 'without doubt one of the loveliest princesses in Europe, accomplished as well as virtuous'.[7]

The announcement of Anna's engagement had to be postponed because of Peter's death, but her wedding to Charles Frederick took place on 21 May of the same year. Catherine marked it by announcing that she had decided to support her son-in-law's claim to Schleswig to the extent of ensuring that he be paid compensation for its loss. Infuriated by her stand, Louis XV instructed his ambassador to St Petersburg, in a despatch dated 15 October 1725, to break off diplomatic relations with Russia and he also ordered his ambassador to the Porte to do everything in his power to dissuade the sultan from fulfilling his treaty obligations to Russia.

Schleswig-Holstein was not the only duchy over which the great powers were to contend during Elizabeth's lifetime. Courland was to prove almost as fertile ground for mistrust. Ever since 1561, though governed by a hereditary grand duke ostensibly living under Polish protection, it had in reality been little more than a Polish fief. During Peter's reign Russian influence had, however, started to make itself increasingly felt there so that, by 1710, the tsar had had no difficulty in arranging for his half-niece Anna Ivanovna to marry its reigning grand duke. Though – as we have seen – the unfortunate bridegroom had died travelling home from his wedding, his widow had established herself in Mittau and although the throne had passed to her late husband's nephew and ward, Ferdinand, the political dissensions which had obliged him to emigrate to Danzig enabled him to act as the Duchy's ruler. As Frederick was both elderly and childless, Poland, Prussia and Russia all felt entitled to nominate his and Anna Ivanovna's eventual successor.

None had foreseen that so glamorous a figure as the brave, fascinating and thoroughly unscrupulous Maurice de Saxe would try to obtain that position for himself. Maurice (1696–1750) was the illegitimate son of Augustus II of Saxony and the perplexing Countess Aurora von Königsmark. When still a youth he had served with distinction in Prince Eugen's service, but in 1720 he had left to join the French army. Now, in 1726, he suddenly appeared in Mittau and virtually overnight he became the most popular man there.

It was as much by chance as by design that Maurice de Saxe found himself in Mittau. His presence there was due indirectly to Elizabeth, for when all hope of a French marriage for her had been finally abandoned, a courtier had foolishly suggested that she should marry Peter's grandson, the schoolboy Grand Duke Peter Alexeeicevich. Johann Lefort – a nephew of Peter the Great's old friend and boon companion of the same name – had countered the proposal by naming Maurice de Saxe as a possible suitor. At the suggestion, de Saxe had abandoned both his regiment and his mistress, Adrienne Lecouvreur, and had hopefully set off on the long journey to Russia. It seems probable that he heard of the possibility of the Dukedom of Courland falling vacant on his arrival in Warsaw and that, preferring a ducal crown and revenue to the position of husband to a Russian grand duchess, he had instantly changed his plans and hurried to Mittau. Only twenty-nine, he epitomized all that was most gallant and

1. Portrait of Peter the Great by J. M. Nattier. The tsar holds a field marshal's baton and wears armour and decorations. There is a scene from the battle of Poltava in the background.

3. Tanauer's portrait of Prince A. D. Menshikov in field marshal's uniform. A scene from the battle of Poltava is included in the background.

2. Portrait of Peter the Great's second wife, the future empress Catherine, by J. M. Nattier.

4. A bronze sculpture by Rastrelli the Elder of the empress Anna Ivanovna and her blackamoor.

5. A portrait by an unknown artist of Anna Leopoldovna as a young girl. She became regent of Russia ruling the country on behalf of her infant son Ivan VI.

dashing in a soldier. His wit, his extreme good looks, his courage and sparkle, and also his reputation as a lady-killer, could not be resisted. Mittau was enchanted by him; the ladies adored him. Stout, unattractive and staid Anna Ivanovna fell madly in love with him. Maurice proposed marriage and was accepted. In a haze of happiness the Duchess of Courland sat down to write to the tsaritsa for permission to marry her suitor. Her letter came as an unpleasant surprise to Catherine who had just promised Menshikov that she would confer the Dukedom of Courland upon him. She hurried to refuse poor Anna's request, doing so with some tartness, but on 18 June the nobles of Courland, meeting in plenary session in the Landstag, had already elected Maurice Duke of Courland. Their decision outraged the Polish Diet and Prussia quite as much as it did Menshikov. The latter gave vent to his feelings by employing troops to dislodge Maurice. The young man began also to assemble a force, using funds for the purpose which had been sent to him both by his mother and by Adrienne Lecouvreur, as well as by the Abbess of Quedlimburg, who had sold her jewels in order to help him. Fearing that Maurice would unleash a full-scale war, his father hastened to disown him; so too did Cardinal de Fleury, France's Minister for Foreign Affairs. Maurice found himself obliged to face Menshikov's Regiment of Dragoons under the command of Marshal Lacy with a force of only 247 men. It is hardly surprising that the future victor of Fontenoy, perhaps the greatest military commander of the Seven Years War, was routed on this occasion and obliged to escape from the island of Usmaüs by swimming to the mainland. Meanwhile Poland talked of dividing Courland into palatinates, and Anna was left to pick up the threads of her lonely life in Mittau.

In Russia Maurice's name continued to be linked with that of Elizabeth even after this escapade. Irked beyond bearing, in a moment of unguarded petulance, the young girl was heard hotly to exclaim: 'I don't want to be like all those princesses who become victims of state considerations. I want to marry according to my inclinations in order to experience the delights of loving the man I marry.'[8]

Such a man had in fact recently come into her life. Ever since the collapse of plans of a French marriage for Elizabeth her brother-in-law, Charles Frederick had been pressing the suit of his cousin Charles Augustus of Holstein, a brother of the King of Sweden and of the Princess Anhalt Zerbs. The Emperor of Austria had already arranged for the young man to marry Elizabeth's half-niece, Natalia Alexeevna, the delightful eleven-year-old sister of the Grand Duke Peter, and although Charles Frederick had expressed himself in favour of that union, in 1725 he persuaded the empress to consider Charles Augustus as a suitor for Elizabeth's hand. Catherine agreed to invite the young man to visit her.

Charles Augustus reached Kronstadt on 16 October 1726. Rather surprisingly the twenty-year-old youth appealed to Elizabeth. He had charm, he was related by marriage to her adored sister, and, above all, he was the first of all her various suitors whom she had actually met. Elizabeth was seventeen years old and extremely attractive. Her gaiety and manners delighted everyone. By early December the French chargé d'affaires informed Versailles that he believed that, regardless of the Church's objections on religious grounds, the marriage had been agreed to. Catherine's decision to confer the Order of St Andrew on the young man seemed to confirm this view. Fearing that a second Holstinian son-in-law would encourage Catherine to press for the return of Schleswig to Holstein, Denmark begged France to prevent the marriage. Meanwhile Christmas was being celebrated at the Russian court with the solemn pomp and serene majesty customary in the Orthodox world. The new year was seen in very gaily. Even Maurice de Saxe's future prospects seemed to take a turn for the better for, on receiving favourable reports of his character, the tsaritsa had relented and agreed to recognize his election to the Dukedom of Courland if he married her niece, Sophia Skavronskaya.

But while Elizabeth and her future husband were savouring their wholly unexpected happiness, the empress, weary of state affairs and the complex problems they presented, had been seeking distraction in love, food and wine. Indulging to excess in all three she had made it possible for Menshikov to overrule the Council of State and make himself omnipotent. His arrogance kept pace with his growing powers till it became boundless. Public opinion had begun to turn against him and people were starting to look to the Grand Duke Peter as their rightful ruler. Menshikov ignored these feelings and dared to ask the empress to consent to the marriage of his daughter Marie to the Grand Duke regardless of the fact that she was seventeen years older than young Peter, and that she was engaged and genuinely attached to the Polish Count Sapieha. Catherine could never stand up to Menshikov or refuse even his most outrageous requests. This time her consent shocked Petersburgian society, yet of all the courtiers only the elderly Count Peter Tolstoy had the courage to take the empress's two daughters by the hand and lead them to their mother. On gaining admittance to the tsaritsa he drew himself up to his full height and bluntly told her that the proposed marriage would endanger the happiness, possibly even the lives, of her household, even of her daughters. He vowed that he would kill himself if it took place and begged her to appoint Elizabeth her successor to the throne.[9] At these words the two Grand Duchesses fell on their knees at their mother's feet; sobbing, they begged her to withdraw her consent. Catherine also burst into tears, but averred that she could not go back on her words.

Catherine's health had begun to fail. She started to suffer from frequent nose bleeding and fainting fits. However, a few days after this harrowing scene, on 6 January 1727, she attended the traditional ceremony of the blessing of the Neva's waters. She wore a riding habit made of cloth of silver trimmed with Spanish braid, and a hat with a white plume. She carried a marshal's baton and looked magnificent. On the same evening she was suddenly taken ill. Elizabeth's engagement to Charles Augustus was to have been made official on the following day, but it was decided to postpone the announcement until the empress had recovered her health. Catherine was seriously ill for two months, then she rallied, but only to collapse again in April. This time her doctors realized that they could do little more for her. They informed her family and close advisers that the empress had not long to live. On hearing their verdict Menshikov placed himself at the dying woman's bedside, it is thought in order to persuade her to proclaim the Grand Duke Peter her heir on condition that he married Marie Menshikova. The French chargé d'affaires informed Versailles that the empress had implored Menshikov to let her nominate Elizabeth, but that he had refused to do so. Catherine held out till she felt death to be at hand. Then she managed to sign her will nominating Peter the next holder of the throne.

Catherine hovered at death's door for another two days before finally succumbing. According to her will and political testament Peter was to come of age at sixteen and, in the meantime, Russia was to be governed by a State Council of nine. Her daughters Anna and Elizabeth ranked as its foremost members and also came first and second in the order of succession to the throne if Peter were to die childless. The other seven members of the State Council consisted of the Duke of Holstein, Prince Menshikov, Rear-Admiral Apraxin, the Chancellor Golovkin, Prince Dmitri Galitzire, Prince Vassili Lukich Dolgoruky and the Vice-Chancellor, Count Ostermann. Ostermann assumed responsibility for the young tsar's education. In addition, Catherine left a million roubles to each of her daughters, with an additional dowry of thirty thousand roubles to Elizabeth, that being the sum which Peter had given their daughter Anna at her marriage to the

Duke of Holstein. Both her daughters also received an annuity of a hundred thousand roubles in compensation for relinquishing their right to the throne to Peter and his descendants. Finally Catherine wished her silver, jewels, furniture and carriages to be shared equally by Anna and Elizabeth.

2

A Disrupted Life

The announcement of Elizabeth's engagement to Charles Augustus had once again to be postponed. Elizabeth was not troubled by the delay. Though her grief for her mother was genuine she was not obliged to bear it in solitude. In addition to her sister and brother-in-law she now had Charles Augustus to confide in, for he could share her sorrow no less than her pleasures. She grew ever fonder of him and both were content, as long as they could spend their days together. Elizabeth seemed to feel no regret or resentment at having been deprived of the throne, but both she and her sister were startled and dismayed to discover that they had an enemy in Menshikov. Although Menshikov owed his wealth, position and power to Peter the Great he ceased to show any concern for the feelings or welfare of the late tsar's daughters. Within a month of Catherine's death he persuaded the boy tsar to become engaged to his daughter Marie. His future prospects made him so arrogant that he offended Anna and Elizabeth, antagonized a large number of the nobility and made enemies of the members of the powerful Dolgoruky clan.

Russia had lost two sovereigns in the space of twenty-eight months. Now, with a twelve-year-old boy occupying the throne, Menshikov became the real ruler of Russia. Though the new tsar was tall and in some ways old for his age, he had not been fitted for his difficult role. His childhood had been a grim and solitary one. Peter the Great had not been able to bring himself to see much of his grandson, for the child was a painful reminder to him of his own ill-starred son, the Tsarevich Alexei. Nevertheless, Peter did not altogether ignore him; he tried to ensure that the boy should receive a proper education by appointing as his tutor a Hungarian called Sevan who had also been tutor in the household of his relatives, the Naryshkins. It was unfortunate for young Peter that Menshikov was able to persuade Catherine to banish the Naryshkins, for

Sevan preferred to share their exile rather than to remain in St Petersburg to supervise the young Grand Duke's studies. Catherine replaced Sevan by Count Ostermann. The choice was not a bad one. Ostermann was the second son of a poor Westphalian pastor. Born in Germany in 1686 he had studied at Jena University and travelled in Europe. He arrived in Russia in 1704 having, it was rumoured, sought sanctuary there after killing an opponent in a duel. He enlisted in the Russian navy and was sent to serve Vice-Admiral Cruys as either a batman or secretary. The admiral was so impressed by the young man's abilities that, shortly afterwards, he advised the Vice-Chancellor, Baron Shafirov, to transfer Ostermann to the College for Foreign Affairs. There too Ostermann was quick to make his mark and was soon acting as secretary to Peter the Great. In 1722 the tsar conferred a barony on him as a reward for his zeal and intelligence. Ostermann remained hard-working, loyal and reliable, and promotion followed at short intervals. Catherine came to rely so greatly on his advice that she appointed him Minister for Foreign Affairs.

Young Peter took to Ostermann, but his affections centred in his childhood on his young sister Natalia. She was a year older than Peter, but although still just a child her marriage to Charles Augustus, Elizabeth's future husband, had been discussed in several European courts. The charming girl was wise and good beyond her years. She was plain, but triumphed over this through courtesy and good sense. Foreigners living in Russia spoke of her with particular admiration and warmth for she was always ready to befriend and protect them. Her intervention had saved more than one of them from ill-treatment at the hands of suspicious Russians. Her death in November 1728 deprived Russia of a princess of true warmth of heart and of singularly liberal outlook.

Elizabeth was eighteen years old at the time of her mother's death. The decision to announce her engagement to Charles Augustus at the end of May, barely a month later was probably due to Menshikov's desire to rid himself of a spirited regent. On 27 May, on the eve of the announcement, Charles Augustus complained of feeling ill and retired to bed. Several hours later his doctors diagnosed smallpox. He died four days later and with him Elizabeth's hopes for a normal, happy married life also died.

In her first access of anguish Elizabeth sought refuge with her sister and brother-in-law at Ekaterinhof, a residence built by Peter the Great for Catherine on the outskirts of the capital. It was as well that she did so for

no one at court spared a thought for her. With quite remarkable callous-
ness Menshikov did not even consider postponing the great reception he
had arranged for the very evening of Charles Augustus's death for the
purpose of announcing the young tsar's engagement to his daughter
Marie. Within a matter of days Menshikov had started to compile a fresh
list of suitors for Elizabeth's hand. The Prussian ambassador, Baron
Mardefeld, again suggested that Charles, the son of the Margrave of
Brandenburg, be included, but Menshikov refused on political grounds.
While Menshikov was busying himself in disposing of Elizabeth she
mastered her grief and took steps to ensure that the legacies listed in
Charles Augustus's will were faithfully discharged. She found that she
possessed few resources, for Menshikov had deprived both her and her
sister of the greater part of their mother's bequests. Nevertheless, she
managed to set herself up with a household of her own in apartments
which the young tsar provided for her in the Summer Palace.

Burglaries were a regular feature of life in St Petersburg. The robbers
were so numerous[1] and so daring that the night watchmen were unable to
control them. Elizabeth lived in such terror of thieves that she could not
rest till she had procured weapons with which to arm some of her servants.
This done, she got some fine pieces of furniture; finally, she acquired some
musicians and a monkey; she believed that reading was an unhealthy
occupation and she hoped that they would divert her and help to pass
the time away.

Menshikov's dislike of Peter the Great's daughters developed into a
hatred which he made no effort to conceal. He never missed an opportunity
to offend or inconvenience them, and watchful courtiers were quick to
adjust their behaviour to his. When Elizabeth eventually succeeded in
obtaining an annuity for herself it proved so small that she was often
without funds. She was never to forget the poverty to which she was
reduced after her mother's death, although it was to become more acute
in the reign of Anna Ivanovna. Some eighteen years later, stung to anger
by the extravagance of the future empress Catherine, Elizabeth sharply
reprimanded the younger woman, telling her that 'the reign of the
Empress Anna had taught her that, having little, she should avoid spending; had she incurred debts she would have feared being damned, for had
she died leaving debts no one would have settled them and her soul would
have gone to hell, which she dreaded; for that reason, when at home, and
on all other possible occasions, she wore simple clothes consisting of a
white taffeta top and an under robe of black. By doing so she saved

money for she took care never to wear expensive clothes in the country or when travelling.'[2]

Worse than the lack of money and the misappropriation of their mother's legacies were the taunts which the Grand Duchesses had to endure from Menshikov and most courtiers. By August, when barely three months had elapsed since Catherine's death, Anna and her husband could no longer tolerate these conditions. In Catherine's day the Duke of Holstein's name had taken precedence even over young Peter's in the official prayer for the reigning family, but now life had been made unbearable for him and his wife. In July 1729, though Anna was pregnant, they decided to leave Russia and to settle in Kiel.

Elizabeth was intensely lonely after their departure but she concealed her feelings, came out of mourning and started seeing a great deal of Peter and Natalia. She began to teach the tsar to ride and hunt, and did her best to keep him amused. Menshikov and Ostermann were so accustomed to her high spirits that they did not at first attach any importance to her activities. Menshikov was fully occupied in trying to surround the tsar with his own relations and friends, and with his newly formed plan of marrying Natalia to his son Sasha. That dissolute youth induced Peter to spend his days in idleness. Ostermann's efforts to persuade Peter to attend to his studies and even Natalia's entreaties were ignored by Peter, especially since Elizabeth encouraged him to amuse himself. Whatever her reasons for this tactic, Elizabeth kept them secret and it is impossible to tell whether she acted from a desire to drown her own grief by the diversions she invented for Peter, or whether she did so to establish her own influence over the tsar at the expense of Menshikov's, though subsequent events might incline one to the latter view. Even so, if she planned to set the tsar against Menshikov to punish him for her sister's departure, then she was behaving in a manner alien to her character. She was by nature quick-tempered rather than calculating. Later in life her outbursts of anger were directed either against people who were thought to have endangered Russia's security or against women whose beauty rivalled her own.

At no time does she appear to have resented Peter's elevation to the throne or longed to possess it herself. She seems to have been genuinely fond of the tsar and it may well be that, having herself often experienced loneliness in childhood, she was anxious that he should forget the years he had spent in solitude. She made a point of mothering and amusing him. When Peter suddenly fell ill Elizabeth rushed to his bedside and, acting as she was later to do whenever a member of her family fell dangerously ill, she stationed herself there even before his ailment had been diagnosed. Fortunately, the tsar had not contracted either of the two most dreaded diseases of the day, smallpox or cholera. He was suffering from an acute attack of either pleurisy or bronchitis, aggravated by the debauchery that he had been indulging in. Some historians blame Elizabeth for the deterioration in his health, but the responsibility rests with the depraved youths with whom Menshikov had surrounded the tsar.

Peter had to keep to his bed for several weeks. When he was at last able to leave it his lungs had become affected and his doctors therefore prescribed a long convalescence to be spent at Peterhof. Elizabeth stayed with him and mingled jollity with pleas that the tsar should dispense with Menshikov. The Dolgorukys seconded her in this, especially Prince Alexei Grigorievich, who was ardently jealous of Menshikov. It was for this purpose that he encouraged his profligate twenty-year-old son Ivan and his daughter Catherine to gain admittance to Peter's circle of intimate friends. Sensing danger, Menshikov drove out to Peterhof intending to reassert his authority over the tsar. Their meeting proved stormy and its outcome unfavourable to Menshikov. He left determined to challenge Elizabeth's ascendency over the tsar. As a first step he decided to celebrate the tsar's birthday on 17 June by holding a reception of unparalleled magnificence in the Palace of Oranienbaum. Elizabeth set out to defy him and managed to persuade Peter to go hunting with her on that day even though, according to protocol, it was his duty to welcome his host's guests and receive their birthday greetings. The tsar did not notify Menshikov of his decision and it was not until the following morning that Menshikov discovered that Peter had not only spent the day hunting, but that instead of returning to Peterhof he had installed himself in the Summer Palace, in apartments adjacent to Elizabeth's.

Menshikov was still wondering how he should handle the tsar when, on 25 September, Major General Saltykov, acting by order of the tsar and Privy Council, entered Menshikov's bedroom in the early hours of the morning, woke him, and placed him together with his wife, son and daughters under arrest. Saltykov informed his prisoners that they had been dispossessed, and even though Marie was still officially engaged to the tsar he requisitioned her engagement ring. When they had packed the bare essentials the prisoners were driven to Tver, where they were at last charged. Menshikov was accused of being in Sweden's pay and he and his family were to be banished to Siberia. Shortly afterwards they were transferred to Riazan and then moved to Beresov. The journey to Siberia was made in such harsh conditions that Menshikov's wife died before reaching Beresov; Marie was to die there some months later and Menshikov within the year.

In St Petersburg courtiers were surprised to notice that Menshikov's fall coincided with a marked coolness in the relationship between Peter and Elizabeth. It lasted for a very short time and the Dolgorukys were annoyed when Peter's affection for Elizabeth revived. It seemed to them to verge on the amorous. Ostermann was anxious for the tsar to marry his young aunt.[3] Others felt that Peter's feelings required curbing. Since Peter was reputed to take more interest in his own sex than in women, Prince Dmitri Galitzine's suggestion that the preference be encouraged was welcomed by Elizabeth's enemies. A young officer called Alexander Buturlin was therefore appointed a member of Peter's suite. It was hoped that he might turn the tsar's thoughts from Elizabeth, but before he could do so Ivan Dolgoruky, Peter's boon companion, was stricken with consumption. Peter was heartbroken and insisted on spending most of his free time at his friend's bedside. As a result, Elizabeth and Buturlin often found themselves thrown together. From the start they took pleasure in each other's company. That pleasure developed into a mutual infatuation. Soon after, Buturlin became Elizabeth's first lover.

By January 1728 the court was ready to move to Moscow for the coronation of Tsar Peter II. The tsar, Natalia, Elizabeth, Ivan Dolgoruky, whose health had improved, and Alexander Buturlin were to travel together. They set out as planned, but Peter was taken ill on the journey and, on reaching Tver, they were obliged to put him to bed and await his recovery before proceeding further. In Moscow Elizabeth busied herself with arranging the semi-official entertainments for the sovereign's guests. The reports which the foreign envoys sent back to their governments often refer to her remarkable beauty, charm and gaiety. While everyone in Moscow was involved in some aspect of the coronation, the imperial family learnt that, in Kiel, Anna Petrovna had given birth to a son on 10 February. Though estranged, the child's parents were overjoyed to have a boy, for he became heir both to the dukedom of Holstein and the kingdom of Sweden. They called him Karl Ulrich Peter and as soon as Anna was on her feet again they decided to celebrate his birth by a court ball. On the same night his birth was to be celebrated in Moscow by a similar ball. In Kiel the event was also to be marked by a spectacular display of fireworks. To enjoy them to the full Anna opened one of the ballroom's windows and, heedless of the treacherous northern spring, stood in front of it without a wrap. She seemed not to notice the cold night air, but on the next day she developed a severe chill. Ten days later, on 4 May, she died of it, aged only twenty-six. The news reached Moscow when the coronation festivities were at their height. Elizabeth was plunged in grief by her sister's death, but only she and Buturlin seemed to spare a thought for Peter the Great's dead daughter during the three months of official court mourning. Anna had asked to be buried beside her parents, and her body was accordingly brought to St Petersburg. After the funeral Elizabeth's sense of loss was so acute that she withdrew from court life. Naïvely, she became convinced that Anna's death had been caused by her fondness for reading.

The tsar missed Elizabeth's company, but the Dolgorukys took advantage of her absence to attack her. Finding that their words were having no effect they tried to discredit her by informing him of her feelings for Buturlin. They found to their dismay that they had made Peter violently jealous of Buturlin and therefore decided to use Alexei Dolgoruky's daughter Catherine to distract Peter's thoughts from Elizabeth. Catherine was beautiful, charming and eighteen years old. Her name had already been coupled with a young courtier's, but more recently she had fallen in love with and become engaged to Count Millesimo, an Austro-Italian diplomat accredited to the Russian court. Disregarding her feelings and that fact that Peter was still officially engaged to Marie Menshikov, Prince Alexei encouraged the tsar to fall in love with his daughter, constantly inviting Peter to his country house, Gorenki, to spend his days hunting and his evenings talking to Catherine. Peter did not protest at the arrangement and pretended not to miss Elizabeth's company, yet his jealousy of Buturlin reached such dimensions that he gave orders for the young man to be posted to the army which was to be sent to the Ukraine to fight the Crimea Tartars.

Buturlin's departure increased Elizabeth's unhappiness. Hurt by what she regarded as Peter's heartlessness, she decided to seek consolation by undertaking a pilgrimage to several of Moscow's most venerated monasteries. It was the first time that she planned to make such a long pilgrimage, but the decision conformed with the ideas she had been used to in her childhood, and she must have derived considerable comfort from the experience. From then on, whenever she felt overwhelmed by difficult problems confronting her, she sought the seclusion of a monastic retreat.

In 1729 news of Marie Menshikov's death in exile left the tsar free to marry Catherine Dolgoruky. Her father considered them already engaged but decided that the court should return to Moscow on 30 November to make their engagement public. He too had become anxious to find Elizabeth a husband. The search for one was carried on so openly that a foreign observer reported that 'various ways of mating the Princess Elizabeth are being considered' and that, in order to induce her to do so, she was 'being deprived of everything, including beer for her household'.[4] But Elizabeth was proving difficult; nothing would induce her to accept the Prince of Bayreuth as a suitor. She was affronted when the Dolgorukys suggested that she should marry the debauched, ailing Ivan Dolgoruky, and the anger she felt for them increased when Natalia's death on 3 December did not alter their decision to celebrate the engagement of Peter and Catherine on 18 December as had been previously arranged. The betrothal was celebrated with all the pomp prescribed by tradition. Mastering her feelings, Elizabeth was the first to approach the platform on which the young couple were seated side by side on sumptuous thrones. Curtsying to each in turn she mounted the dais and respectfully kissed her sovereign's hand; then she moved on and with complete composure did the same to Catherine's. She betrayed no emotion. But none failed to notice the deep unhappiness on Catherine's face and the expression of profound dejection on Peter's. When Count Millesimo approached the dais to pay his respects Catherine came near to fainting and the rejected diplomat seemed on the point of doing likewise; indeed, he left Russia two days later. Lady Rondeau, the widow of Thomas Ward, England's Consul General to Russia, who had recently married the British Resident Charles Rondeau, remarked in a letter on how sorry she felt for him 'who becomes Imperial Highness of Russia'.[5] The day was made even more painful for Elizabeth by Ivan Dolgoruky. Acting in a manner designed to insult her, he chose to announce his own engagement to Helen Sheremetieva and to celebrate the event by seizing the jewels which Natalia had bequeathed to Elizabeth so as to share them with his sister.

Scorned and lonely Elizabeth was often to be seen in the company of Count Semeon Naryshkin,[6] her close contemporary and a relation on her father's side. After a while, tiring of Moscow, she announced her intention of retiring to live at Ismailovo with a small household of her own choosing. It included Mavra Chepeleva, a clever and amusing childhood friend, Mikhail Vorontsov, Alexander and Peter Shuvalov, her French doctor, Armand Lestocq and, naturally, Semeon Naryshkin. Ten years later four of these men were to place her on the throne. Peter went to Ismailovo to visit her shortly after, ostensibly in order to wish her a happy birthday. She took advantage of his visit to complain bitterly of her lack of funds. Peter passionately denied being in any way responsible for her poverty and they parted as friends. Soon afterwards, however, Naryshkin found himself forced to leave Russia. He moved to Paris and remained there till recalled by Elizabeth in 1742.

The tsar's wedding was to take place in Moscow on 30 January 1730. Everyone therefore stayed on in Moscow after the official proclamation of his engagement to get ready for the wedding. The regiments which had been brought to Moscow to officiate at the first ceremony were retained there to do so at the second. Additional guests poured into Moscow from all parts of Russia while courtiers and officials busied themselves with the final arrangements. On 6 January they watched the tsar officiate at the ceremony of the Blessing of the Waters. For the next few days he was left much alone; with no one to divert him he felt bored almost beyond endurance. On 28 January the weather was bitterly cold, but it was the day chosen for him to review the regiments which were to take part in his wedding celebrations. The parade lasted for several hours and on the following day Peter fell ill. It was assumed that he had caught a chill at the review; he was put to bed and physicians summoned. They failed to diagnose his complaint till the following morning when they found that he had contracted smallpox. By then he was so desperately ill that nothing could be done for him. Although it was night Lestocq hurried to inform Elizabeth. He went to her bedroom, woke her and tried to persuade her to make a bid for the throne. She refused to listen to him, even to rise before morning.[7] Meanwhile at the very hour at which he was to have married, his life slipped from him. According to the French envoy, Magnan,[8] Elizabeth was not in Moscow at the time, having refused to attend Peter's wedding, nor was she present at his burial. Her unconventional, independent way of life had already given rise to much unfavourable comment. Magnan's report contains some of the earliest references to her lax morals, remarking that her passions were being fully satisfied at Ismailovo. Lady Rondeau's letters also imply that the Grand Duchess's behaviour was not above criticism, yet Elizabeth's absence from Peter's funeral can be better explained by her reluctance to become involved in the political issues raised by the tsar's death.

The male line of the Romanov dynasty now became extinct, and for the third time within five years the throne fell vacant. According to the will of Catherine I Elizabeth became the only person legally entitled to occupy it, and, like the majority of the nation, she must have expected the crown either to be offered to her outright or, if offered to her sister Anna's infant son, that she would find herself appointed regent. Her subsequent behaviour seems to suggest that she considered the latter course to be more correct constitutionally but the issue was complicated by Prince Alexei Dolgoruky. On the grounds that his daughter was on the verge of becoming empress by her marriage to the late tsar he staked her claim to the throne. The desirability of selecting an adult as ruler, without further delay, became evident to all. A Council of State was hurriedly assembled for the purpose and the names of Tsar Ivan's two elder daughters added to the list of candidates. The younger of the two, Ekaterina Ivanovna, had found her marriage to the Duke of Mecklenburg so unbearable that she had left her husband after four years and returned to Russia bringing her three-year-old daughter, Elizabeth Catherine Christina, with her. Her candidature was quickly set aside for it was feared that her husband would return to her if she were appointed empress and that the infiltration of Germans into Russia would follow. Ostermann is supposed to have prevented Elizabeth's election, because he knew that she disapproved of his harshness. There remained Anna Ivanovna's right to the throne to consider. She was still living in Mittau where she had now fallen in love with her secretary, Count Ernest Johann Bühren. He was a grandson of Mathias Bühren of Mecklenburg, groom to James, third Duke of Courland, who had so endeared himself to his master that he had received a barony and a small estate from him. Ernest Johann was so ardent an admirer of France and all things French that he had gallicized his name to that of Biron, and had adopted the arms of the extinct Birons of France. Perhaps misled by the docility with which Anna Ivanovna had submitted to Catherine I's refusal to allow her to marry Maurice de Saxe, the Councillors of State decided to offer her the throne. They would have done well to recall a sally of her jester who, when Anna Ivanovna was still a girl, nicknamed her Tsar Ivan the Terrible. Ostermann, though a leading statesman, took to his bed. Months later he was to admit to Finch, Britain's ambassador,[9] that 'he feigned sickness so as not to sign the document on the succession', Finch adding the acid comment that 'he will always lie by, when the going is not settled'. Manstein confirmed this device of Ostermann's, noting that[10] 'it was by the trick of these sicknesses, occasionally pretended at the proper times, that this minister kept his ground so long in the empire'. Ostermann was, therefore, able to conceal his objections from Elizabeth, and Magnan was probably acting in good faith when he ascribed the State Council's failure to elect her to moral considerations.[11]

Anna Ivanovna was to be crowned in Moscow in the spring of 1730. Tradition obliged a sovereign entering Moscow for a coronation to spend a week in the village of Vsesviatskoe, situated scarcely two miles from Moscow, in order to prepare for that solemn event by prayer and fasting. Anna Ivanovna reached it on 20 February and took advantage of her stay to ask Elizabeth to call on her. Anna lacked education and was often gross in her tastes, but she was far from being a fool. The knowledge that her young relative had a better right to the throne than she must have made her anxious to discover for herself whether Elizabeth was resentful and likely to become a dangerous rival. Elizabeth's serene, open countenance must have convinced the empress that her fears were groundless. Elizabeth told her frankly of her grievances and of the way in which Menshikov had deprived her of her mother's bequests. Anna Ivanovna was gracious and encouraging; she undertook to right these wrongs but her promise to restore Elizabeth's inheritance was to prove an empty one, and so far as is known the subject was never mentioned again by the two women.

Anna Ivanovna was thirty-seven years old when she became empress of Russia. During the nineteen years of her widowhood she had experienced few joys and Catherine I's refusal to agree to her marriage to Maurice de Saxe had ended her hopes of family happiness. Now that she was empress she was determined to make up for all the fun she had missed in her youth. To please those courtiers who longed to revert to the old, indolent way of life and to see Moscow reinstated as the country's capital she stayed in Moscow for two years, spending much of her time at Ismailovo for lack of a more comfortable residence. Yet it is unlikely that she ever contemplated abandoning St Petersburg and all that it represented. The years she had spent in Mittau had taught her to enjoy western customs and western culture.

Anna Ivanovna had insisted that her lover, Count Biron, come to Russia with her. After her coronation she conferred the Dukedom of Courland upon him, but kept him at her side instead of allowing him to go to Mittau to govern his duchy. Her courtiers soon discovered that Biron was the real power in the land; if he looked displeased, so did the empress; if he seemed happy, so was she. On his advice the empress got rid of the powerful Dolgorukys and Galitzines by charging them with the crime of having debauched the young tsar, thereby fatally undermining his health. They were found guilty and exiled to Siberia. The age of Biron, the Bironovshchina, had set in.

With Biron in constant attendance, Anna Ivanovna launched out on a round of seemingly unending gaieties. Some of her diversions were harmless, legitimate, even beneficial to a society which had but recently adopted the western way of life. Others reflected the coarse and cruel streaks in her nature, and were far from pleasant. The 'ice wedding' which Anna Ivanovna desired in 1739 as a punishment for a Prince Galitzine serves as an example. Displeased by his change of religion, she turned him into a buffoon and ordered him to marry a peasant girl of her choice. She invited representatives of all the country's racial groups to come to the wedding dressing them in their national costumes, and arranged for a two-roomed ice house to be built on the frozen Neva. Its furniture, including the bridal bed, was of ice; so too were the four small cannons firing half-ounce charges of powder as well as the two firing small wooden grenades mounted at its entrance. The newly wedded pair were conveyed to it in a cage borne by an elephant. The three hundred guests from the provinces were mounted in pairs on reindeer, dogs, oxen, goats, camels and other beasts and formed into a procession. The prince and his wife were forced to spend the night in the ice house, while their guests feasted in Biron's Riding School.

When Elizabeth realized that the empress had no intention of fulfilling the promises she had made to her at Vsesviatskoe, she decided that it would be wise for her to withdraw from court life. Anna Ivanovna raised no objections to her desire to live permanently in a wing of Ismailovo, and Elizabeth was able to return there when the coronation festivities were over.

Elizabeth loved Ismailovo and adored the Russian countryside with its primaeval forests and wide expanses. She felt free there. In the evenings she amused herself and her household by organizing amateur theatricals and games of many kinds. She particularly enjoyed the hours she was able to spend in the open air. She was passionately fond of hunting and delighted in expeditions lasting several days. On such occasions she took a tent, often instructing her servants to erect it close to some large country house or attractive village. After the day's sport she enjoyed inviting the local residents to it for a party. Her vivid accounts of the day's events and her successes in hunting such dangerous animals as wolves and hyenas enthralled her guests. When she was not engaged in hunting the Grand Duchess involved herself with the lives of her peasants, encouraging them to breed better cattle and to plant orchards. Though desperately short of funds she helped to finance these ventures as well as to build more and better cottages for them. She delighted in sharing her peasants' rustic amusements, tobogganing or skating with them in the winter months, mushrooming in the late summer and joining in their dances and sing-songs. Nevertheless, hunting remained her favourite occupation. She was a magnificent horsewoman and since her legs were shapely and her figure good she could appear to advantage dressed as a man seated astride a spirited horse. However, she did not neglect her own estate but insisted that it should be well farmed. She was one of the first landowners to sell her surplus sheep and farm produce. Her bailiff was expected to keep detailed records and accounts, and to enter the prices he obtained. Even so, her income remained far from adequate.[12]

It is hardly surprising that Elizabeth should have fallen in love again as she lived this idyllic life. This time she lost her heart to a young sergeant called Alexei Shubin. Like her father before her, Elizabeth set little store by lineage and a great deal by personal merit. She had no hesitations in taking Shubin as a lover, but when Anna Ivanovna heard of her romance she was furious. Forgetting that her own conduct was not beyond reproach the empress banished the young man to Kamchatka and ordered Elizabeth to return to Moscow immediately. Elizabeth was obliged to comply. Outwardly calm, yet inwardly angry and miserable, she installed herself in part of Anna Ivanovna's palace of Annenhof, situated on the banks of the Yauza, and gave vent to her feelings by writing verses in both French and Russian. She started observing the tsaritsa silently, yet very attentively, taking careful note of her behaviour.

There was much for her to record. Anna Ivanovna had become obsessed by the trappings of grandeur and spared no expense to satisfy her longing for them. She had a horror of anything sad or sombre and her hatred of black led her to forbid it being worn in her presence. She instructed her courtiers to dress in brightly coloured stuffs cut on western lines. The first set of liveries which she chose for her servants were in green laced with gold; later she changed them to yellow laced with silver. She drew up precise instructions regarding the clothes her courtiers were to wear on ceremonial occasions, expecting even ambassadors to comply with them. Thus when, in January 1732, the court moved back to St Petersburg, those entitled to assemble on Mondays, Wednesdays and Saturdays in Biron's new, vast, covered riding-school were expected to wear yellow buffalo-hide jerkins embroidered in silver over a blue vest. These regulations made it necessary for courtiers to spend two to three thousand roubles a year on clothes – the equivalent then of five to six hundred pounds. Hence many contracted debts which they were in some cases unable to repay with the result that their heirs were harassed by creditors till they in their turn proceeded to fleece their peasants in order to discharge these loans and pay their way at court.

Although opposed to gambling Anna Ivanovna encouraged it, playing quinze or pharaoh for such huge stakes that it was by no means unusual for twenty thousand roubles to change hands at her court in the course of an evening. She was equally fond of music and capable of appreciating it. She sent to Italy for musicians and often employed them to give court concerts. She also delighted in theatrical performances, using actors brought from Germany and Italy to appear in her favourite German and Italian comedies. She was the first ruler to send to Italy 'for all that is necessary in order to provide these performances' and as a result Russians heard their first opera in 1736. Biron's love of horsemanship was also beneficial to the country, for he imported stallions from Spain, Germany, Naples, Persia, Turkey and Arabia to improve the native breeds. Both he and the empress, incidentally, made attempts to curb drunkenness in the capital.

Although Anna Ivanovna's extravagance proved a financial burden to the country, it was perhaps not quite as harmful as the patronage which, largely as a result of Biron's influence, she made a point of extending to foreigners, and more particularly to those of German birth. The latter poured into Russia in an unending stream. They were bent on making their fortunes there. In contrast to Peter the Great who had seldom appointed foreigners to the highest office, Anna Ivanovna assigned them to key posts in every walk of life. Men such as Baron Brevern, Baron Mengden, the Löwenwolde brothers and General Manstein were among those who made spectacular careers. As their numbers increased so did Russia's innate distrust of them.

When the court moved to St Petersburg in 1732 Elizabeth was able to return to her old apartments in the Summer Palace. It may have been due to her frankly voiced disapproval of Germans being allowed to hold key posts in the administration and the army that Anna Ivanovna started to mistrust her. Whatever the cause, she now took steps to have the princess watched, ordering her spies to report personally on all Elizabeth's activities. Courtiers were quick to notice the change in the empress's attitude and many dared openly to slight the Grand Duchess. Biron was among the very few who continued to treat Elizabeth with consideration and courtesy. Elizabeth ignored the insults and made a point of attending all court functions looking gay and serene. But her good temper broke down at all attempts to find her a husband. The names of fresh suitors were being constantly submitted to her. She would consider none of them, for soon after the court's return to St Petersburg, sometime, it is thought, towards the end of 1731, Elizabeth met the man whom she was first to love passionately and then to remain permanently attached to.

Like her father before her, Elizabeth was to find personal happiness with a companion of quite humble origin. Known to begin with as Alexei Razum, he was born into a Cossack household on 17 March 1709. At best his father may have been a smallholder; his mother kept an inn at Lemeshi, a village situated on the post road from Kozolets to Chernigov. When he was old enough for the purpose Alexei became the village shepherd. He grew to be an exceptionally handsome lad, one universally liked for his kindliness and good nature. Admiration for his eminent good sense was acknowledged by a pun: he was spoken of as Razumovsky – The Man of Reason – which came to serve as his surname. Alexei was attracted by books, and the priest of Tchemer, a neighbouring townlet, secretly taught him to read. Alexei's father, a fierce man given to drunkenness, was infuriated by his son's scholarly tastes. One day he gave him such a severe beating as a punishment for his addiction to reading that Alexei fled his home and went to live with his teacher, the priest. The latter discovered that his pupil possessed a singularly beautiful singing voice. According to the French ambassador, the Marquis de la Chétardie, it resembled that of the popular French court singer Benoist. Razumovsky was to owe his good fortune to the sweetness of his voice, for the priest made him sing in his church choir. One day a Colonel Vishnevsky spent a night at Tchemer when travelling back to St Petersburg from Hungary with a consignment of Tokay for Anna Ivanovna. On hearing Alexei sing he decided to take the youth to St Petersburg with him to become a chorister in the Imperial chapel. Elizabeth must have heard him sing there in 1731 or 1732. She fell in love with him and knew no peace till she had obtained the empress's permission to attach Razumovsky to her household. He entered it in the capacity of major domo. There his instinctive understanding of human nature, his sensitivity and tact won him the affection and devotion of her staff. Writing of him and his younger brother Kyril many years later the empress Catherine II asserted 'she knew no other family enjoying the sovereign's favours to a like degree, who were so much loved by so many people as the two brothers'.[13]

Elizabeth's beauty, obvious happiness and increasing popularity roused Anna Ivanovna's jealousy, and her refusal to marry angered her. These feelings were played upon by her sister, Catherine, Duchess of Mecklenburg, who had been begging the empress ever since her coronation to proclaim her daughter Catherine Elizabeth Christina her heir and to arrange for the girl to be fittingly educated. Christina was now fifteen. Encouraged by Ostermann, Anna Ivanovna arranged for her to become a member of the Orthodox Church under the name of Anna Leopoldovna and, at her mother's death a month later, the empress provided the girl with a household of her own and installed her in a mansion situated close to her own palace. Observers rightly concluded that the empress would in due course appoint her niece her heir.

Once again there is no record of Elizabeth's reaction to the ceding of her right to the throne to the empress's niece. However, when the Austrian ambassador decided that the moment had come to bring Don Manuel of Portugal to St Petersburg as a suitor for Elizabeth's hand or, failing hers, for Anna Leopoldovna's, both young women found Don Manuel so unprepossessing that they firmly refused to consider him as a prospective husband. In fact, Anna Leopoldovna had already fallen deeply in love with the thirty-one-year-old Count Linar, Saxon ambassador to the Russian court. To begin with no one attached much importance to her feelings, dismissing them as a youthful infatuation, but when the young girl refused to consider Prussia's suggestion that she should marry Prince Anton Ulrich of Brunswick Bevern, the situation was seen in a new light. The prince was a cousin of Marie Theresa of Austria, and that sufficed to win him Ostermann's support. Anna Leopoldovna's obstinate refusal to marry Anton Ulrich had at first surprised Ostermann and the empress. They then discovered that Anna Leopoldovna's French governess, Madame D'Anderkass, had encouraged her romance with Linar and had enabled them to carry it further than was desirable. Though it was too late to undo the harm which had been done, Madame D'Anderkass was dismissed and expelled from Russia and attempts made to obtain Linar's recall. It only remained to hope that Anna Leopoldovna would soon forget him. Biron thought of achieving this by persuading Anna Ivanovna to allow the girl to marry his own son, but the empress had decided in favour of Anton Ulrich. She refused to listen to her niece's objections and imposed a strict routine upon her, allowing her to appear at court only on state occasions. As a result Anna Leopoldovna became dependent upon her lady-in-waiting, young Julie Mengden, and soon the two girls became devoted to each other.

In her determination to get her own way and in her anxiety not to offend the emperor of Austria, Anna Ivanovna invited Anton Ulrich to visit her. Anna Leopoldovna was changing from a lively, engaging and not unattractive child into a plain, silent, almost glum young woman. She was bitterly resentful of her aunt's decision to marry her to a prince whom she found uncongenial. In contrast Elizabeth appeared happy and her beauty seemed to increase. Both the empress and her niece were irritated to find that at every gathering it was Elizabeth, not her younger rival, who became the focus of admiration and attention. Even the Swedish officers who had been captured when the Russians defeated the Poles at Danzig, and who were being treated as distinguished guests rather than as prisoners of war, did not hesitate openly to proclaim Elizabeth the most beautiful and delightful lady at court. Her love of France had not suffered from the failure of the plan that she should marry a Frenchman. Her mastery of the French language helped her to become the centre of attraction at gatherings which included an increasing number of foreigners and also of Russians who had been abroad, and who had made a point of visiting Paris and seeing Versailles.

Although Anna Ivanovna's thoughts were largely centred on amusements and on finding husbands for both Grand Duchesses, she had many pressing state affairs to deal with. Much though she relied on Ostermann's help and advice, she remained wholly responsible for all the decisions taken. Her reign was marred by a series of peasant revolts and political conspiracies which turned public opinion against her, while the diplomatic problems confronting her became increasingly complex and difficult to handle. Between 1733 and 1735 the need to find a suitable heir for the Polish throne seemed especially important. The choice was rendered all the more difficult because Britain, France, Austria, Russia and even Prussia were concerned in the outcome, since each believed that her country's security depended on it. The interests of each conflicted with those of the others. Each determined to ensure her candidate's success.

Russians thought that it would be to their advantage if the Polish throne passed either to a ruler well disposed towards them or to so weak a man that they would be able to exert their influence over Poland and Courland. Austria, on the other hand, needed Poland to be strong enough to act as a buffer against the Turks. France, naturally enough, wanted Stanislas

Leczinsky, Louis xv's father-in-law, to regain his throne, but Austria and Britain favoured a Bourbon candidate and would not agree to this. While Austria and Russia were hesitating over the choice of Augustus's successor, France engineered the election of her candidate. By then, however, Anna Ivanovna had pledged her support to Augustus's son – another Augustus – and she therefore refused to recognize Stanislas Leczinsky as king. To add force to her words she sent an army to Poland to depose him. France retaliated by recalling her ambassador to Russia. Undeterred, the Russian troops pressed on to Warsaw. Leczinsky retreated to Danzig in what was more of a flight than an organized withdrawal. Russia's Field Marshal Münnich pursued him with an army of twenty thousand men and besieged the town. A French squadron hurried to Leczinsky's relief, but Münnich succeeded in cutting the citadel off from the sea. On 9 July 1734 he defeated the joint Franco-Swedish attack. Though Münnich could not prevent Leczinsky from escaping and eventually making his way to France, Danzig capitulated and Augustus iii succeeded his father as Elector of Saxony and King of Poland, while the Russian army pressed on towards the Rhine under Lacy's command.

The Polish question was becoming increasingly complicated by the political changes resulting from the War of the Spanish Succession. In 1726, when it still seemed possible that Elizabeth might marry a French prince of royal blood, the pattern of international relations built up in Europe over recent decades, though already severely impaired, still held together. Hence French diplomats still strove to encircle Russia by a band of unfriendly nations, using Constantinople as the centre from which to do so. Russia's short-term treaty of alliance with Austria, contracted in 1726, had to some extent been directed against Turkey. In 1737 Austria proposed the renewal of the treaty and Ostermann had pressed Anna Ivanovna to agree to this. To include Denmark in the treaty, the Emperor of Austria acted as mediator between Russia and Denmark and eventually succeeded in persuading Russia and Holstein to agree to Denmark's retention of Schleswig in return for the payment of a large indemnity to the Duke of Holstein. However, there was no resulting change in the political outlook.

Though Elizabeth was happy in her love for Razumovsky, she felt vexed to find, in the spring of 1738, that the empress had decided, with Ostermann's encouragement, that her niece was to marry Anton Ulrich. The engagement was made official in June and the marriage announced for 3 July of the following year. Elizabeth naturally attended the reception held in honour of the newly engaged couple. Her appearance invited comparison with that of the unattractive duke and his plain, inert, obviously unhappy bride to be. Even Anna Ivanovna noticed the difference and became increasingly suspicious of Elizabeth. She gave orders for ever closer watch to be kept on her movements, but Elizabeth continued to go about as much as ever, and wherever she went gained general admiration. The carefree months she had spent at Ismailovo hunting and sharing in the villagers occupations had given her insight into the lives of the poor. On coming to live in St Petersburg she had made a point of getting to know the men serving in the Guards regiments stationed in the capital. She had stood godmother to many of their children and it was by no means unusual to see a couple of guardsmen jump on to the runners of her sledge as she drove through the town, and lean over her shoulders the better to talk to her or to find them being shown into her drawing room, to be welcomed as warmly there as more illustrious guests. Had Elizabeth an ulterior motive for cultivating their friendship? Many think so, but there is no evidence to support their case. Anna Ivanovna appeared to be in perfect health and there was no reason for thinking that she would not live to reach old age. Elizabeth had readily accepted her as her sovereign because Anna Ivanovna had been constitutionally elected tsaritsa; the idea of dislodging her from the throne does not seem to have occurred to Elizabeth. She was spontaneous, generous and hospitable by nature; she loved people and she adored being surrounded by those who admired her. She was probably acting in good faith when befriending the soldiers but, in the absence of contrary evidence, all that can be said was that she was constantly to be seen in the streets of St Petersburg, and that the more she moved about them, the more popular she became.

Anna Leopoldovna's wedding failed to stimulate the people's imagination. At the time everyone's thoughts were turned towards the Turkish front where the campaign had entered a decisive phase. The war which had started so brilliantly for Russia with Münnich's troops capturing the fortresses of Azov and Ochakov had become bogged down. It was not until the spring of 1739 that the badly equipped and provisioned army had managed to capture the key fortress of Chotin and the town of Jassy. These victories were hailed as triumphs by the Russians, perhaps deservedly so since they had been won from the strongest military power of the day. As such they seemed to herald the end of the age-old danger of Tartar incursions. The defeated Turks retreated across the Danube, the Moldavians asked to be incorporated into Russia and the British started to regret that in 1734 they had refused to consider a Russian alliance. Austria meanwhile chose flagrantly to disregard her treaty obligations to Russia, startling the Russians by opening separate peace negotiations with the Turks. Her action was based on the sudden fear that if Russia were able to press her advance she might end by becoming Austria's close – and unwelcome – neighbour. Russia had lost a hundred thousand men in the war and was in no position to continue fighting the Turks unaided. Now, with victory so close, Austria's action was to deprive the Russians of all their conquests and all they had hoped to obtain at the conference table, first and foremost of the right to maintain a navy in the Black Sea.

Russia had scored a point in having the candidate of her choice elected to the Polish throne, but it was France, together with Russia's faint-hearted ally Austria, who was to emerge victorious at the Belgrade peace talks. However, the conflict did not end there. It was resumed in diplomatic circles, mainly at the Russian court, but also at the court of Turkey and in the major European capitals. Louis xv entrusted Baron Jacques Joachim Trotti de la Chétardie with the task of putting his policy into effect in St Petersburg. The ambassador set out for his new post in the spring of 1739. He was accompanied by twelve secretaries, eight chaplains, fifty liveried servants, five cooks who were to assist Bariotte (a lesser master than his distinguished colleague Duval, but nevertheless a superb chef). De la Chétardie's luggage included a hundred thousand bottles of choice wines and so overall it is hardly surprising that he made slow progress. However, he eventually arrived in St Petersburg and a few days later a court carriage called for him and drove him to his audience with the tsaritsa. She received him with marked affability yet, on leaving her presence, the ambassador called on Elizabeth before paying his respects to Anna Leopoldovna. When reprimanded by Ostermann he stoutly maintained that he had acted according to etiquette since the Princess Elizabeth's imperial lineage gave her precedence over the Grand Duchess Anna Leopoldovna.

Anna Ivanovna had not been well during the winter of 1738–9. Was de la Chétardie aware of it? Had he considered the possibility of her early death or wondered whether the future might not lie with Elizabeth? Such thoughts would have been no more than natural, for during the decade which followed Peter the Great's death many observers thought that the throne was so unstable that a palace revolution might at any moment dislodge its holder. Many also believed that every political decision taken by Anna Ivanovna's advisers could be reversed at her whim.

De la Chétardie may well have decided to win Elizabeth's friendship in order to use it to further French interests. If so, his task was to prove easy, for both he and the Grand Duchess took an instant liking to each other. Indeed, there was much in de la Chétardie's character to appeal to Elizabeth. Though he was distrusted and disliked by his British colleagues, de la Chétardie was very much a man of the world, an experienced courtier and an accomplished diplomat. He could fascinate people by his wit, intelligence and taste.

On 24 August 1740 Anna Leopoldovna gave birth to a son. The empress was so delighted that the child was a boy that she could think of little else. She insisted that the boy be called Ivan after her father and gave orders for him to be moved from his parent's residence to her own, where he was to have apartments adjacent to hers to enable her to keep constant watch over him. Society was shocked by this decision. Elizabeth said nothing, but time was to reveal that she had taken careful note of it. Scarcely a month later Anna Ivanovna had a stroke. She made a quick recovery, but her illness had made her fear for the future. Acting hurriedly she proclaimed the baby her heir in place of his mother, whom she appointed regent if the boy were to inherit the crown while still a minor. Manstein[14] believed that Field Marshal Münnich was responsible for these decisions and also for insisting that the baby's parents and Elizabeth should in the presence of the empress swear allegiance to the child immediately. This may well have been the case since Münnich was probably anxious to express his gratitude to the empress for his appointment as Governor General of St Petersburg and his promotion from general to field marshal. Anna Ivanovna and Münnich had become real friends, for the empress had never been able to resist his wit and his persuasive powers; she found such pleasure in his company that Biron and Ostermann feared leaving them alone together. If it was indeed Münnich who had on this occasion encouraged the empress to act according to her inclinations, it was Ostermann who actually summoned the child's parents, the Grand Duchess Elizabeth and the senior officers of the realm to swear the desired oath.[15] Anna Leopoldovna was unable to conceal her disappointment at finding herself supplanted by her son.

On 16 October Anna Ivanovna had a second stroke. This time her physicians pronounced her condition hopeless. According to Manstein[16] Biron hurried to her bedside and would not move from it until he had persuaded her to revoke the appointment of Anna Leopoldovna as regent in order to nominate him to that exalted post. His request had received the backing of Ostermann, Münnich and Alexei Bestuzhev, all of whom knew themselves to be disliked by Anna Leopoldovna. By the time that the empress had agreed to their entreaties she was no longer able to sign the statement which had been hurriedly taken down. She died on 26 October aged forty-seven.

As soon as the empress's heart had stopped beating Biron insisted that Anna Leopoldovna, Anton Ulrich and Elizabeth should once again swear allegiance to the infant Tsar Ivan. On the following day the late empress's unsigned will and last testament were read out to the nobles who had been summoned to the Summer Palace for that purpose by Ostermann. They were dismayed to learn that the throne had passed to a baby, that if he died without issue he was to be succeeded by any brothers he might have in their order of seniority and that Biron was to be regent during his minority. The nation as a whole was equally perturbed by the news, for all realized that if Anna Ivanovna's wishes were carried out Russia would come under the rule of German princes of the houses of Mecklenburg and Brunswick. The prospect was an odious one, yet the alternative was hardly better since the election of a sovereign would inevitably result in court intrigues and encourage the Guards regiments to riot in order to place the candidate of their choice on the throne.

3

The Great Decision

The nation swore allegiance to the infant Tsar Ivan – the sixth ruler of that name though only the third to hold the title of tsar – with resentment and dread. Fears were quickly justified, for within a few hours Biron had set his spies to work, to eavesdrop on conversations, to report on the growing volume of criticisms directed against him in his capacity of regent and to record the anger felt by Anna Leopoldovna and her husband at having been set aside. When the grand ducal couple ventured to question the validity of Anna Ivanovna's will on the grounds that the dying woman had been too weak to sign it, Biron did not scruple to silence them with the threat of exile. Biron was not wholly convinced that he was in any danger, but the fear of being deposed seems to have haunted him often. He embarked on a reign of terror in which anyone suspected of disloyalty was liable to find himself arrested and harshly dealt with. Not even Anton Ulrich escaped Biron's vigilance; he had to submit to a gruelling examination and, though granted a liberal income, was obliged to resign from the army and to live with his family in complete seclusion. On the other hand Biron endeavoured to retain Elizabeth's regard, largely because he was planning to marry her to his eldest son whilst at the same time arranging for his daughter to marry the young Duke of Holstein. Ignoring the fact that, in the natural order of things, the infant tsar should outlive both Elizabeth and the Grand Duke, Biron hoped by these moves to ensure that the crown remained within his own family. Foreign envoys to Russia believed that Biron even settled Elizabeth's debts for her.[1] Although Elizabeth had no intention of marrying young Biron or any other politically desirable suitor, she always remained grateful to the regent for the consideration with which he treated her.

The dislike which Anna Leopoldovna had always felt for Biron flared into hatred now that her own fate and that of her family had come to depend on his good will. General Münnich detested him likewise, although he concealed his feelings during Anna Ivanovna's reign. He had even persuaded Anna to nominate Biron regent in the mistaken belief that the favourite would be satisfied with the trappings of his office and willingly delegate the task of governing Russia to others. Indeed, Münnich had felt so certain of this that he had already put out feelers for the Hospodarship of Moldavia and the Dukedom of the Ukraine, even for the Dukedom of Courland, which he assumed that the regent would gladly confer on him.[2]

Münnich was not the only courtier to feel jealous of Biron. Anna Ivanovna's Master of the Horse, Count Löwenwolde, and especially Ostermann coveted his position. In that respect at any rate, all three men were allies and each could rely on the other's support. In the space of only three weeks Münnich felt himself to be in a sufficiently strong position to belittle Biron in Anna Leopoldovna's eyes. By 7 November he was convinced that she would welcome the regent's removal from office. On the evening of that day he therefore summoned Lieutenant-Colonel Manstein and instructed him to arrest Biron on a charge of conspiring to usurp the throne. Manstein was yet another German who had come to Russia in search of fame and wealth. He had done well in the Russian army and his services there had been rewarded at short and regular intervals by promotions to the rank which he now held.

Manstein had no hesitation in carrying out Münnich's orders. He selected forty grenadiers from those doing guard duty in the Winter Palace and marched them to the Summer Palace where Biron had installed himself. It was guarded that night by men from Münnich's regiment of the Preobrazhensky Guards. Entering the palace he led his unit to Biron's bedroom. Though Biron had felt unaccountably depressed earlier in the evening he had had no suspicion of what lay in store for him and was sleeping peacefully. Manstein woke him, charged him with his offence and placed him under arrest. As soon as Biron had dressed he was transferred under escort to the Winter Palace, while Manstein hurried to the house of Biron's brother-in-law, Gustavus, colonel of the Izmailovsky Guards. He was much loved by his men, but Manstein's action was so unexpected that he was able to arrest Gustavus before the Izmailovtzy could intervene.[3] Manstein proceeded next to the house of Alexei Bestuzhev, Biron's henchman in the Ministry for Foreign Affairs, to apprehend him. All those arrested that night were taken to the Winter Palace. They were joined there by the nation's senior officials, all of whom had been hastily summoned from their beds. Acting in the name of the infant Tsar Ivan, Anna Leopoldovna presented herself to them as regent. She invested herself with the title of Serene Imperial Highness and announced her intention of governing Russia during her son's minority. The traditional *Te Deum* was then sung and the oath of allegiance administered. A palace revolution had been quietly accomplished. Anna Leopoldovna celebrated the occasion by appointing her husband Commander-in-Chief of the army; Münnich became her chief minister, while Ostermann remained in charge of foreign affairs. The new regent also issued instructions for the debts of all noblemen to be settled by the crown. When morning broke the capital's inhabitants learnt that their future was to be moulded by new hands.

To begin with, the new regent was considered more acceptable than the old one. Russians had grown accustomed to being governed by a woman so that it seemed but right that the tsar's mother should rule on behalf of her son. Yet, at court, the change was providing courtiers with an opportunity for jockeying for advancement. Ostermann concentrated on supplanting Münnich – an ambition which he achieved within three months by convincing Anna Leopoldovna that the general was in the pay of the Elector of Saxony; ignoring the fact that she owed her position of regent to Münnich, Anna Leopoldovna divested him of all his dignities and duties. Münnich realized that he was lucky to escape with his freedom of movement and his material possessions unaffected, even though his wife and children did not share his relief and felt deeply aggrieved.

Saxony's decision to re-appoint Count Linar as envoy to Russia was received with anxiety in St Petersburg, and rightly so since, at her first sight of him, Anna Leopoldovna's love for him revived. This time she was determined to express it. When Linar was with her she firmly refused her husband entry to her apartments, a situation which Anton Ulrich rebelled against. This passion for Linar led to frequent quarrels between husband and wife. Few courtiers were genuinely attached to Anna Leopoldovna. The majority were angry to find that there was once again a powerful, interfering foreigner at court whose every wish received the regent's approval. They had at first assumed that the sentence of exile which had been passed on Biron and his entire family marked the end of Russia's domination by foreigners. It was with bitterness that they realized their mistake. Officers in the crack Preobrazhensky, Semenovsky and Izmailovsky regiments of the Guards made little effort to conceal their disappointment and disapproval. However, Anna Leopoldovna, happy perhaps for the first time in her life, paid scant attention to them.

She appointed Count Linar a Gentleman of the Bedchamber; she let herself savour her good fortune to the full, preferring to do so in the presence of only a small circle of intimates. She therefore remained unaware of the growing hostility at home and of the new political currents developing in a Europe torn by bitter dissensions and conflicting interests.

The death of Charles vi of Austria on 20 October 1740, just four days after Anna Ivanovna's (allowing for the difference in calendar), had disrupted the old, traditional system of European alliances and endangered Austria's future. Having no son to succeed him, the emperor had tried to secure the throne for his daughter Marie Theresa by persuading Britain and Holland to recognize the indivisibility of his kingdom under her rule in an agreement known as the Pragmatic Sanction. Spain subscribed to it and so too did the Scandinavian countries, but at Charles vi's death none of the signatory powers felt inclined to adhere to what now seemed an unprofitable undertaking. The seizure of Naples and Sicily by Don Carlos of Parma and Piacenza by the Hapsburgs, and of Lorraine by France encouraged Spain to set her sights on Hungary. Similarly Frederick of Prussia now hoped to gain Silesia and Louis of France dreamt of weakening Austria by supporting the claims to the Austrian throne put forward by the Elector of Bavaria and the Elector of Saxony, both of whom were married to nieces of Charles v.

Russia had also undertaken to abide by the Pragmatic Sanction, but Anna Ivanovna's sudden death raised doubts in Europe about Russia's intentions. Early in December, when the situation was still fluid, Frederick of Prussia stole a march on Europe by invading Silesia without first declaring war on Austria, and entrenched himself there. His action unleashed the War of the Austrian Succession, a conflict which was to divide the great European powers for fifteen years and eventually propelled them into the Seven Years War. Frederick's invasion of Silesia stunned Europe. It placed Russia in a particularly awkward position since, in accordance with Ostermann's advice,[4] Anna Ivanovna had promised to assist Austria if she were ever attacked. At that time the clause was unlikely to antagonize the French, but in May 1741 France had signed with Bavaria an agreement at Nymphenburg which was directed against Austria and which was soon to include Saxony, Spain and Sardinia.

It was fortunate for Anna Leopoldovna that she was on good terms with Elizabeth during the difficult start to her regency. Although Elizabeth had lost a valuable protector in Biron, she did not try to weaken the new regent's position nor did she alter her way of life. She was still often seen in the streets of St Petersburg, and went for frequent walks in the grounds of the Preobrazhensky Guards' barracks close to the palace which her father had built for her in 1720 at Smolny.[5] Finch was perhaps the most observant of the undistinguished diplomats who succeeded each other as British envoys to Russia in Elizabeth's lifetime. In a despatch dated June 1741[6] he tried to assess the internal situation there and the stability of Anna Leopoldovna's position. Whereas Frederick of Prussia[7] angrily dubbed the regent as 'capricious and unkind' and Elizabeth as 'secretive but amenable; both loathing work, neither being fitted for governing' and Manstein[8] considered Anna Leopoldovna 'extremely capricious, passionate, indolent, hating work, lacking the necessary gifts for governing so great an empire in a time of trouble and difficulty', Finch described the regent in his despatch as 'handsome with a pretty figure with a good shape. She spoke with feeling and had always a melancholy and rather fretful air'; Elizabeth, on the other hand, was

exceedingly obliging and affable, and in consequence much personally beloved and extremely popular. She has also the additional advantage of being the daughter of Peter I, who though he was more feared than any former prince of this century was at the same time more beloved also. The last appeared in a most memorable manner at his funeral and the first most necessarily real at the end. This love certainly descends to his posterity and gives a general bent to the minds of the common people and of the soldiery too, in their favour a remarkable instance of which there was among the last when the Duke of Courland [Biron] was seized and the Grand Duchess was declared regent, for when three regiments of the Guards were assembled and marched to the palace a general notion prevailed with strong appearance of all general satisfaction that they were going hither in favour of their Matushka Elizaveta Petrovna. The same spirit appeared in the garrison regiment in the island called Wassili Ostrov, which makes part of the town, and at Cronstadt; at both which places a mutiny was feared for they called out aloud, would nobody act themselves at their head in favour of their Matushka Elizabeth.

Elizabeth's French doctor, Armand Lestocq, had wanted Elizabeth to play on her popularity by making a bid for the throne. According to Manstein[9] the doctor had hurried to her bedroom; she was asleep but

waking her, he pressed her greatly to assemble the Guards, show herself to the people, and going directly to the Senate assert her right to the crown. But she could not be prevailed upon to stir out of her room. . . . Just then she preferred her amusement to the glory of reigning, and very certain it is that if she had not been molested in the reign of Queen Anna she would have continued to prefer the tranquillity of a private life to the burden of a crown.

Many years later, when empress of Russia, Elizabeth replied to a question of General Keith by frankly saying, 'I am very glad that I did not [assert my right to the throne earlier]; I was too young and my people would never have borne with me.'

Manstein states that,[10] to begin with, Anna Leopoldovna and Elizabeth 'visited each other without acrimony and lived on terms of familiarity'. But soon 'the princess Elizabeth became more reserved and no longer went to the Grand Duchess unless upon days of ceremony or on such occasions as she could not well avoid paying her visits'. Elizabeth's displeasure was aggravated by Anna Leopoldovna's desire that she should marry the regent's brother-in-law, Prince Ludwig of Brunswick. Elizabeth refused to consider the idea; even so, Anna Leopoldovna invited the prince to Russia with the intention of making him Duke of Courland.

The first of Finch's despatches that mention Elizabeth is dated 14 February 1741. It makes it clear that the pleasant relationship which had existed between the regent and the Grand Duchess had already begun to deteriorate. The reference takes the form of a postscript in which Finch reported that 'the Princess Elizabeth was this afternoon to the Great Duchess on a visit. Her Highness said to me that she believed I had a rendezvous with the princess because she was there the last time when I had the honour to play [cards] with the regent for the first time.'[11] Anna Leopoldovna was not given to joking and Finch was wise to attach some importance to her remark for it revealed the distrust which the regent had begun to feel in Elizabeth. Had she also begun to fear her? If so, Anna Leopoldovna concealed her apprehension even from herself, for although she gave orders for Elizabeth to be more closely spied on than ever, she yet disregarded the warnings of Linar, of her ministers and her secret agents, all of whom advised her to take note of Elizabeth's popularity.

Throughout the remainder of Elizabeth's life the Russian court was to be the setting for the most ruthless, shameless and persistent scheming by foreign envoys to be met with in the annals of eighteenth-century diplomacy. Versailles was generally responsible for the efforts made by the diplomats to interfere in Russia's internal affairs, for French policy required a weak yet friendly Russia. Ignoring the insulting manner in which his government had handled the Russian suggestion of a French bridegroom for Elizabeth, Louis determined to win Russia's friendship whilst setting

6. Portrait of the tsarevna Elizabeth in the guise of a little Venus. Painted by Caravaque when she was seven years old.

7. Portrait of the tsarevna Elizabeth as a young girl, painted by Ivan Nikitin, one of the most talented of Peter the Great's 'fledgelings', 1716.

8. Portrait by an unknown artist of Peter II the boy tsar.

9. Count Ostermann, tutor to Peter II, civil servant and Minister for Foreign Affairs, by an unknown artist.

his allies against her. He therefore instructed de la Chétardie to do every-thing in his power to bring Elizabeth to the throne, for he was convinced that she would always act in accordance with her well known love of France.

De la Chétardie was conceited, frivolous, mischievous, and foolish. In a court turned almost entirely towards Germany he found that few oppor-tunities existed for furthering France's interests. He appears to have concluded quite soon after his arrival that Elizabeth's friends would eventually establish her on the throne and he seems to have set himself deliberately to vex Anna Leopoldovna, doing so even at the cost of his own acceptance at court. He refused to present the letters accrediting him to his post to any one other than the two-year-old tsar. The foolish point of etiquette on which he justified his conduct gave rise to endless discussions. While they lasted de la Chétardie was forbidden to appear at court even though it was the only place where he could meet Elizabeth without arousing suspicion. In April, when still forbidden to court, de la Chétardie withdrew to a house on the outskirts of the capital that overlooks the Neva, and lived there in seclusion.[12] Cut off from court circles he found that he needed a trustworthy person to act as messenger between Elizabeth and himself. He found the ideal go-between in Armand Lestocq, the gay and gallant doctor. Nevertheless, in May Elizabeth felt that they should meet; after much thought she decided to take advantage of the light nights, when the sun seems scarcely to set, to sail down the Neva, when she planned to attract de la Chétardie's attention by blowing her hunting horn as she passed his villa, and then to send a boat to bring him aboard. The plan miscarried either because de la Chétardie did not hear the sounds of the horn or did not appreciate their importance.

Elizabeth's intimate circle of friends consisted of Lestocq, her German music master Schwartz, who often acted as her secretary, Mikhail Vorontzov, Alexei Razumovsky and Peter and Alexander Shuvalov. She was more closely watched than ever before, but continued to appear in public just as often. Nevertheless for the first time in her life she often seemed unsettled and dissatisfied. There is no evidence to show that she had by then already begun discussing the possibility of seizing the throne with de la Chétardie, though she had probably done so by June, when Lestocq was at last able to arrange for them to meet in private. The ambassador hastened to inform Versailles that 'in her capacity of daughter of Peter the Great she believes that she will be acting in accordance with her father's wishes in placing her trust in France's friendship and in turning

C

to France for aid in claiming her legal rights'.[13] Though de la Chétardie therefore asked Versailles for funds with which to win supporters to her cause, he gave his government no hint of Elizabeth's popularity with the regiments of the Guards and the inhabitants of St Petersburg. Foreign observers were subsequently inclined to consider Lestocq chiefly responsible for Elizabeth's bid for power, with Schwartz acting as no more than the latter's lieutenant and de la Chétardie as his banker. De la Chétardie and Lestocq undoubtedly spurred Elizabeth to action, but there is as yet no evidence to prove that the Russians who carried Elizabeth to power had been bribed to do so by the French. Finch's reference in his June despatch to Elizabeth's wide popularity shows that there was little need for bribery. Also, though the Russian court was the most extravagant and luxurious in Europe, the French ambassador's way of life was a source of constant comment there. It seems probable that de la Chétardie was personally short of money, but wished to conceal his financial difficulties from his government and continue to live in great style.

If de la Chétardie did indeed use the funds sent to him from France to bribe Elizabeth's supporters it seems probable that most of the money strayed into Lestocq's pocket. He was not a man of high principles and had paid for this failing in the past. Peter the Great had banished him to Kazan for a time, primarily for seducing a nobleman's daughter. Both Frenchmen were too wily to keep accounts and there are no records to show how de la Chétardie spent the considerable sums which reached him from Versailles. Manstein's statement[14] that he supplied Elizabeth with funds with which to form a party seem no more accurate than his unfounded assertion that she entered into correspondence with the Swedish authorities to secure their help in winning the throne. Versailles was misinformed on this point by de la Chétardie, and unintentionally misled Sweden into believing that Elizabeth was ready to restore her father's Finnish conquests to Sweden if the latter attacked Russia for the purpose of placing her on the throne. De la Chétardie had more than once assured both his own government and that of Sweden that Elizabeth would regard a Swedish attack on Russia helpful to her cause. Though Elizabeth was later to admit that she had known France was pressing Sweden to attack Russia in order to undermine Anna Leopoldovna's position, she steadily denied having been told that the price demanded by Sweden for doing so was the return to her of Peter the Great's Finnish conquests. This assertion is borne out by de la Chétardie's efforts throughout July and August to persuade Elizabeth to give him what amounted to no more than a written expression of her good feelings towards Sweden, a harmless request which she nevertheless refused.

Was Finch aware of de la Chétardie's hopes? In a secret despatch dated June 1741[15] he expressed the opinion that 'a revolution can be thought of now or even certainly foreseen at a distance', yet he felt that Elizabeth's chances of becoming empress were of the slenderest for, 'if she married there was little probability of her having children on account of her fatness'. This is the first indication that Elizabeth had already by then put on much weight. However, Finch believed that 'her popularity would be greatly serviceable to her nephew, the Duke of Holstein, who at the same time is prior to herself in the natural order of succession, he being the son of her elder sister, and it would appear that Her Highness herself is sensible of this since immediately upon the demise of the late tsar she hung her nephew's picture in her apartment and kept it there publicly during the late Duke of Courland's regency, though immediately after the present (regency) was settled, she took it down again'. The fact that Finch thought it necessary to make these observations is a clear indication of his doubts in the stability of Anna Leopoldovna's rule, but his despatch is also important because of the light which it throws on Elizabeth's character. She has been much maligned by historians, who have tended to stress her failings at the expense of her qualities. Thus Kluchevsky dubbed her 'a clever and kind but disordered and wilful madam' and took no account of her courage. Finch's remark indicates that she was brave morally as well as physically for she risked alienating Biron by displaying the portrait of the member of the imperial family whose claim to the throne was greater than that of Tsar Ivan; the consequences for doing so might well have been very serious. Finch's statement also indicates that Elizabeth agreed with popular opinion in thinking that Tsar Ivan's mother was the right person to act as regent during his minority and suggests that, at any rate during the summer of 1741, she had no intention of claiming the throne for herself, even of challenging Anna Leopoldovna's authority.

Elizabeth's feelings towards the regent hardened in July when Prince Ludwig of Brunswick arrived in St Petersburg to receive the Dukedom of Courland and formally to ask for her hand. The proposal was repugnant to her, but although she consistently refused his offer the prince renewed it more than once. So too did the twenty-year-old Prince de Conti – with similar results. Fortunately her mind was distracted several days later by the arrival in St Petersburg of the Turkish ambassador with a vast, picturesquely attired retinue. At the peace talks which had recently been held in

Constantinople much time had been spent in defining the honours to be paid to the ambassadors of both countries in their respective posts. The Russians had insisted on their representative to the Porte being treated as the equal of Austria's; in return the sultan's envoy was to be paid similar honours in the Russian capital. The Turkish ambassador was the first of the diplomats to reach his post after this agreement had been concluded and particular care was therefore taken in St Petersburg to implement it. His arrival in the capital attracted huge crowds. They were enchanted by the spectacle presented by the magnificently attired ambassador, riding a splendidly caparisoned horse and accompanied by a large colourful retinue of his own, and a Russian guard of honour.

A few days later Petersburgians were entertained by an even more enthralling spectacle. On 30 July Nadir Shah's brother, the Master of his horse, entered St Petersburg as his sovereign's envoy. He too came on horseback, but he was accompanied by two thousand mounted retainers and sixteen elephants laden with the Shah's presents. His arrival had been timed for the previous year, but the Shah's plan had miscarried because the envoy advanced towards the Russian border unannounced, yet at the head of sixteen thousand followers equipped with twenty cannons. News of the approach of so considerable a body of armed men was sent to St Petersburg, where it was thought to herald an invasion. Count Apraxin, the commander of sixteen regiments stationed near Astrakhan was hurriedly ordered to investigate. The two forces met on the banks of the river Kizlar and it was fortunate that Apraxin asked the Persians to account for their presence there before engaging them in battle. He was astonished to hear that Nadir Shah, wishing the Grand Duchess Elizabeth of Russia to marry his son,[16] had assembled the embassy which Apraxin saw drawn up before him for the purpose of discussing the matter with the ruler of Russia. Acting with considerable presence of mind, Apraxin convinced the shah's envoy that a desert separated Astrakhan from Moscow and that the journey across it was fraught with such difficulties that the Russians could not undertake to supply provisions and lodgings for an embassy more than two thousand strong. Fourteen thousand Persians and all twenty cannon had accordingly remained in Persia while the envoy pursued his journey with a greatly reduced retinue.

The gifts carried by one of the elephants accompanying the Persians were intended for the regent, those on eleven of the others for the young tsar and for Russia's leading notables, but the loads on the four remaining ones were for Elizabeth. According to Finch[17] all the presents were infinitely 'more magnificent than the Turkish ones'. Though Elizabeth had no intention of marrying the Persian she was as intrigued by the new arrivals as were all the inhabitants of St Petersburg. Her anger and consternation can well be appreciated when she learnt that she was not to be permitted to receive the Persian envoy, nor even to meet him and that the shah's gifts were to be transmitted to her by Count Apraxin. Finch[18] reported that the words in which she openly expressed her annoyance 'struck and surprised everyone' by their bitterness. She made no secret of her belief that Ostermann was responsible for the affront. 'Tell Count Ostermann from me,' she instructed her messenger, 'that he thinks he can deceive the world but I know full well that he tries to humiliate me on every occasion, and that, on his advice, measures are being taken against me which the regent is too kind hearted to think of. He forgets what he was and what I am; he forgets how much he owes to my father, who found him a mere clerk and made him what he is now.'[19]

Encouraged by her anger Lestocq and de la Chétardie redoubled their efforts to persuade Elizabeth to make a bid for the throne. According to Manstein[20] 'Count Ostermann, who took normal precautions, was informed that the princess Elizabeth was hatching something against the regency. Lestocq, the most giddy man alive and the least capable of keeping a secret, had often said, in a coffee house, before a great many people, that there would soon be great changes in Petersburg. The minister did not fail to report this to the regent, who only laughed', and perhaps rightly so, for even though Elizabeth was very angry and unsettled, she was still not contemplating anything drastic. Nevertheless Finch sensed the regime's underlying instability. He may even have voiced his doubts to Ostermann, with whom he was on such good terms that, in June, he was able frankly to discuss the situation with him. Ostermann admitted that he suspected de la Chétardie, who was being encouraged by Lestocq and the Swedish envoy, Baron Nolken, of plotting in Elizabeth's favour and added that the French ambassador had taken to visiting the Grand Duchess 'even at night and in disguise'.[21] In the despatches which he sent to Versailles, de la Chétardie confirms that he was resorting to both measures, for although he had at last won his point and had presented his credentials to the two-year-old tsar and was therefore able to meet Elizabeth at court functions, yet he dared not converse with her in public for fear of arousing suspicions. He implied, and many have believed him, that Elizabeth was not indifferent to his charms and that their secret meetings were not wholly political. This suggestion is unlikely to be true and Ostermann, who had no great love of Elizabeth, was surely right when he told Finch that 'there being no indication of gallantry in the case the motive must surely be political', adding ominously that if Elizabeth's 'conduct should clearly appear equivocal she would not be the first in Russia who had been shut up in a monastery' which, 'of all things in the world' – commented Finch – 'should not please her and might be a dangerous expedient for she has not one bit of nun's flesh about her, and is extremely well loved and very popular'.[22] The months that followed were to be dangerous and difficult ones for Elizabeth.

By the early autumn Elizabeth had come to believe that she was in danger of losing her liberty. Anna Leopoldovna had more than once been heard to say that if Elizabeth did not marry the Duke of Courland it might be as well to oblige her to take the veil. The mere thought of such a thing terrified Elizabeth; Schwartz tried to comfort her by offering to kill anyone who attempted to harm her[23] whilst Lestocq and de la Chétardie played on her fears in an effort to persuade her to attempt a *coup d'état*.

Earlier in the year France had become an ally of Prussia, Bavaria and Saxony, yet Louis wished Sweden to regain her former strength and therefore urged her king to invade Russia. He argued that a Swedish attack would oblige the regent to send the regiments stationed in St Petersburg to the front, that Elizabeth would then find it easy to secure the throne for herself and, having done so, that she would willingly return the lost Finnish territories to Sweden. Frederick of Sweden was reluctant to go to war unless Elizabeth undertook in writing to restore the land in question. De la Chétardie could not persuade Elizabeth to do so yet dared not tell his own government this. While Sweden hesitated, Finch asked Ostermann for his view on the situation.[24] The minister replied by assuring the ambassador that Elizabeth's 'sentiments of love and affection for Russia were too great to allow her to give in to any of the rumoured projects'.[25] Commenting on this and on the stability of the regency, Finch once again remarked that 'it is certain that the princess is extremely popular and well loved, whilst I am afraid that the regent does not take proper methods of being so, neither is the interior of the court perfectly calm since the princess and the favourite have opposite interests and work in different ways'.

De la Chétardie was in his element. He devised a rather simple code for use when corresponding with Elizabeth; in it 'hero' stood for her name, 'confidant' for Lestocq's, 'intermediary' for Schwartz and Mikhail Vorontzov. His visits to her, still conducted at night and in disguise, increased in number; his demands for funds from France with which to finance the rising became ever more insistent[26] and France reluctantly complied whilst continuing to pour money and advice into Sweden, which, under pressure from the Hats faction, was now at war with Russia. When the Swedish army started meeting with reverses it was Louis who advised the king to invite the Duke of Holstein, though still a mere child, to visit his army headquarters in the belief that the youth's presence there would prevent the Russians charging. In Russia the war and the possibility of its spreading to other fronts, coupled with the nation's fear of being governed by Germans, quickened the people's sense of patriotism. The old spirit of isolationism revived and an increasing number of politicians began to press for Russia's complete withdrawal from European affairs and the concentration of its armies along its own borders for purely defensive purposes. Finch reacted by redoubling his efforts to obtain an alliance, and in October at last succeeded. But in a despatch dated 14 November he felt bound to warn his government that 'the internal situation at court was by no means such as would be wished . . . Anna Leopoldovna's party being formed in a great number by Mr Botta's [the Austrian ambassador] intrigues, with Count Golovkin at the head in a declared opposition to Count Ostermann with such success that [the regent's] confidences and diffidences are both much greater than they ought to be for her own service'.[27]

Indeed, the regent was behaving with surprising carelessness. Her liaison with Count Linar was giving rise to so much criticism among her courtiers that she decided to end the gossip by a truly astonishing plan of her own invention. It consisted in Linar's resignation from his post in order to assume Russian nationality. Then, while continuing the liaison with Anna, he would save appearances by marrying her favourite lady-in-waiting, Julie de Mengden. Enchanted by the idea, Linar set out for Dresden to do as she asked, but events moved faster than he did and he was not destined to return to St Petersburg. Preoccupied as she was by her plan, Anna Leopoldovna refused to pay any attention either to her husband or to Count Linar when they warned her that de la Chétardie and Lestocq were plotting her downfall. Count Golovkin urged her to declare herself empress and, after hesitating for a few days, she decided to do so on her birthday, on 7 December. Yet although Anna Leopoldovna did not act on the danger signals she received from her friends, she was much affected by them and, at night, she was often too frightened to sleep. Elizabeth was equally unsettled and as reluctant to act. With irresolution that was to prove characteristic, she refused to commit herself when pressed by the two

Frenchmen and constantly found some fresh excuse for postponing any decision. According to Manstein[28] she was still constantly to be seen in the streets of St Petersburg, often in the company of admiring soldiers. Ostermann recognized the gravity of the situation and repeatedly warned the regent of it. Before departing for Dresden, Count Linar urged the regent to order Elizabeth's arrest. A servant happened to overhear him and reported his words to Elizabeth. Still nothing happened. Then, on 20 November, while holding a court, Anna Leopoldovna beckoned to Elizabeth to withdraw in order that they might speak in private. When they were alone the regent charged the Grand Duchess with conspiracy, with visiting the French embassy for the purpose and with maintaining a correspondence with the nation's Swedish enemies. The last two charges were unfounded, for Elizabeth had never set foot in the French embassy nor, for all Manstein's assertions to the contrary,* is there any evidence that she communicated direct with the Swedes or encouraged them to attack Russia. Though she knew that France had persuaded Sweden to attack Russia in order to provide her with an opportunity for making a bid for the throne, she was able hotly to deny the last two charges. Her tears, the result of fear rather than contrition, helped to convince the regent of her innocence, but she informed Elizabeth that she intended to have Lestocq arrested on the following day. When both ladies rejoined their courtiers all noticed that Elizabeth was extremely agitated. Tension mounted rapidly at court. Anton Ulrich, whom Manstein described as having 'the best heart and the best temper imaginable, with an intrepidity and courage that could be wished in military affairs, but too timid, too embarrassed in affairs of state',[29] wished Lestocq to be arrested immediately and the town to be picketed. There was talk of raiding the French embassy, and although the regent refused to sanction these measures, de la Chétardie hastened to arm his household. He also insisted that Elizabeth should settle on a day for her bid for the throne. Cornered, she decided on Twelfth Night, still some six weeks distant, but the day on which the regiments which were wholly devoted to her would be assembled in the capital for the traditional ceremony of the blessing of the Neva's waters.

Both Frenchmen realized that action could not be postponed till Twelfth Night. On the morning of 24 November Lestocq therefore entered Elizabeth's bedroom, woke her and handed her a card. She saw that on one side he had drawn a picture of herself seated crowned and enthroned but on the other she appeared dressed as a nun, with a rack and gibbet in the

* He was in no position to know the true facts, and had, in this instance, to rely on hearsay.

background. 'Your Highness, Madam,' he said to her, 'you must choose finally now between these two issues – whether to be empress or to be relegated to a convent and see your servants perish under torture.'[30] The drawing, and the news that four thousand guardsmen were to leave the capital for the front immediately, made a deep impression on Elizabeth. While she was considering these issues seven young Guards' officers burst into her room and told her that instant action had become imperative as their regiment was to leave for the front on the following day. Elizabeth realized that the moment she dreaded had come. Hesitation was no longer possible. She decided to act at midnight.

The conspirators had less than twelve hours in which to make ready. Time did not allow for elaborate plans. Elizabeth had no organized party to back her and her active supporters numbered no more than thirty, none of whom appears to have been bribed by the French or to have plotted with them. Although their number was so small, Elizabeth believed that she was popular and that knowledge, together with the trust she placed in God, sufficed her. No records exist to reveal the way in which she spent the hours of that fateful day, but it is very probable that she spent them in the same way as she did other difficult moments in her life – at prayer before her favourite icon of the Saviour. A little before midnight she is known to have turned to it and sworn that if she became empress no Russian would die by her orders. Then, carrying the icon and accompanied by Lestocq, Schwartz, Mikhail Vorontzov, the brothers Shuvalov and two young Guards' officers, she set out for the barracks of the Preobrazhensky Grenadiers.

It was a bitterly cold night but the conspirators were too excited to notice the weather. On reaching the barracks[31] Elizabeth walked into the guardroom and cried: 'Lads! You know whose daughter I am. Follow me.' 'Ma'am,' cried the soldiers, 'we are ready. We will kill them all.' 'If that is what you intend doing,' retorted Elizabeth, 'I won't go with you.' 'We will die for you,' they shouted. 'No Russian blood is to be spilt on my account,' Elizabeth commanded. Three hundred men rallied round her. Entering the sledge with her seven companions she made for the centre of St Petersburg. The Nevsky Perspective already possessed some fine mansions. They paused at the gates of those belonging to notables known to be unfavourably disposed to Elizabeth and silently stationed pickets beside them. Small groups of soldiers were also sent to arrest Ostermann, Münnich and other prominent men, while Elizabeth and the bulk of her supporters hurried to the Admiralty. Time was running out, yet they decided to abandon their horses there as the sound of their hooves might raise the alarm. They proceeded to the Winter Palace on foot. All begged Elizabeth to hurry, but the snow was so deep that, tall though she was, she had difficulty in doing so. Impulsively some of the soldiers raised her in their arms and carried her. On reaching the Winter Palace she hurried to the guard-room. Surprising the men on duty, she told them to lay down their arms and follow her. She led them to Anna Leopoldovna's bedroom. Entering it with her seven companions she personally woke the sleeping woman, saying 'Little sister, it is time to rise.' One glance sufficed to convince poor Anna Leopoldovna that all was lost and that it only remained for her to beg Elizabeth for mercy. She showed particular concern for the safety of her son, Tsar Ivan. Elizabeth assured her that no harm would befall any of them. She meant it at the time. Raising the young tsar in her arms she carried him out to the soldiers, kissed him and, in all sincerity, affirmed that all would be well with him. It was one of the few perfidious actions that mar her life.[32]

When Anna Leopoldovna and Anton Ulrich had dressed they were led to a waiting sledge; their son and infant daughter were placed with their nurses in another sledge and the family was then driven to Elizabeth's apartments in the Summer Palace. They found assembled there the men whose arrest Elizabeth had ordered as she hurried to the Admiralty – Ostermann, the Chancellor Golovkin, the Löwenwolde brothers, Baron Mengden and Field Marshal Münnich who, of them all, had alone attempted to resist arrest. The others had been too surprised even to protest. Throughout the night Elizabeth had sent messengers to inform de la Chétardie of her successes. Now, while her prisoners waited for her to tell them what lay in store for them, she sent messengers to such senior officials as Field Marshal Lacy to tell them that they had nothing to fear. Then she sat down to draft her first manifesto. Only when she had finished it did she summon her prisoners and inform them that they would be charged with the crime of having deprived her of her hereditary rights.

Elizabeth's manifesto was presented to the nation at eight o'clock that morning. It informed the people that she 'had ascended her father's throne by virtue of her hereditary rights and that she had caused the usurpers to be apprehended'.[33] She also assured the nation that the Brunswick family would be safe under her care. The news was acclaimed with satisfaction. People of distinction hurried to the palace to swear allegiance to Elizabeth and the troops stationed in the capital joyfully took the oath. Elizabeth left her apartments in the Summer Palace and at three o'clock on the afternoon of 25 November 1741 she entered the Winter Palace as empress of Russia. De la Chétardie came to pay his respects to her there at six o'clock, bearing a song of praise composed for the occasion by his secretary Valdancourt.[34] He found Elizabeth much excited, wondering with amusement how Finch and Botta, representatives of countries ill-disposed to France, were reacting to the *coup d'état*. Later that evening she gave orders for all foreign monarchs to be notified of her accession, but two days later she wrote personally to Louis xv to inform him that she had assumed control of her country's affairs and to assure him of the warmth of her feelings for France.[35]

4

The Start of a Reign

The new empress was thirty-two years old. She was of striking appearance. Tall like her father, heavily built like her mother, her magnificent carriage, lively blue eyes, clear skin with naturally pink cheeks and shining auburn hair, which she was soon to dye black to conform with the prevailing fashion, made her widely admired; yet what sort of person was she? No one quite knew? Although the problem of providing her with a suitable husband had served as an amusing conversational topic in many of Europe's most fashionable drawing rooms, kings and diplomats suddenly realized that their knowledge of her amounted to very little. She had a reputation for affability, gaiety and flirtatiousness bordering on the amorous, but her political opinions were unknown to the world and no one could predict how much her rule would reflect them nor how stable her hold on the country would prove. Since the removal of Menshikov many of the most influential people in the country had been foreigners, generally men of German extraction. Indeed, under Anna Ivanovna, someone had remarked that the court was ruled by Biron, the administration by Ostermann and the army by Münnich. Elizabeth's love of France was widely known; de la Chétardie and Lestocq's roles in the recent palace revolution tended to be exaggerated and most foreigners therefore concluded that French influence would prevail in Russia under the new empress's rule. Russians hoped that nationalism would triumph. In the sermon which he preached on receiving the news of Elizabeth's accession, the Archbishop of Novgorod reflected popular sentiment; he described the event as a victory over the devil's emissaries, and Lomonosov proclaimed that 'like Moses Elizabeth had come to release Russia from the night of Egyptian servitude; like Noah she had saved Russia from an alien flood'.[1]

During the first few days of her reign Elizabeth gave Europe no indication of her intentions. She was too preoccupied with domestic matters to spare a thought for the international situation. Almost her first acts as sovereign took the form of tangible expressions of her gratitude to those who had helped her and stood with her in harsher times. She showered gifts on her supporters, giving titles to every one of the Preobrazhensky Grenadiers who had marched with her to the Winter Palace, endowing each with from twenty-nine to forty-five male serfs[2] and promoting privates to lieutenants, corporals to majors, armourers and quartermasters to lieutenant colonels and so on. She formed them into a special unit of the Imperial bodyguard and appointed herself their colonel. Lestocq, whose role had been largely limited to that of a go-between, was generously rewarded. Although he hoped for financial benefits and permission to return to France, Elizabeth refused to part with him. Instead she made him a Privy Councillor, appointed him Physician in Chief to the sovereign, President of the Imperial College of Physicians and gave him her portrait set in gems valued at twenty thousand roubles as well as an annuity of seven thousand roubles. De la Chétardie received the Order of St Andrew mounted in fine quality diamonds, a ring set with a very large diamond, a gold snuff box adorned with the empress's portrait, some loose diamonds and twelve thousand roubles in cash. Mikhail Vorontzov became a count and was appointed to the College of Foreign Affairs, where he later rose to the highest rank. The five officers who had supported Elizabeth from the start became court chamberlains. Schwartz, a man of violent and jealous temperament, felt that he had been inadequately rewarded by his appointment as colonel; as messenger he had in fact been in some danger and his complaint was therefore not unjustified. On finding that Elizabeth was not prepared to do more for him he took his departure and was not heard of again. Elizabeth expressed her love for Alexei Razumovsky by making him a count and appointing him court chamberlain as well as Grand Master of her hunt. He retained a sense of proportion and when the empress told him that she wished to make him a field marshal – a post for which he knew himself to be unfit – he gently replied, 'Your majesty may create me a field marshal if you so desire, but I defy you or anybody else to make even a tolerable captain out of me.'

Having expressed her gratitude to those who had helped her to the throne Elizabeth addressed a second manifesto to the nation. In it she undertook to deliver her subjects from the control of foreigners. Her words raised nationalist hopes to fever pitch, many interpreting them as a licence for resorting to violence. A mob collected in the capital's streets and dealt roughly with the foreigners who fell into its hands. Hatred of foreigners expressed itself with particular violence among the troops fighting in Finland and even more so among the recently promoted soldiers, who molested many foreigners so seriously that the empress was forced to punish them. She expelled from the capital for ever those Grenadiers who were found guilty, posting them to serve as officers in regiments stationed in the provinces, no two culprits being assigned to the same unit. Nevertheless, dislike of foreigners did not abate, and, since it was essential for the empress to secure the loyalty of the entire nobility, she found herself obliged to expel certain foreigners from Russia, even though it was the last thing she had ever thought of doing. Nevertheless, ill-feeling ran high, at any rate until her coronation, causing much resentment among the country's foreign residents.

The pleasant task of rewarding her friends was inevitably followed by the distasteful one of dealing with the ministers who had been arrested on the night of the *coup d'état* as well as with the courtiers who had scorned Elizabeth when she counted for little. Like most quick-tempered people Elizabeth was kind and forgiving, traits which Catherine II was quick to recognize and put to her own use. Had it not been for de la Chétardie's insistence that she 'should erase all traces of the previous reign'[3] Elizabeth would probably have dealt less harshly with Anna Leopoldovna and her family and in return she would doubtless have received fairer treatment from historians. It was unfortunate that she had no one but her two French friends to turn to for advice during those first, breathless all important moments of sovereignty. De la Chétardie played on her dislike of Ostermann in order to vent his own anger against that minister for being on good terms with Finch and for engineering the Anglo-Russian alliance so distasteful to France. He urged the empress to show no clemency to those who had treated her inconsiderately in the past. Elizabeth accepted his advice because she was herself acutely conscious of the danger arising from the presence in the capital of two sovereigns, even though one of them was still a baby.

On this occasion the woman whom historians describe as too irresolute for governing recognized the need for swift action. Although the fact that Ivan had been proclaimed tsarevich at birth and was, as a result, legally entitled to reign, weighed heavily on Elizabeth's conscience yet, now that she had seized the throne, she was resolved to retain it. She was equally determined to put an end to the king-making activities of the aristocracy and the Guards' regiments, hoping to turn both into loyal supporters of

the legitimate sovereign. On the third day of her reign the empress therefore issued yet another manifesto. In it she again stressed her right to reign
and informed the nation that Anna Leopoldovna, together with her
husband and children, were to be evicted from Russia and that all those
who had served in the regent's government would be tried for disloyalty.
At the same time the empress gave orders for all edicts, manifestoes, coins,
documents and objects bearing either the names or portraits of Tsar Ivan
and his mother to be destroyed.

On 13 December 1740 Tsar Ivan, his parents and baby sister, accompanied by their entire household, set out for Germany under a strong
military guard. If Anna Leopoldovna rejoiced at the thought of living in
freedom in Germany she was doomed to disappointment. When they
reached Riga the prisoners learnt that they could go no further until the
arrival of an order from the empress permitting them to do so. While
waiting for further instructions they were to live in the fortress of
Dünemünde. They were fated to remain in it, living under constant
supervision, till 13 January 1744. Prince Ludwig of Brunswick, who had
come to Russia as their guest, fared only slightly better. Elizabeth must
have taken an especially violent dislike to him for, although she did not
ill-treat him, she made him stay in Russia for almost a year, keeping him
in miserable lodgings and under constant surveillance.

Elizabeth was poised between two worlds. The old Muscovite world
was one where Tartar barbarity had developed under Ivan the Terrible
into a policy of calculated cruelty.[4] Anna Ivanovna had been caught in its
wake, but had nevertheless obtained a foothold in that more enlightened
world which was nebulously reflected for Elizabeth in her father's dreams
and aspirations, if not in his conduct. Like her father Elizabeth ranged
herself with Europe by instinct, inclination and conscious choice, yet she
could not wholly escape from her medieval heritage. The simultaneous
existence of these two incompatible worlds, each of which was firmly
rooted in her being, placed her in a dilemma which she was never able
fully to resolve, though she did succeed in building the road which was to
lead Russia out of the labyrinth. Conscious of her need for an able and
experienced adviser the empress fell in with Lestocq's suggestion that she
should employ as her secretary – to give him the full title of his later
years – Count Alexei Petrovich Bestuzhev-Riumen.

In an age when people's lives were apt to follow unpredictable courses,
his took many surprising turns. He appears to have been a descendant of a
certain Gabriel Best of Kent, who came to Russia in 1412 and so greatly

distinguished himself that he was given a title by Ivan III. If this was indeed so, it would help to explain certain actions of Alexei Bestuzhev's when Grand Chancellor of Russia. He was born in Moscow in 1693 and as a youth he was sent, together with his brother Mikhail, to complete his education at his father's expense first in Copenhagen, then in Berlin. From Berlin Alexei Bestuzhev made his way to Hanover where, on obtaining Peter the Great's permission, he entered the services of the Elector, remaining in his employ when the latter became king of Britain. In 1717 he was as a result appointed Hanoverian ambassador to Russia, but he reverted to Russia's service in 1720 in order to comply with Peter the Great's wishes that he should become Russian ambassador to Copenhagen. He was still serving in that capacity in 1730 when he gained Biron's confidence by extracting Catherine I's will from the Kiel archives. As a reward for this service he was recalled to Russia soon after to act as assistant to Ostermann in the Ministry for Foreign Affairs. He was as a result involved in Biron's fall, but though condemned to sentence of death, the sentence was commuted to one of exile, and he was close at hand when Elizabeth became empress. Ostermann's enemies, especially Count Golovkin and Prince Nikita Yurievich Trubetskoy, Procurator to the Senate, took advantage of this to hurry him back to the capital, and within a matter of days he was acting as secretary to the empress and as her adviser on foreign affairs. Very soon afterwards he became vice-chancellor of Russia. He was a secretive and moody man. Though an experienced statesman and devoted to Russia's interest he was far more drawn to science than to politics and derived much satisfaction from his discovery of a sedative which, under the name of *tintura tonica nervina Bestuzhev*, was widely used. His marriage to a Lutheran, though disapproved of at court, probably helped him to understand the working of the western mind. At all events he was to prove invaluable to the empress. His first task, she told him, was to bring about peace with Sweden.

Apart from home affairs there were several pressing European problems for Elizabeth to consider. The most urgent resulted from Prussia's invasion of Silesia, for Elizabeth feared that the alliance which Russia had entered into with Austria in 1726 might oblige her to go to Austria's assistance. She realized that this could lead to her fighting France. The mere thought of it horrified Elizabeth, increasing her dislike of the emperor of Prussia. Though many of her courtiers were indifferent to him they were opposed to Russia becoming involved in a western war.

Frederick of Prussia had, for his part, always instinctively feared and disliked Russia. As early as 1741 he had warned his ambassador to Russia, Baron Axel Mardefeld, to beware of the country and instructed him to persuade Lestocq to act as his paid informer, an offer which the doctor accepted though, from 1742, he was also to receive a pension from France. Frederick dreaded having Russia as an enemy yet he did not really want her as a friend. He realized, however, that merely by favouring his French ally the empress could hinder Prussia's expansion and that she might well prevent it if she went to Austria's assistance. Frederick had no reason for supposing that Louis intended to trick Elizabeth throughout her life into thinking that he was well disposed towards her when the reverse was true. Frederick was convinced that Elizabeth owed her crown to France. He frequently asserted that the Preobrazhensky Guards had been 'corrupted by French money';[5] he believed that Elizabeth had already rewarded the two Frenchmen who had acted as her advisers by bestowing her favours upon them and felt convinced that she would remain grateful and loyal to that country for years to come. Therefore his fear of Russia persisted. It left him determined to win Elizabeth's friendship.

Although Louis was no lover of peace he now needed it in Europe, if only temporarily, for France had exhausted herself in the War of the Spanish Succession. Nevertheless, Louis pressed Sweden to regain the territory lost to Peter the Great by encouraging that country to regard Russia as its worst enemy. Elizabeth neither feared nor disliked the Swedes; she hated bloodshed and longed for the Swedish war to end. She knew that Russia had been bled white by wars and mismanagement, that the troops were exhausted and ill-equipped, the navy on the verge of decay, yet she was determined not to cede any of her father's conquests in order to end the war. On 12 December 1741 Finch reported[6] that the empress 'was resolved not to cede any Russian soil being not so afraid of thirty thousand Swedes as to consent to buy peace so dear especially since notwithstanding the small inclination people might think there was among her troops to fight the Swedes (which is but too true and nothing more visible), yet in case of war continuing she was capable of putting herself at the head of her army, when she was sure that every man would do his duty'.

Elizabeth's determination placed de la Chétardie in a most difficult position. Time and again he had assured his government that if she became empress she would end the war by agreeing to Sweden's demands. Now, though she had instructed Alexei Bestuzhev to regard peace as his foremost objective, she proved adamant on this, to her, all-essential point. Her hatred of war was such that she also instructed Bestuzhev to do everything possible to avoid embroiling Russia in the Austro-Prussian war, while at the same time making it clear to Frederick that she would never condone his annexation of Silesia and would do everything in her power to ensure that he returned it to Austria. The empress also instructed Bestuzhev to do his utmost to overcome the reluctance of Europe's sovereigns to accord her her full imperial title; as yet, only Marie Theresa had been willing to do so.

In December Ostermann, Münnich, Golovkin, Mengden, the Löwenwolde brothers with other members of Anna Leopoldovna's government, were brought to trial in the Winter Palace, with Prince N. Trubetskoy presiding. Elizabeth is believed to have followed the proceedings in secret, hidden from view by a curtain, in much the same way as her father had watched the trial of the Tsarevich Alexei. At the same time everything possible was done to trace the unfortunate people who had been banished to Siberia during the two preceding reigns in order to restore their freedom to them. Their number was thought to exceed twenty thousand; many had disappeared without leaving any traces. Biron was among the first to be recalled. Remembering his many kindnesses Elizabeth expressed the desire to reinstate him as Duke of Courland. Her ministers dissuaded her from so quixotic and dangerous a step and, instead, Biron was sent to live in his Yaroslavl estates where he was given considerable freedom and permission to hunt round a radius of eight miles. Nor did Elizabeth forget her former lovers. The search for Shubin lasted for over two years. When he was at last found the empress refused to see him,* but she conferred a decoration on him together with an estate in the district of Nizhni Novgorod. He did not ask for more. Fortune had smiled on him – a rare occurrence in Russia – and that sufficed. He retired to his estate to live a peaceful and contented life, and to die a natural death there. Alexei Buturlin was recalled in 1742 and made a splendid career for himself in the army, becoming a field marshal in 1756 and Commander-in-Chief of the army fighting in Prussia in 1760.

The trial of Anna Leopoldovna's ministers ended at last. All the accused were found guilty and condemned to death. Ostermann was the first to be notified because he had in the past constantly humiliated Elizabeth. He was to be broken on the wheel; Münnich was to die by quartering, the others by decapitation. Elizabeth must have heard the sentences with dread, if without surprise, for she must have clearly remembered her oath before the icon on the night of her bid for power, that no Russian would

* According to some reports he had been physically disfigured and mentally affected by having his tongue torn out.

die by her orders, a promise which she had repeated formally and publicly on the first day of her reign. It was one she had every intention of keeping and she had already attempted to abolish capital punishment for felons, but had been dissuaded by her ministers who feared that such clemency would lead to an increase in crime. It was the death sentence itself rather than the form in which it was to be administered which perturbed Elizabeth for, with the rest of Russia, her sensibilities had become blunted under the tutelage of Anna Ivanovna, when cruelties of the most barbarous nature had been committed. In a manner which was to become habitual to her when in doubt – one which was to madden all the officials who had to deal with her – Elizabeth at first refused either to pass any opinion on the sentences which had been pronounced or to ratify them. She avoided committing herself for as long as possible, but when at last forced to take action she commuted all the death sentences to banishment to Siberia, in each case with the loss of the prisoner's entire personal fortune, but not that of his wife. She also allowed the wives and children of the condemned to choose whether to accompany their men folk into exile or to withdraw to their estates. The majority elected to share their husbands' fortunes. The convoy of exiles set out for Siberia on 19 January 1742. Each prisoner was allowed to take four suits with him as well as two dozen shirts and as many servants as he wished. Each was granted an allowance of a rouble a day for his own needs and a tenth of that sum for those of each of his servants.

The condemned men learnt of their reprieve in the cruellest possible way. On 17 January, the day appointed for their execution, they were led to the platform which had been erected for the purpose in the main square of the Vasilievsky Ostrov district of St Petersburg. Ostermann was too ill to mount it unaided but he managed to stand unassisted to hear his death sentence read. He listened calmly to the announcement that he was to be beheaded instead of torn on the wheel; he undid his shirt collar, removed his wig and placed his head upon the block. Only then was he told that his sentence had been commuted to banishment to Beresov in Siberia. Struggling to his feet, he appeared unperturbed and quietly asked for his wig to be returned to him. Münnich was subjected to a similar experience, but he was told that he was to be sent to Pelim to occupy the quarters recently vacated by Biron, and so were the others. It is impossible to establish precisely who was to blame for the ordeal the condemned men were obliged to undergo, but the empress must be held ultimately responsible for it.

During the reigns of the two Annas, Elizabeth had been taught the dangers of outspokenness, and the safety that lies in concealment and discretion. No one, with the probable exception of Alexei Razumovsky, had realized the depth of her devotion to Russia, the extent to which her seizure of the throne troubled her conscience or the problem of the choice of a successor occupied her thoughts. The memory of Tsar Ivan was to haunt her throughout her life, causing her many a sleepless night. By birth he had almost as much right to the throne as her own nephew, and a far stronger one by the terms of Anna Ivanovna's will, yet Elizabeth had always made it abundantly clear that she gave her allegiance to her nephew because he was descended from Peter the Great. The young Duke of Holstein was known to Europe as 'the child of Kiel', but Anna Ivanovna had always referred to him as 'the little Holstein devil'. His father had taught him to think of himself as heir to the crown of Sweden as well as to the Dukedom of Holstein. The luckless boy knew little of Russia and the fact that he was expected to learn Russia's language and religion* had made him hate everything connected with that country. His father had been more concerned with making a soldier of him, disciplining and hardening him, than in ensuring that he received an education befitting a ruler. At his father's death in 1739 the eleven-year-old boy was sent to live with his cousin and guardian, Frederick Augustus Bishop of Lübeck. The latter chose as his tutor Baron Brümmer, an obtuse man and a rigid disciplinarian with a sadistic streak. The boy was desperately lonely and neglected while under his charge, and often hungry. He was thirteen when Elizabeth became empress of Russia. Soon after, her thoughts began to turn to the son of her beloved sister Anna. Finally she announced that she considered it fit that Peter the Great's only surviving grandchild should come to Russia to pursue his education.

Frederick Augustus dared not risk offending Elizabeth, and Peter was therefore informed that he was to go to Russia with Baron Brümmer and a suitable suite. The boy was appalled by the decision, but had to comply with it. He arrived in St Petersburg in January. Elizabeth was distressed by his unattractive appearance and awkward manners; she was also horrified by his ignorance. Concealing her disappointment, comforting herself with the thought that he was young enough to change, she went to great trouble to find men of ability and gentle temperament to tutor him.

After a short stay at Tsarskoe Selo the court set out for Moscow on 22 March. The move followed a pattern which was to become all too familiar and hateful to those involved in it. Although Elizabeth loved

* He was by birth a Lutheran.

luxury she neither minded, nor indeed noticed, discomfort. She was as restless as her father had been and her moves from town to town and palace to palace were frequent. In the manner of a medieval monarch she was always accompanied on them by her entire court and household, and she invariably took with her all her clothes, furniture, tableware and other possessions; so too did her courtiers. When the court transferred from Petersburg to Moscow the government moved with it. Twenty-four thousand people – a quarter of the new capital's entire population – were affected. Nineteen thousand horses were needed to transport them with their luggage and other possessions from one capital to the other, a distance of some four hundred miles.

The journey was more difficult in summer than in winter, when a sledge harnessed to a team of fast horses could cover the distance in three days and nights. In summer a week or so was needed to complete a journey rendered odious by dust, swamps and gnats. Elizabeth abominated slow travel. Abandoning her household, leaving them to deal with her clothes and chattels, she moved at speed, covering the distance between Petersburg and Moscow in forty-eight hours of continuous travel. Both her travelling coach and her sledge were so large that they needed twelve horses to draw them; the interior of each was fitted out to resemble a small room, furnished with a sofa, armchairs and card table. The sledge was upholstered in green cloth and heated by a stove. The speed was such that her horses often fell exhausted and died on the wayside. Their places were filled from the twelve horses which galloped loose beside the coach and fresh relays were always kept in readiness for her at the staging posts, Elizabeth paying lavish compensation for those which had failed to survive the journey. Few comforts were available to the weary travellers when they reached Moscow. Even the empress's personal apartments were often in a state of such disrepair that the rain came through the roof and the doors would not close properly. Once the Grand Duchess Catherine found that even the stove in her bedroom was unusable; Elizabeth seemed oblivious.

When travelling to Moscow for her coronation Elizabeth conformed with tradition and broke her journey at Vsesviatskoe to prepare her soul for that solemn event. She entered Moscow on 28 March 1742 and was welcomed by salvos of guns firing from the Red Square and the sound of bells being rung from Moscow's five hundred churches. She made her way on foot to the Cathedral of the Assumption where she was met by the Archbishop of Novgorod who conducted her to the Cathedral of the Archangel to attend a *Te Deum*. After the service the empress drove to the

Annenhof Palace where students from the Slavo-Graeco-Latin Academy, wearing garlands in their hair and carrying laurel leaves, greeted her with hymns of welcome. As soon as she had installed herself in the Preobrazhensky Palace Elizabeth sent for her relations on her mother's side, the Skavronskys, Hendrikovs and Efimovskys. They arrived in time to attend a reception of great magnificence. Though the first of the palace fires Elizabeth was to experience had broken out on the preceding day in the Palace it was held there as planned, with its splendour undiminished.

Two days before her coronation heralds toured Moscow announcing the details of the forthcoming festivities. Triumphal arches, made according to designs by I. Y. Blank* and Ukhitomsky, were set up at key points on the procession's route. On the morning of 25 April twenty-one salvos were fired from the Red Square. By six o'clock the soldiers lining the route of the procession were in their places and the empress's guests had assembled in the Cathedral of the Assumption. At eight o'clock the clergy entered the cathedral and soon after the empress appeared, her train supported by twenty pages dressed in white and cloth of gold. She mounted the dais and the long service began. It was conducted by Amfrosy, Archbishop of Novgorod, assisted by the Archbishop of Pskov. A week of feasting and rejoicing followed, the populace dining nightly on roasted oxen and wine discharged from fountains while the sky above was irradiated by fireworks made to Blank's designs. The decorations had cost nineteen thousand roubles, the festivities fifty thousand. Reymish provided the design for the medal struck on that auspicious day. Elizabeth seemed carefree and it was not until twenty years later that Catherine II, herself just become empress, learnt from Father Dubiansky, Elizabeth's confessor and the priest whom she chose to instruct Catherine in Orthodoxy, that on the day of her coronation Elizabeth had handed him a small sealed packet which she had asked him to conceal in the cathedral's altar. He had done so without knowing what it contained and the packet was still in its hiding place. Catherine sent for it and opened it in private. It contained a sheet of paper on which Elizabeth had written, 'For the health of her Highness, the autocratic great ruler, the Empress Elizaveta Petrovna and for her heir, the nephew of Peter I, Sire and Grand Duke Peter Feodorovich'.[7] At the time the young Duke of Holstein was still not a member of the Orthodox Church nor had he been declared heir to the throne. Catherine was surely right in thinking, as she gazed at the note, that Elizabeth had written it to ensure the throne's continuity in the event

* Kokorinov's teacher.

of her sudden death. Writing in her Reminiscences, Catherine commented that Elizabeth

was deeply religious, [she] must have named her heir on the day of her coronation, describing him as such for the first time in writing, and confiding her decision to God alone; superstitiously she had the note concealed in the altar. Indeed, it was her custom, whenever she had a document of importance to sign, to place it, prior to signing it, at the foot of an icon of the Vernicle which she especially revered. After it had been there for some time she would either sign it or not sign it, according to the promptings of her heart.[8]

The coronation festivities extended through May. At court a masked ball, the first of many given by Elizabeth, proved one of the gayest events, but from the artistic point of view, the opening on the banks of the Yauza of a public theatre with a seating capacity of three thousand was more important. Lestocq and de la Chétardie, each imagining himself to be indispensable to the empress and each aspiring to assume the duties of a prime minister, were in constant attendance. De la Chétardie was still a privileged person at court; Elizabeth continued to place complete trust in him even though the clever and astute Prince Kantemir, Russia's ambassador to France, a lover of France and a close friend of Montesquieu, advised her to be cautious.

In his efforts to end the Swedish war, de la Chétardie attempted to bribe Bestuzhev to support him. Bestuzhev refused, and he decided to bypass the vice-chancellor and deal direct with the empress. With Lestocq's help he persuaded Elizabeth to write personally to the king of France to ask him to mediate in negotiations for a truce. In due course hostilities were halted and peace discussions began. French insistence on the return to Sweden of large areas which Peter the Great had conquered so astonished the empress that she refused to use France as an intermediary any more. The talks broke down and hostilities were resumed.

It was unfortunate for de la Chétardie that a letter sent on 12 January by Amelot de Chaillon, French Minister for Foreign Affairs, to de Castellane, France's ambassador to the Porte, was intercepted in Vienna. It was based on some disparaging references to Elizabeth and a disturbing comment from a despatch which de la Chétardie had sent from Russia the previous April. The offensive passage read as follows:

the last revolution (in Russia) marks the end of Muscovy's greatness. Since the princess Elizabeth intends ceasing to appoint foreigners to senior posts in Russia, with only herself to rely on, the country will flounder in its original morass; to hasten Russia's fall while freeing itself of a troublesome neighbour the Porte cannot be too quick in adopting a more forceful attitude and, by taking advantage of its agreements with Sweden, join that country in attacking Russia.[9]

But the sultan was too concerned by Nadir Shah's threatening attitude to do so.

Marie Theresa fully understood that Austria's safety depended in no small measure on her ability to renew the Austro-Russian treaty of alliance. She assumed that it would help her to do so if the intercepted letter were shown to Elizabeth. In May a copy of the incriminating document reached her ambassador, the Marquis de Botta, with instructions to present it to the empress. Lestocq, as always well informed, got wind of the affair and hastened to warn de la Chétardie. When questioned by the distressed and angry empress the ambassador therefore had his answers ready; he managed to convince her that he had been maligned and that he had never made the statements attributed to him. The very fact that his position at court had been endangered seem to spur the ambassador to behave with astonishing presumption. He started making a habit of entering the empress's apartments unannounced; he stationed himself beside her at all official functions and he treated her courtiers with increasing superciliousness. His behaviour fanned the dislike and distrust felt for him by Bestuzhev and caused so much displeasure among the courtiers that their sympathies veered away from France towards Austria. Elizabeth ignored the situation and made a point of treating de la Chétardie with courtesy, though she gradually ceased asking him for his advice. On learning that France still expected her to restore Peter the Great's Finnish conquests to Sweden, she informed de la Chétardie that Russia would negotiate with Sweden direct, without using France as an intermediary. Deeply slighted the ambassador asked for his recall. His request was granted, though his departure was timed for some months ahead. In her anxiety to part with him on the best possible terms the empress encouraged him to spend much of his time in her presence. Sir Cyril Wich, Britain's new ambassador, complained somewhat bitterly because the Frenchman was able to see the empress whenever he wished, without having formally to apply for an audience.

Frederick of Prussia's attitude to France was always to remain as equivocal as Louis xv's treatment of Elizabeth. He resented de la Chétardie's presence at Elizabeth's court quite as much as Wich for he thought that the Frenchman was encouraging the empress to offset the loss of the Finnish territories desired by Sweden by the seizure of Pomerania. To counteract de la Chétardie's influence Frederick enlisted Lestocq's help in return for the down payment of fifteen thousand roubles and an annuity of four hundred. Frederick was one of the very few foreigners who never underestimated Elizabeth's intelligence. Though he believed that she 'had no great liking for any of the major powers and that she had taken a particular dislike to the courts of Vienna and Prussia', yet he maintained that 'she was sufficiently astute to hoodwink both the French and the commander of the Swedish army fighting in Finland for the purpose of gaining a respite in which to strengthen her own army'.[10] Naturally enough, Elizabeth had devoted much attention to the situation on the Swedish front where, if hostilities were to be resumed, she intended retaining the upper hand. Much concerned about the well being of her troops, she did everything possible to improve the conditions in which they lived and fought, and it was entirely due to her that, when the war flared up again, they were well equipped and so well clothed that few suffered from frost bite.[11]

In June – at the very time when his French ally was being severely defeated in Bavaria – Frederick surprised Europe by declaring himself satisfied with his military gains and ready to enter into peace talks with Austria. In an effort to redress the balance in favour of France, de la Chétardie suggested that the empress should seek a French bride for the Duke of Holstein and that she should also invite Maurice de Saxe to visit her in Russia, ostensibly to confer the Dukedom of Courland upon him, but really in the hope that the empress, whose name was still linked to that of Maurice, might decide to marry him. Elizabeth was amused and attracted by the idea of meeting the French marshal and Maurice was equally pleased by the thought of visiting Russia. Abandoning the regiment with which he had laid siege to Prague some seven months earlier, he hastened to Moscow where he was to stay in the French embassy. De la Chétardie presented him to the empress: the meeting was an unqualified success. Elizabeth and Maurice had many tastes in common. They became inseparable and wherever they went de la Chétardie followed. Public opinion was ruffled. Then, on 18 June, during a firework display, the Muscovites were startled, indeed shocked, to see their empress, dressed as a man, riding gaily between Marshal de Saxe and the ambassador of France. A sudden storm obliged the trio laughingly to gallop to the Kremlin for shelter. Elizabeth hastened to change into one of her magnificent dresses and reappeared in great spirits. With equal gaiety her companions persuaded her to accompany them back to the French embassy for an improvised supper. She offended public opinion by staying there till six o'clock in the morning. Maurice's visit lasted a month; it was probably the gayest month in Elizabeth's life. At the end of it he departed as he had come, leaving Elizabeth the richer by a gallant letter of farewell and a parting poem.

Some six months later it was de la Chétardie's turn to take leave of the empress. She received him alone in her private apartments. No one has discovered what they said to each other, but after the interview it became known that the ambassador was to accompany the empress on the pilgrimage she was on the point of making to the Troitse-Sergieva Lavra (now known as the Monastery of Zagorsk, that of the Trinity and St Sergius of Radonezh). Muscovites were stunned by the news. It seemed inadmissible to them that a Roman Catholic and a foreigner should accompany their sovereign on such an expedition. Foreign observers were scarcely less irritated by a situation which seemed to confirm the rumour that the ambassador had become the empress's lover;[12] some historians support this conclusion on the grounds that both Buturlin and Alexei Razumovsky had in the past accompanied Elizabeth on pilgrimages. The argument is not a convincing one, partly because Buturlin and Razumovsky, being practising members of the Orthodox Church, would have religious reasons for going, quite apart from going as companions to Elizabeth. Moreover, even when no more than a scorned princess, Elizabeth had ample opportunity for meeting her lovers in her own apartments. Now that she was empress she had even less occasion for using a monastery's guest room as a lovers' meeting place, and in any case her deep religious feelings would undoubtedly have made this impossible. Her piety was so profound that one of her severest rebukes to the Grand Duchess Catherine occurred when she was late for morning mass having, so the empress thought, devoted the time set aside for God to the embellishment of her person. Nevertheless, Elizabeth was attached to de la Chétardie; he was amusing, he had been a friend in need, she was grateful to him for it and was sorry to part with him. She was not, however, destined to carry out her pilgrimage in his company.

Elizabeth had decided to make the pilgrimage on foot, although the distance exceeded sixty miles. According to Wich she set out from Moscow on 26 July for an 'exercise which will last five days. Since it has an air of devotion it would be a kind of impiety too nicely to inquire into the motives for it. Mr Chétardie, who had an audience of leave yesterday at noon, is the only foreign minister who has the honour to accompany the tsarina on her progress.'[13] Even so, Wich did not think that the Frenchman would succeed in persuading the empress to choose a French bride for her nephew. Reporting to his government three days later Wich stated that the empress had not been able to carry out her vow of going to Zagorsk on foot. After covering some twenty-eight miles of the journey she was so exhausted that she had to drive back to Moscow. When she recovered she intended driving to the point at which she had had to abandon her walk and complete the rest of the distance by foot in daily stages of eight miles; her coach would pick her up at the end of each stage and drive her back to her last resting place, conveying her in the morning to the point she had reached on the preceding day. Later in life she performed all her pilgrimages in this manner, though she was obliged to reduce the daily distance to six miles.

De la Chétardie had arranged to drive to the monastery in his own coach so that it was only when he arrived there that he discovered that the empress had returned to Moscow. He decided not to accompany her on 2 August when she set out on her pilgrimage for the second time, but he drove with the Saxon minister as far as her first stopping point. In London Lord Carteret was so concerned by the influence which he thought de la Chétardie was able to exercise over Elizabeth that he instructed Wich to secure Bestuzhev's and Lestocq's goodwill by offering both of them a British annuity. Bestuzhev refused the bribe, but Lestocq accepted it even though he cannot really have needed it, since he had only to bleed the empress to earn between three to four thousand roubles, a method which he made too much use of for the good of Elizabeth's health.

On the day of de la Chétardie's departure eighty bottles of Tokay were placed in his carriage at the empress's order. Foreign observers calculated that since he had come to Russia he had accumulated 150,000 roubles. He was sorry to be leaving, but consoled himself with the thought that Elizabeth would miss him enough to ask for his recall. Indeed, shortly afterwards the empress instructed Prince Kantemir to request Versailles to re-appoint de la Chétardie in place of his successor d'Allion, a request which the French Government did not even bother to reply to. Frederick was delighted to learn of de la Chétardie's departure, and when his efforts to win Elizabeth's friendship led her, in March 1743, to enter into a treaty of friendship with Prussia (on condition that note was taken of her disapproval of Frederick's annexation of Silesia) the King conferred the Order of the Black Eagle upon her because he knew this would annoy his French allies.

Through the summer of 1742 Elizabeth had obstinately refused to accept Bestuzhev's advice that she should renew Russia's treaty of friendship with Britain. She was reluctant to side with an enemy of France as she was convinced that the French would soon offer her the treaty of friendship which she so ardently wanted; yet, instinctively, her trust in Lestocq was decreasing. In de la Chétardie's absence the doctor had begun to rely increasingly on the advice of Brümmer and Mardefeld, both of whom were plotting Bestuzhev's fall, for they regarded him as the chief obstacle to Russia's friendship with Prussia. Indeed, Brümmer was so absorbed in politics that he neglected his pupil. Elizabeth failed to notice her nephew's profound loneliness and depression.

In November 1742 Peter was received into the Orthodox Church by Father Semeon Todorsky under the name of Peter Feodorovich. For the young duke this did not represent an act of faith, nor even one of convenience; he was merely submitting to the wishes of those who controlled his life. In December he derived no pleasure from the empress's official announcement that she had chosen him as her heir and successor to the throne.

Wich thought that Elizabeth had issued the proclamation naming Peter her heir in order to distract the nation's attention from Tsar Ivan, but there was probably a more personal reason for the announcement. The proclamation did more than provide the nation with its future tsar; it indicated that the empress had no intention of contracting a royal marriage in the hope of begetting a child of her own to follow her on the throne. Since we know that she had already fixed her choice on Peter at the time of her coronation, and since nothing in the boy's character can have increased her confidence in him, the reason must surely be sought in her relationship with Alexei Razumovsky. Although she was to have several love affairs in the years to come no one has ever questioned the sincerity of her attachment to him, and historians are now united in believing that she was secretly married to Razumovsky some time early in her reign. Some think the marriage was in 1744, at Perovo – a large palace standing in grounds adorned with pavilions, statues, fountains and rare plants which she gave him that year – whilst others think that they were married in the autumn of 1742 at the church of the Presentation of the Virgin, on the Pokrovka in Moscow. All agree that Father Florinsky officiated at their marriage, and some scholars assert that it was he who, on moral grounds, persuaded Elizabeth to marry her lover. His elevation to the rank of archimandrite and his appointment to the Senate seem to support the assumption, 1742 seems the more likely date since because her wedding put an end to any lingering doubts Elizabeth may still have had about marriage to royalty, it was a logical time to proclaim her nephew her heir. Moreover, political unrest within the country rendered the announcement timely. Nevertheless, if the marriage did happen, the secret was kept well enough for no prying diplomats to have any inkling of it. No indiscreet documents were drawn up, but shortly afterwards Elizabeth sent Alexei's young brother Kiril to be educated abroad and invited his mother to visit her at court. She arranged for the worthy woman to be provided with a handsome wardrobe, with the result that when Razumovsky's mother first saw her own elaborately dressed figure reflected in a mirror she failed to recognize herself and dropped a deep curtsy to her own image. Indeed, the sensible creature felt so out of place at court that she begged to be sent home and the empress eventually consented.

On 11 December 1742, King George II of England at last consented to address Elizabeth by her imperial title, and Bestuzhev persuaded the empress to sign the Anglo-Russian treaty of friendship. Although Elizabeth went to the trouble of writing to Louis of France to assure him that the treaty was not directed against his country the news aroused great resentment in France. Concern there became greater with each Russian victory over the Swedes; these culminated in the spring of 1743 with the surrender of over twenty thousand Swedes at Friedrixsham and, shortly afterwards, of a further seventy thousand at Helsinki. As a result the whole of Finland fell to the Russians and, on 27 May, the Swedes sued for peace. Lestocq and Brümmer persuaded Elizabeth not to entrust Bestuzhev with the negotiations. As a result the peace talks made little headway and Russia's relations with Turkey started to suffer from the delay. Finally, disregarding Bestuzhev's advice, Elizabeth decided to restore to Sweden part of the territory captured by her troops, and retained only the areas to the south of the river Kümen and three important fortresses. The Swedish Diet relieved their feelings of resentment by expressing a desire to depose their king in order to offer his throne to the Grand Duke Peter. Elizabeth refused it on her nephew's behalf, since he was heir to the Russian throne, and insisted on the nomination of Peter's uncle, Adolphus Frederick of Holstein, the eldest brother of her dead bridegroom. Finland emerged from the war ruined and devastated. The Swedes denied all responsibility and took no steps to redress the country's situation, but Elizabeth made supplies of seed corn available to the Finnish peasants. She also expressed her desire to end all ill-feeling between Sweden and Russia, and succeeded so well in this endeavour that, when Denmark invaded Karelia as a first step towards the annexation of Sweden and Norway, it was to Elizabeth that the Swedes turned for help and advice.

Many of the foreigners connected with the Russian court had watched de la Chétardie's activities with considerable interest; some were tempted to follow in his steps and intervene in Russia's internal affairs. Elizabeth was to suffer from intrigues. The worst of these occurred both at the start and again at the end of her reign; some almost assumed the dimensions of conspiracies. The first threat to her sovereignty was brought to light less than eight months after she seized power in July 1741, when Turchaninov, a manservant in her service, was seen placing a barrel of gunpowder under her bed. When knouted he remained silent, but it was generally assumed that he was involved in a plot to kill both Elizabeth and her nephew. In a despatch dated July 1743 Wich reported that it was impossible to identify the instigators, but that those who had been arrested were believed to have been heavily bribed; Turchaninov paid for his act by having his tongue and nose removed, the others only their noses. From the winter of 1742 Elizabeth had had to endure a whispering campaign which in order to enlist support for Tsar Ivan played on her illegitimacy. Within a couple of months it had gained such impetus that some young officers were won over by it; they talked, they may even have contemplated murdering the empress and the Grand Duke in order to reinstate Ivan; their wild words were overheard long before the conspirators had reached the stage of planning any acts of violence, and they were arrested and sent for trial. The proceedings dragged on for some months. Eventually all the prisoners were banished to Siberia. Elizabeth was profoundly disturbed by both events and began to fear a *coup d'état*. To avoid it she decided to move the court back to St Petersburg. Under the directorship of Alexander Shuvalov the secret police force was increased and its members instructed to keep close watch on all those overheard making derogatory references to the sovereign. The outlook was rendered more depressing for Elizabeth by her nephew's temperament. Peter was not shaping well. His dislike of Brümmer, which Elizabeth was unaware of, his loneliness, his hatred of Russia, his difficulty in adapting himself to the long hours he was expected to spend at his desk studying subjects which bored him, were all having a disastrous effect on his health. Early in the winter of 1743 he became so weak that he was easily exhausted and his studies had to be curtailed.

At the time Elizabeth could not give him her full attention, for towards the middle of the summer, soon after the ratification of the peace treaty of Abo, her sense of security was shattered by a sensational event. The personalities involved were of the highest standing, among them Countess Lopukhina and her dearest friend, the twenty-six-year-old wife of Alexei Bestuzhev's brother Mikhail, with, worst of all, the Austrian ambassador, the Marquis de Botta.[14] The empress and the countess had become bitter enemies from the first day of Elizabeth's reign, but they had probably felt jealous of each other long before, for Countess Lopukhina was the only lady at court whose beauty could compare with Elizabeth's. Elizabeth had always shown a marked preference for dressing in pastel shades for she thought that they suited her delicate colouring better than darker ones. As empress she intended to outshine all her ladies and she therefore forbade them to wear her favourite colour, pink. Only Lopukhina ventured to flout the empress's wishes. Not content with dressing in pink she dared to appear at court one day with her hair dressed in the same manner as the empress's, and, in addition, with a pink rose pinned to it. Angered beyond endurance Elizabeth had ordered her to kneel before her; in full view of her guests she had proceeded to cut off the offending flower together with the lock of hair to which it was attached, and had then delivered two smart smacks on the culprit's cheeks. Lopukhina's fury became ungovernable when her lover, Count Löwenwolde, was banished to Siberia, leaving her powerless to conceal her feelings from her friends. Her lack of discretion was matched by her lack of caution. When she heard that a young Courlander, a Lieutenant Berger, had been posted to Solikamsk to take command of the unit guarding Löwenwolde she asked him to take a letter to her lover. Though the lieutenant was far from pleased at having to serve in Siberia he agreed to hand the letter to his prisoner. But when the letter was delivered to him Berger could not resist opening it. It ended with the words: 'Your trials are perhaps drawing to an end.'[15] On reading these words it occurred to the lieutenant that, if skilfully used, they might serve to delay, if not cancel, his departure from gay Petersburg. He therefore sought out Lestocq, quoted the words, interpreting them as an indication that people were conspiring against Elizabeth. Lestocq no longer had the wily de la Chétardie to consult but he turned for advice to the latter's successor, D'Allion. The two Frenchmen decided that they needed something more definite than the letter before they could tell the empress of their fears and they therefore instructed Berger to produce more convincing evidence of the existence of a plot. The lieutenant was nonplussed until he remembered

that Countess Lopukhina's son, Ivan, a chamberlain of Anna Leopoldovna's, was given to grumbling in public because he no longer held a
court appointment. Ivan was overfond of drink, and quickly fuddled by
it; he was just the man for Berger. The lieutenant promptly invited him
to dinner and then set himself to compromise his guest. As they sat over
their wine Ivan made some disparaging remarks concerning the empress
and, with a passing reference to Botta, he rashly raised his glass to Tsar
Ivan, adding that Frederick of Prussia intended to reinstate the boy at the
first opportunity. His words and behaviour provided Lestocq with more
evidence than he needed. Bubbling over with excitement the doctor
reported to the empress everything he had learnt from Berger, insisting
that her enemies were conspiring to overthrow her. He hoped that his
words would precipitate the downfall of the Bestuzhevs and their friend
the Austrian ambassador and thus further French interests.

The Austrian ambassador, Antoinette, Marquis de Botta d'Adorno,
had distinguished himself both as a soldier and as a diplomat before his
appointment to Russia. In his youth he had been a companion in arms of
Prince Eugen, but had later forsaken the battlefield for politics, where he
had proved competent. Marie Theresa had felt that no one could serve
Austria's cause at the court of her relative better than Count Botta, nor
had she been mistaken for Botta proved loyal and discerning. He took
Anna Leopoldovna's interests very much to heart both because of her
relationship to his sovereign and also because she had renewed Anna
Ivanovna's treaty of friendship with Austria. He warned her repeatedly
that her hold on the regency was in danger, but he also succeeded in
establishing a friendly relationship with the Grand Duchess Elizabeth.
When Elizabeth came to the throne it fell to Botta to hand her the
intercepted letter sent by d'Amelot to Castellane which had been intercepted in Vienna and found to compromise de la Chétardie: on that
occasion the empress had not attempted to conceal from him the distress
she felt as she read it; indeed, she had frankly admitted to him that she
had herself on certain occasions doubted France's sincerity. Botta had
therefore been trying, with the help and encouragement of Alexei
Bestuzhev, to persuade Elizabeth to renew the Austro-Russian treaty
rendered void by the *coup d'état*.

Botta did not rate Elizabeth's political abilities at all highly nor did he
think it likely that her rule would prove stable or lasting. Nevertheless, it
was on his advice that Marie Theresa promptly agreed to accord Elizabeth
her full imperial title, even though Europe's other sovereigns were

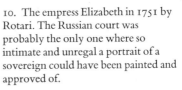

10. The empress Elizabeth in 1751 by Rotari. The Russian court was probably the only one where so intimate and unregal a portrait of a sovereign could have been painted and approved of.

11. Dr Lestocq, Elizabeth's physician, painted by Grooth.

12. The Grand Chancellor of Russia, Count A. P. Bestuzhev, by Grooth.

Ф.С. РОКОТОВ
[1735 — 1808]
А.И. Шувалов
не позже 1760 г.

13. The empress Elizabeth in 1748 wearing a black domino for one of her masked balls, by Grooth.

14. Alexander Ivanovich Shuvalov, the head of the empress Elizabeth's secret chancery, painted by Rokotov.

15. Ivan Shuvalov, the empress's favourite, founder of Moscow University, by Losenko.

refusing to do so. Botta was therefore irritated to find that the Prussian ambassador seemed to be meeting with success, while he himself was making little headway in his effort to obtain the renewal of the Austro-Russian treaty. He became so discouraged that towards the end of 1742 he asked for and obtained his papers of recall. Wich regretted his departure. Now that his integrity was in question it was just as well that he was no longer in St Petersburg to defend it.

Botta had become a friend of the Lopukhins and had often visited them in their house. Had Ivan Lopukhin been bribed? Was it due to the pressure exercised on him by the two Frenchmen and the Prussian ambassador that, when cross-examined, he stated that he had heard the Austrian ambassador remark in his mother's drawing room that Anna Leopoldovna ought not to despair, for better times lay ahead of her. It was well known to the Russians that Marie Theresa felt concerned over the fate of Anna Leopoldovna and her family. Indeed the Austrian empress had not concealed her feelings from Elizabeth and had instructed Botta to defend the princess' interests. On finding that Anna Leopoldovna and her family had been detained in Riga, Marie Theresa had instructed Botta to notify the empress of her hopes that the detainees would be treated leniently. Now, since Botta could not be questioned by the Russian authorities, the charges which had been made against him were forwarded to Marie Theresa together with Elizabeth's demand that a commission of inquiry be set up for the purpose of examining the ambassador's conduct while *en poste* in Russia.

Although Marie Theresa needed Russia as an ally she stoutly denied the charges levelled against her former ambassador and as a token of her good faith in him she appointed him ambassador to Berlin. Elizabeth demanded an inquiry more insistently than ever. Frederick was particularly anxious to avoid a misunderstanding with Russia at that particular moment for he was toying with the idea of a Prussian, Swedish-Russian alliance. He therefore instructed Mardefeld to make what profit he could out of the Botta scandal and informed Marie Theresa that since he did not wish to mar his relations with Russia he would prefer someone other than Botta to represent her in Berlin. Marie Theresa felt obliged to cancel the appointment, but Elizabeth was not satisfied and continued to demand an inquiry, while expressing her appreciation of Frederick's conduct. He availed himself of the opportunity to win her confidence by venturing to advise Elizabeth to transfer Anna Leopoldovna and her family to a safer place of detention than Riga, where they had been imprisoned for well over a year.

Suppressing her distrust of Frederick, Elizabeth expressed her gratitude by agreeing to a treaty of friendship between their two countries. After hesitating for eight months Elizabeth acted on Frederick's hint[16] and on 13 January 1744 the regent and her family left Riga under guard for Riazan, whence they were eventually to proceed to the Solovetsk Monastery on an island to the north of Archangel, to stay there as prisoners. They were accompanied by their entire household but on resuming their journey in late July Anna Leopoldovna's favourite lady, Julie de Mengden, was forbidden to go with the party. Anna Leopoldovna was expecting the birth of another child; the weather was atrocious. Conditions worsened as they moved eastward and eventually became so bad that it proved impossible for them to proceed further northward than Kholmogory. The idea of conveying a party consisting of one hundred and thirty adults and children to the Solovetsk Monastery had to be abandoned and instead the prisoners were installed in the palace of the local archbishop. It was a vast, rambling building surrounded by fairly extensive grounds. A high wall was hurriedly erected round them and the prisoners forbidden to step outside the boundary. It was there that Anna Leopoldovna's three younger children were born and fated to spend the greater part of their adult lives. Anna Leopoldovna died there in 1746, when giving birth to her last child.

After many acrimonious communications had been exchanged between Elizabeth and Marie Theresa the Austrian empress finally appointed a commission to inquire into the charges levied against Botta. When the commission failed to bring anything definite to light the Russian ambassador was invited to question Botta. He fervently refused, on the grounds that he had not been instructed to do so. In reality, he refrained from fear of being implicated and even went to the length of sounding the Austrian authorities about his chances of being granted political asylum there.

Was Botta guilty of anything worse than loose talk based on his feelings of loyalty towards Anna Leopoldovna? It seems unlikely that he ever contemplated conspiring against Elizabeth. Although exhaustive inquiries were made both in Russia and in Austria no evidence was found either in his favour or against him, and the case remains not proven. In Vienna the commission floundered on. Bestuzhev continued to press Elizabeth to renew the Russo-Austrian treaty of friendship. Elizabeth lost her temper and threatened to break off diplomatic relations with Austria if Botta went unpunished. Marie Theresa dared not risk a breach with Russia yet, in the absence of incriminating evidence, was reluctant to punish her ambassador. Inevitably the situation reached a point where someone had to concede. Marie Theresa therefore wrote to inform Elizabeth that, even though proof of Botta's guilt was lacking, she would pass a six months or rather longer sentence of banishment on Botta purely in order to please the empress. In fact she sent him to the charming and healthy resort of Graz for a few months and ignored Elizabeth's further demands that he should either be returned to Russia for trial or indicted.

The inquiry which was being simultaneously held in Russia developed along very different lines. Proceedings were conducted in the Winter Palace before a tribunal which included Lestocq as well as the nation's senators and three representatives of the Church. The empress often attended the proceedings, though hidden from view by a hanging, yet although the Countess Lopukhina and some of the other accused compromised Botta the inquiry failed to produce any definite written evidence of a plot either to dethrone the empress or to endanger her life. It did show that there had been much loose talk of a dangerous kind and that Botta had often contributed to it. The empress came to feel that Countess Lopukhina had shown lack of respect for her own person and also that her behaviour constituted an insult to the memory of Peter the Great. Eventually all the prisoners were pronounced guilty and were sentenced to death by quartering or decapitation. Once again the empress was faced with a cruel dilemma and once again she delayed making her decision known. It was only on her return to her apartments early on the fatal morning after attending a court ball held on the eve of their execution that the empress issued the edict commuting the death sentence. Instead of losing their lives the prisoners were to be viciously beaten in public with the knout and to have their tongues torn out. Then they were to be exiled to Siberia. The decision appeared in the form of a manifesto in which Botta was once again charged with participation in the crime.

On 31 May 1744 a large platform was erected in front of the lovely building Tressini had designed to house the nation's Twelve Administrative Colleges. At the appointed hour the prisoners were led to it. A vast crowd had collected to watch the sentences being carried out. Mikhail Bestuzhev's wife was very calm, the Countess Lopukhina seemed demented by fear. With considerable courage and presence of mind Bestuzheva succeeded in slipping a diamond crucifix into the executioner's hand. He grasped both the bribe and its purpose and, whilst seeming to cut out the prisoner's tongue, managed to inflict only superficial damage to it. Nevertheless, years later, at the very time when her husband, with their daughter acting as hostess, was living in ambassadorial gaiety and splendour in Paris, she was slowly dying of hunger and pain in Siberia. When Lopukhina was led onto the platform she could not control the terror which possessed her. She had to be dragged to the block. Her struggles were so violent that her clothes were torn from her body in full view of the crowd and her tongue so cruelly wrenched out that she lay in a dead faint whilst her husband's bones were being so mercilessly broken on the rack that he never recovered their use. At his death in Siberia in 1758 the countess implored the empress to pardon her and permit her to return to western Russia, but Elizabeth remained adamant and the unfortunate exile was obliged to stay in Siberia. However, at Elizabeth's death Peter III, acting less out of magnanimity than a desire to dissent from the dead empress's wishes, allowed her to return to St Petersburg.

Alexei Razumovsky cannot have approved of the tortures inflicted on the prisoners. Though he made a point of never interfering in affairs of state he invariably tried to help the people whom he either loved or respected. He must have interceded for the families of those convicted, for the mother of one retained her position of lady in waiting to the empress, and the brothers Bestuzhev remained in office with their influence unaffected. If Lestocq had set this violent and distressing sequence of events in motion for the purpose of obtaining the dismissal of the Bestuzhevs he had to conceal his disappointment at the failure of his plan. Elizabeth never again behaved in so cruel and barbarous a manner. As her hold on the throne became firmer her punishments lost much of the brutality she had learnt from her predecessors.

5

Years of Hope
and Disillusion (1743-7)

Elizabeth was not lacking in courage. Though she was so distressed by
death that she would go to almost inhuman lengths to prevent any one
dying in one of her palaces she was a fearless sportswoman, a reckless rider
and, until she became empress, showed no regard for her own safety. Even
after becoming empress she was prepared to risk her life and appearance
of which she was extremely proud, in order to nurse those whom she
loved through such a fearful and loathsome disease as smallpox. Nevertheless, during the opening years of her reign she quailed at the mere thought
of assassination. Her contemporaries made much play of her frightened
reactions to reported plots against her person and of the sleepless and
tormented nights which resulted from them. Yet her dread of assassination
did not stem so much from a fear of death, real though that was, as from
her dread of vacating the throne before Russia had been provided with a
capable successor.

The great importance which Elizabeth attached to the task of ensuring
the continuity of the monarchy did not mean that she set small store on
her possession of it. On the contrary, she enjoyed being empress. She knew
that she had inherited much of her father's sense of kingship and therefore
felt justified in preserving her life for the benefit of her people. At the same
time she felt no scruples in enjoying the good things of this world now
that they had at last come within her reach; she felt that she was entitled
to them, but she also thought that her pleasure in splendour and display
would serve to cheer and invigorate the nation. In the past her subjects
had, like herself, been frequently obliged to accept a harsh and circum-
scribed existence; she wished them to forget the sterility of the old way of

life, the cruelty which had taken root in Muscovy following the Mongol occupation of Russia; she wanted them to realize that life could be gay, stimulating and absorbing. Unfortunately Elizabeth was herself too in-nured in the past to know how to complete the transformation which she desired and which had been set in motion by her father. Her eyes could not see beyond the boundaries of the small world made up of her courtiers, her servants, her armies and the inhabitants of Moscow and St Petersburg together with the latter's respective belts of country palaces and great rural monasteries. With the sole exception of Alexei Razumovsky's native Ukraine she had few thoughts to spare for the inhabitants of Russia's vast expanses and heavily wooded regions. This is hard to understand in a princess who had entered so closely into the life of the peasants as had Elizabeth when she lived at Izmailovo. Russia was to suffer from the effects of her oversight for a century or so to come for Catherine II, as in so much else, seems to have based her own attitude to the peasantry on that of Elizabeth.

The Botta affair upset Elizabeth's equilibrium and self-confidence. She had until then firmly believed that the success of her *coup d'état* indicated that she was generally popular, not merely loved by a number of men serving in the Guards' regiments. In the months which followed Elizabeth became a prey to fears and grim forebodings. She was probably also often haunted by the memory of foolish, inoffensive Anna Leopoldovna's stricken face on the night of the coup. Elizabeth developed a dread of sleeping in her bedroom. Night after night she would send her maids scurrying from one apartment to another in whichever of the vast, ramb-ling, decaying palaces she happened to be living, to choose the room in which she thought she would be able to sleep, to find that she could endure it for only a night or two. She would postpone the hour for retiring ever later, at times disregarding the exhaustion of her older courtiers and insisting on staying up till dawn. Or again she would summon her ladies to her bedside and, believing as she still did that reading was unhealthy, she would instruct some six of them, forming a special group of ticklers, to talk to her while tickling the soles of her feet. She encouraged them to gossip and report the day's sayings and events to her, relying on their talk for keeping in touch with public opinion. She depended especially on a mysterious and rather questionable old lady known only by her name and patronymic Elizaveta Ivanovna, who had been aptly nicknamed by Count Stroganov 'le ministre des affaires étranges'. When the group included Mavra Egorovna Bestuzheva and Anna Karlovna Vorontzova, by birth a Skavronskaya and thus a cousin of the empress's, the three favourites were referred to as 'Elizaveta Petrovna's Cabinet'. A former stoker called Shulkov was generally present at these gatherings. Elizabeth had appointed him chamberlain and he was her guardian at night. He slept at the foot of her bed, and left his post only at dawn to make way for the empress's favourite.

If it was fear rather than a troubled conscience which kept the empress awake at night there were grounds for it. Whether true or fabricated – and neither the empress nor those who were attached to her ever questioned the reality of the reported plots – each conspiracy helped to keep alive the memory of Tsar Ivan. Elizabeth was not herself in need of such reminders, for her thoughts often turned to him, never permitting her to forget how necessary it was to ensure the throne's continuity. Although the number of amorous adventures with which Elizabeth has been credited is vastly exaggerated* she must long ago have realized that there was little likelihood of her ever being able to bear the children in whom she would have found such delight. Even court scandal† ascribed only one child to her – the mysterious young woman who, under the name of Princess Tarakanova, claimed to be her daughter. Historians are now united in regarding her as an adventuress who had succeeded in convincing herself of the validity of her claim, one whom even her contemporaries supposed to be the daughter either of a sultan, of a Nüremberg baker or of a French innkeeper. In a Europe which saw no difficulty in accepting bastards of royal birth Elizabeth would have had no reason to conceal the existence of a child of her own, and even if convention had made secrecy desirable she would probably have refused to comply with it, so fervent was her love of children.

Elizabeth must have realized almost from the start that her fourteen-year-old nephew, the boy whom she longed to love, cherish and train for his high office, was unfit to govern her people. She could not at the time admit this even to herself. She smothered her apprehensions in the comforting thought that he was still young enough to change and develop. His appearance had in fact improved since his arrival, and in her anxiety to ensure the succession to the throne Elizabeth's thoughts turned to the problem of finding him a suitable bride. It was not altogether easy to do so.

---

* Seven can be confirmed.

† Gossips accredited her with eight children, including Marfa Filipovna Bekhteieva and Olga Petrovna Soupaiera among her daughters. Aff. Etr. Memories et Documents Russie, vol. 9, folio 146, d'Aubigny papers.

France would probably refuse to provide one of the king's daughters for the purpose. Bestuzhev suggested Princess Louisa, daughter of Britain's king, but Elizabeth was opposed to this and so as an alternative he put forward the name of Princess Marianna, a daughter of Augustus III, Elector of Saxony. The proposal displeased Frederick of Prussia, who was also unwilling to see his sister Ulrique, later queen of Sweden, married to Peter. However, he undertook to provide Elizabeth with a suitable bride.

His choice rested on Sophia of Anhalt Zerbst, the fifteen-year-old daughter of an impoverished German princeling. Her name had some years earlier already been linked with Peter. Frederick spoke so well of the girl that, in the absence of a more eligible candidate, Elizabeth agreed to see her. Though the matter was treated with great secrecy Lord Tyrawley, who had succeeded Wich as British ambassador to Russia, was able to inform London of the plan as early as 21 July 1743, but it was not until the autumn that loneliness, boredom and the long hours he was expected to spend at his studies affected Peter's health to such an extent that the empress decided to send for the young girl.

Versailles was beginning to realize that it had acted unwisely in not being represented in Russia by an ambassador capable of winning the empress's regard. After giving the matter some thought the king reached no better decision than that of re-appointing de la Chétardie to the post, but he continued obstinately to adhere to the refusal, first given to Peter the Great in 1721, to address Russia's ruler by his imperial title. Even though de la Chétardie claimed to have placed Elizabeth on the throne, and although she had let it be widely known that she would not accept an ambassador whose sovereign refused to address her as empress, the king forbade de la Chétardie to accord her her full title.

The difficulties arising from Louis' refusal were discussed at great length by Versailles. Finally, in late September, a solution was found which reflects the duplicity of Louis' treatment of Elizabeth. De la Chétardie was given two letters neither of which had the full value of a letter of credence. One was a document known as a 'lettre d'amitié', in which the empress was not addressed by her full title; the other was a personal communication which addressed her by her title, but only unofficially. Acting in the belief that the empress was sufficiently devoted to him for him not to require either document de la Chétardie decided to appear before her in the private capacity of an old and trusted friend. He relied on their earlier intimacy to gain ready admittance to her presence and invitations to dine with her in private. D'Allion was furious when he heard of de la

Chétardie's appointment and informed Versailles that it was mistaken. His disapproval was shared by the British ambassador, in his case through fear of de la Chétardie's influence over the empress. Both their letters were intercepted by Bestuzhev's spies and copies submitted to Elizabeth.

De la Chétardie planned to arrive in St Petersburg early in November to attend the celebrations marking the anniversary of the empress's accession but he was delayed by bad weather. Hence he covered the last stage of the journey at great speed and risked his life in a dangerous crossing of the only partially frozen Neva. (The river still lacked a permanent bridge.) Even so, he reached the capital on the very day of the empress's anniversary. He had notified no one of his arrival and so he drove to Lestocq's house where he planned to stay till d'Allion had vacated the embassy. Then, having had time for only a brief rest, he set out for the reception being held in Elizabeth's honour. Elizabeth greeted him affably, but without any marked warmth.

Things did not go well for de la Chétardie on this second visit. To begin with he and d'Allion became so uncontrollably jealous of each other that on one occasion they even exchanged blows in public. Far worse for the French was Elizabeth's determination not to discuss affairs of state with de la Chétardie, on the grounds that he was visiting Russia in a private capacity. She proceeded to make good use of her ability to stall – an ability which irked foreign diplomats almost beyond endurance, angering them more than her hot temper or her laziness. To force de la Chétardie to negotiate direct with Bestuzhev Elizabeth gave the impression of being wholly preoccupied with her social engagements. The Frenchman was equally determined not to discuss Franco-Russian relations with a man who was unsympathetic to France and who believed that Russia's interests would best be favoured by friendship with Austria and Britain. Vanity also influenced de la Chétardie's attitude for he was incapable of believing that the empress had lost confidence in him. He was convinced that he had only to see her in private to obtain her agreement to a French alliance.

The Princess of Zerbst and her young daughter left their home in January 1744 on the first stage of their journey to Russia. At Frederick of Prussia's request they broke their journey in Berlin where the king persuaded the princess to act as his secret agent. In Berlin Sophia parted from her meek and considerate father. She was never to see him again, nor was she ever to return to her native land.

Cares of state and concern over the succession to the throne had begun to leave their mark on Elizabeth. Plays had now to be performed for her entertainment with increasing frequency, balls to be more numerous and sumptuous than ever. Even then they proved less delightful than before till in 1744 Elizabeth hit on the idea of asking all her guests to attend one such ball un-masked, with the men dressed as women and the women as men. The evening gave her such pleasure that she decided that balls of this type, known as 'metamorphoses', should occur at regular intervals. Although they proved extremely unpopular with her male guests many of her ladies enjoyed them almost as much as the empress herself. Though Elizabeth was steadily putting on weight her legs remained beautiful and her dancing light and graceful so that male dress suited her. She still enjoyed dancing so much that she seldom sat out and often found it necessary to change her costume three times in the course of a single evening.

The fact was that neurasthenia was gaining a hold over the empress. As yet its symptoms lay concealed, yet there were signs that the quite harmless interest which Elizabeth had formerly taken in clothes was turning into a mania. The exaggerated importance which Anna Ivanovna had attached to expensive, elaborate dresses and flashing jewels was more than outmatched by Elizabeth. Her life was spent amidst the discomforts of medieval palaces and hastily, often shoddily refurbished dwellings where leaking roofs and broken pieces of furniture aroused no feelings of surprise. Even the largest of these residences were so overcrowded that, during one of the court's visits to Moscow, seventeen of the Grand Duchess Catherine's ladies were obliged to sleep in a closet the only exit of which led to Catherine's bedroom. In such conditions as these innumerable servants were expected to deal with veritable mountains of the empress's clothes. In a disastrous fire in Moscow in 1744 Elizabeth asserted that she had lost four thousand dresses, countless pieces of jewellery and a large jewel-encrusted bowl which Prince Rumiantzev had acquired for her in Constantinople at a cost of eight thousand chervontzy.* Since Elizabeth seldom wore the same dress twice it is scarcely surprising that, at her death seventeen years later, she left fifteen thousand dresses hanging in her cupboards, two trunks filled with stockings, and immense debts. Courtiers felt obliged to keep in step. When Sophia was still only engaged to Peter, within days of returning from the state visit to Kiev, the sixteen-year-old girl had contracted debts amounting to seventeen thousand roubles. Fortunately Elizabeth had given her fifteen thousand roubles and a trunk filled with exquisite materials to ensure that she

---

* From 1701 a gold coin worth three roubles, equal in value to the ducat.

should be suitably attired for the state visit to the Ukraine and, on this occasion, she was therefore able to settle the majority. Most of Elizabeth's courtiers incurred debts which they increased in the reign of Catherine II. The need for finery fostered jealousies, the existence of debts intrigue and corruption. If any consolation can be drawn from this senseless way of life it is to be found in the personal rather than political nature of the court's intrigues. The change was brought about by Elizabeth who was determined to put an end to the dynastic factions which had divided courtiers since her father's death and in which lay the root of many conspiracies.

The court had moved to Moscow by the time the Princess of Zerbst and her daughter arrived in St Petersburg, but the empress had left careful instructions about their reception. She had also arranged for their wardrobes to be examined and supplemented with everything necessary to ensure that they appeared at her court fittingly attired. Both were found to need many extra dresses, particularly Sophia. While these were being made for them Sophia was shown all the sights of St Petersburg, and there was already much for her to admire there. In the meantime de la Chétardie and Mardefeld paid court to her mother, both diplomats having stayed in St Petersburg for the purpose. Since they were all anxious to be in Moscow in time for Peter's birthday celebrations they decided to travel there together. They managed to reach Moscow by ten o'clock in the evening of 9 February, the day before Peter's birthday. Elizabeth received Sophia and her mother that very evening. She welcomed them on the threshold to her apartments with extreme affability. Her ample bosom was smothered in great diamonds and splendid jewels, and she wore a large black feather in her hair. The girl was dazzled by her regal air, her astonishing beauty and impressive carriage. As the empress gazed at the young girl's intelligent, anxious face some trait in it may have reminded her of Charles Augustus of Holstein, Sophia's dead uncle, the man she had hoped to marry, for tears filled her eyes. She controlled them and talked to her guests for half an hour, then she sent them to rest and to prepare for the next day's ceremonies. She was enchanted by Sophia. The child was far more prepossessing than she had dared to hope. The impression which the empress made on the young bride-to-be was equally favourable, at any rate at this stage. Its effect was to prove far more lasting and profound than is generally realized, for Catherine (as Sophia came to be called) was to copy Elizabeth in many ways. It was from her that she acquired the fervent sense of patriotism, the respect and love of Russia which were later to carry her to the throne.

On the morning of 10 February Elizabeth sent for the Princess of Zerbst and her daughter. In honour of Peter's birthday the empress was dressed no less richly than on the previous night. She was an impressive figure when she rose to invest mother and daughter with the Order of St Catherine, the decoration which her father had created in honour of her mother. The day's festivities proved a revelation to Sophia. She had never imagined that such splendour could exist and the sight of it aroused in her an almost insatiable desire for luxury and magnificence. In the days which followed, the valuable and beautiful objects which the empress lavished upon her served to strengthen Sophia's determination to make the best of the uncouth and temperamental youth she was to marry. From the start she treated him with astonishing tact. Surrounded as they were by adults their youth formed a bond between them and they were soon on good terms.

Sophia was determined to please the empress. Her remarkable intelligence and keen perceptions enabled her rapidly to appreciate the sincerity and depth of Elizabeth's love of Russia. She quickly came to recognize the importance of following the empress's example. The ardour with which she applied herself to the task of mastering the country's language, customs and church ritual delighted the empress. Elizabeth's heart warmed to Sophia, but she could not bring herself to like her mother. Nevertheless, she treated the Princess of Zerbst with affability, at any rate until early March, when their relationship became strained. The trouble arose over Sophia. Elizabeth had left Moscow for a few days to take a short retreat in the Troitse-Sergieva Lavra when Sophia, having woken early one morning, left her bed and sat down in her nightdress to learn the lesson set by her Russian tutor Vasili Adadurov. As a result she caught a chill and was soon dangerously ill with pleurisy. Her doctors failed to diagnose her illness and became alarmed by her condition, but the princess of Zerbst seemed unconcerned and seldom went too near her daughter's sick bed. When Sophia's condition worsened she refused to help the nurse who was attending her lest the girl were suffering from smallpox, but Elizabeth considered her refusal to allow Sophia to be bled almost as reprehensible as her lack of feeling. Sophia became so ill that a messenger was finally sent to inform the empress of her condition, and to warn her that the girl had possibly caught smallpox. The mere thought of Sophia dying was appalling. Without a moment's hesitation or a thought for her own health and appearance the empress hastened back to Moscow. Her swiftest horses were harnessed to her carriage and, with Lestocq seated beside her,

Elizabeth drove there at break-neck speed. On arrival she sprang from the carriage and hurried to Sophia's bedside. She found the girl unconscious, though alive. Taking her in her arms she ordered Lestocq to examine and bleed her. The treatment answered. On regaining consciousness Sophia was astonished to find herself held by the empress. Her life remained in danger during seventeen more days and during that time Elizabeth scarcely left her. Her devoted nursing undoubtedly saved Sophia's life. The incident increased the empress's affection for the girl, but she failed to realize that Sophia was as calculating as she was fascinating. Even when still very ill and weak she often pretended to be asleep so as to overhear the empress's conversation and thus adjusted her own behaviour to the latter's wishes. Elizabeth never discovered the deception and was deeply touched when told that Sophia's illness had been caused by her desire to master Russian and that, when her life was thought to be in danger, she had asked for Father Semeon Todorsky, the priest who was preparing her for entry into the Orthodox Church, in preference to a Lutheran pastor.[1] On the other hand the empress took a most unfavourable view of the way in which the princess of Zerbst had reacted to her daughter's illness.

On 21 April, though still very thin and weak, Sophia was able to appear at her own birthday celebrations. Elizabeth presented her with a snuffbox studded with diamonds and kept referring to her as 'her adorable child'. On the same day, partly to indicate that she considered the princess of Zerbst unfit to look after her own daughter, she also provided Sophia with a household of her own. The princess failed to realize that she had forfeited the empress's regard. She was by nature self-assured and obtuse, but she was also at the time so much absorbed in plotting Alexei Bestuzhev's disgrace with de la Chétardie and Mardefeld that she failed to notice the change in Elizabeth's manner. In accordance with Frederick's wishes the princess had turned her drawing room into a rallying point for all Bestuzhev's enemies and for those opposed to any accord between Russia, Austria and Britain. Mardefeld and de la Chétardie were among her most active assistants in this, but they were warmly seconded by Lestocq, who had been drawing a Prussian pension since 1742 and who now went to the length of threatening the empress with his resignation should Bestuzhev remain in office. Though Elizabeth has been labelled weak and wayward by historians her confidence in her vice-chancellor never wavered under these pressures. Angered by her firmness, irritated by the aloofness with which she treated him no less than by his own ill-defined position at court, de la Chétardie became embittered. He began venting his spleen in his despatches, deriding the empress, referring to her in disparaging terms, often even alluding to her 'deplorable behaviour', her 'voluptuous lethargy', her vanity, inconstancy and licentiousness. Typical of these reports is a passage in a despatch which he sent to Versailles on 2 April 1744. He stated in it that 'her love of trifles, her delight in seeing herself when in the privacy of her apartments surrounded by riff-raff, wholly occupies the tsarina's mind. Intoxicated by this setting she deludes herself into believing that the greater her personal contentment the more do her subjects adore her and the less has she to fear. The thought of work scares her, and her indolence and laziness invariably result in her permitting events to take their course.'[2]

Bestuzhev knew that he was hated by the French and the Prussians, and that they were hoping to disgrace him; he was convinced that a French alliance would prove disastrous to Russia; he mistrusted de la Chétardie. On becoming Vice-Chancellor and Minister for Foreign Affairs he had followed the example set by Frederick of Prussia and had provided himself with an efficient intelligence service. When de la Chétardie arrived in Russia for the second time Bestuzhev instructed his spies to keep a close watch over the Frenchman. They had as a result intercepted a number of his despatches, but at first they were unable to break the French cypher. By March 1744 Bestuzhev already possessed a considerable number of these documents; in April his men succeeded in decoding them. They found all the evidence needed by Bestuzhev to convince the empress of de la Chétardie's duplicity, but the minister preferred to hold his hand. It was not until 6 June that he handed fifty-seven of the decoded despatches to the empress and informed her of their contents. At first Elizabeth was so stunned by his words that she was unable to take in their full meaning. She was especially outraged to discover that the Princess of Zerbst was spying for Frederick, sending the King of Prussia regular reports on all that occurred at her court. 'It can't be true,' she shouted; 'it is a fabrication of my enemies, and you are one of them.'[3] Scarcely two years earlier her confidence in de la Chétardie had been shaken by Austria, but it had emerged from the test almost unharmed; now that she could not doubt the evidence submitted to her she was as distressed by his interference in Russia's domestic affairs as she was by the way in which he had pictured her to the King of France. She felt bitter regret at having quarrelled with Marie Theresa. Profoundly disturbed she withdrew to her apartments and shut herself in for twenty-four hours. Lestocq, however, discovered what had taken place and hastened to inform Mardefeld, but the latter made no

effort to warn de la Chétardie. Lestocq believed that he too was implicated and was terrified. He contemplated suicide, but was dissuaded by his
wife. Sensing the danger Brümmer cautioned the Princess of Zerbst, but
she seemed incapable of appreciating her peril.

The reports of foreign diplomats contained numerous references to
Elizabeth's reluctance to make up her mind or deal with the state's affairs;
they remarked on her innate laziness and incapacity for sustained thought
due, so they believed, to lack of training in concentration. But although
Elizabeth could overcome her indolence when she considered it necessary
she often made use of it throughout her reign to conceal her lack of
experience in international affairs. When she was obliged to make a major
decision she became hesitant, and frequently changed her mind while the
documents awaiting her signature piled up on her desk, often for weeks
on end. In cases of extreme consequence she was apt to withdraw to a
monastery, where prayers and privacy finally directed her on a definite
course. Nevertheless her hesitations were neither as frequent nor as intense
as foreigners believed. When urged to act against her inclinations she often
feigned indecision in order to achieve her own ends. Now, in the privacy
of her room, the empress had little difficulty in deciding how to act –
de la Chétardie was to leave Moscow within two hours and Russia within
eight days. An officer was sent to inform the Frenchman of her wishes,
but de la Chétardie had gone to dine with Mardefeld. He did not return to
his rooms till the early hours of the morning and the empress's orders took
him by surprise. He went to his room and packed. Two hours later he
got into the carriage which had been provided for him and set out for the
frontier under a strong guard. At the border the officer in command of it
insisted on the return of the empress's portrait and the ribbon of the Order
of St Andrew which Elizabeth had conferred on him to mark the start of
her reign, adding as a final insult that de la Chétardie could retain the
precious stones which had been set in them.

While de la Chétardie was travelling westward Elizabeth had rushed to
the Troitse-Sergieva Lavra, leaving orders for the Princess of Zerbst,
Sophia, Peter, Lestocq and certain courtiers to follow her there. She gave
no inkling of her feelings or intentions but sent for them soon after their
arrival. On entering her ante-room Peter and Sophia were told to wait
while the Princess of Zerbst was conducted to an inner room. At the time
Peter and Sophia were at ease together and even took pleasure in each
other's company for the girl was handling him with tact and Peter seemed
well disposed towards her. They therefore gaily clambered onto a high

window seat and, as they swung their legs, chatted contentedly. They felt carefree and when the inner door suddenly opened and Lestocq burst into the room they were unperturbed. Advancing menacingly towards them the doctor turned to Sophia and said abruptly, 'Go off and pack your bags; you are to return home at once.' The young people were too startled to rebuke him for his rudeness. Both realized that the Princess of Zerbst had offended the empress. Sophia sensed that her future was at stake. Scared and bewildered they were sitting silent and motionless when the door was flung open for the second time and Elizabeth appeared, her face flushed with anger, her expression unusually stern. Behind her stood the princess of Zerbst, her eyes red rimmed, her white cheeks wet with tears. Like the frightened children that they were, Peter and Sophia scrambled down from the window seat. They looked so young and so anxious that Elizabeth was both touched and amused. She could seldom bring herself to be angry with children or young people. Bending down the empress kissed Sophia, indicating thereby that her marriage would take place as planned. Sophia was never to forget how easy it was to touch and disarm the empress, and was often to win her forgiveness by merely saying 'Vinovata, Matushka' – I am at fault Ma'am. Deceit and disloyalty were the two faults which Elizabeth found most difficult to condone and on this occasion she could not bring herself to overlook the princess of Zerbst's behaviour. She announced her intention of immediately evicting the princess from Russia. Finally she relented sufficiently to permit her to stay on for her daughter's wedding, though forbidding her to appear at court on other than the most formal occasions.

Elizabeth had never come really to like Bestuzhev, but from the start she had appreciated and relied on his advice. Now that his opinion of de la Chétardie had been proved correct, her trust in him increased and she decided to appoint him Grand Chancellor of Russia. Simultaneously she promoted Mikhail Vorontzov to the post of Vice-Chancellor even though she knew perfectly well that the two men held opposing views about Russia's foreign policy. In contrast to Bestuzhev, Vorontzov advocated closer links with France; his policy appealed to Elizabeth yet she accepted Bestuzhev's advice that she should try to link Russia's future to those of Austria and Britain. She finally agreed to an alliance with Britain chiefly because it was directed against Prussia. It was ratified at the end of the year and a Russian army was sent to the country's western frontier to wait there till needed by Britain.

During the summer of 1744 Elizabeth devoted more attention to personal and family matters than to foreign affairs. On 29 June Sophia was received into the Orthodox Church as Catherine. Since the name of Sophia figures in the Orthodox calendar of saints there was no reason why she should not have kept it on accepting orthodoxy, but it was one which Elizabeth associated so closely with her father's half-sister that it had become hateful to her and she therefore insisted on the young girl adopting the name of her own, dearly loved mother. She went to immense trouble to ensure that the girl looked her best on that day, choosing a dress of white Tours silk trimmed with silver for her, arranging for her unpowdered hair to be tied back with a white ribbon, and limiting her jewellery to a large pendant and brooch which she had herself given to her. Sophia was determined to make a good impression and fully succeeded in doing so. The empress was especially pleased by her conduct during the long and complicated ceremony. As a sign of her approval she presented Catherine, as Sophia was now to be called, with a diamond brooch and necklace valued at 150,000 roubles, intending that she should wear it at the great state banquet arranged in her honour for the same evening, but in the event Catherine felt too tired by the morning's religious ceremony to attend it.

On the following day Catherine became officially engaged to Peter. She was invested with the rank of grand duchess, which carried with it the title of an imperial highness. Their betrothal was celebrated in the Cathedral of the Assumption. Wearing her crown and mantle of state the empress accompanied the young couple as they walked from the palace to the cathedral beneath a canopy of silver carried by eight generals, along a route lined with guardsmen. The ceremony was conducted with all possible pomp and magnificence, the Archbishop of Novgorod officiating. The service lasted for four hours. In the course of it the young couple exchanged rings, standing on a dais covered in velvet. Salvos of guns were fired at regular intervals and the remainder of the day was spent in universal rejoicing. Elizabeth showered gifts on Catherine, including a miniature of herself and another of Peter, both studded with diamonds. The day's happiness was, however, marred by the Princess of Zerbst. On finding that she was not to sit on a raised platform beside the empress and the newly engaged pair at the state banquet, she refused to mingle with the other guests and insisted on dining alone on a small balcony overlooking the banqueting hall, nor would she appear at the ball which concluded the day's events.

Alexei Razumovsky may well have been the first to suggest to Elizabeth that she should take the grand ducal couple on a journey across Russia to visit Kiev. He adored his native Ukraine and always promoted its welfare. As Russia's first capital Kiev was the kernel of Elizabeth's kingdom; its great and glorious Monastery of the Caves was the oldest and most deeply venerated in the country; Elizabeth wanted her heirs to grow to know Russia intimately in order to come to love the country and have faith in it; she longed herself to visit Russia's oldest monastery as a pilgrim and, finally, she delighted in pleasing Alexei Razumovsky. She therefore decided to undertake the long and tiring journey across Russia in the company of Peter, Catherine, the Princess of Zerbst, 230 courtiers and retainers and, naturally enough, Alexei Razumovsky. They were all to leave Moscow on 26 July; she herself was to follow a day later since she intended to travel faster than they could.

Roads had been repaved and new bridges built for the benefit of the royal travellers. Some of the villages through which they were to pass were smartened up with fresh coats of whitewash, but nothing in the nature of the sham constructions which Prince Potiemkin erected some forty years later for Catherine's journey to the Crimea. Elizabeth knew Russia in all its poverty and backwardness far too well to have countenanced such a deception. She wanted Catherine and Peter to see Russia as it really was, with its shabbiness and simplicity unmasked. The Grand Duchess was, however, so disturbed by the sight that she did not notice the sober majesty of the landscape or appreciate the dignity and warmth with which the peasants welcomed them at each stopping place, offering them the black bread and salt which symbolized hospitality. During the early stages of the journey she commented on their poverty and was keenly critical of it. Soon after she ceased to notice it and years later, at the time when her intelligence, powers of observation and expression had come to be widely admired in the West, she did not recognize Potiemkin's sham villages and dolled-up peasants as counterfeits; and she was unaffected by the misery of the countryside although it was even more pronounced than in Elizabeth's day.

Elizabeth's journey to the Ukraine was often tiring and uncomfortable. The Princess of Zerbst was permanently on edge and her outbursts of bad temper were so frequent and so violent that her future son-in-law took an intense and permanent dislike to her, and nicknamed her 'the vixen'. Peter was profoundly bored throughout the journey and behaved in an even more childish manner than usual. Catherine whiled away the tedium of the long stages by chattering and joking with the handsome young gentlemen attached to Peter's suite. The empress, however, was in splendid spirits. Her delight in the journey persisted even after the discovery at Glukov of a plot to overthrow her. Once again it is impossible to establish whether the conspiracy was real or imagined, but suspects were produced and two of them were found guilty and banished to Siberia. The inquiry which followed lasted three weeks. Elizabeth spent them there and the rest of the court waited for her at Kozeltse.[4] The empress would not permit the incident to affect existing arrangements and no additional measures were taken to protect her or her heirs when the party resumed their journey to Kiev.

It was not until August that they reached the outskirts of Kiev. The students of the Theological Academy, at the time the most advanced centre of religious learning in the country, had assembled to meet them, some dressed as Greek gods, others as heroes of antiquity, others as imaginary beasts. A group of clerics carrying the city's most venerated icon stood beside them singing the Liturgy in unison. A bearded old man, in a golden crown and royal robes, and representing Kiev's legendary founder, prince Kij, presented the empress with the city's keys, while the students intoned hymns of welcome. The empress was then asked to transfer from her own carriage to one drawn by a pair of horses adorned with the emblem of Pegasus, driven by a man masquerading as Phaeton. The grand ducal pair entered a second carriage while the rest of the royal party joined the clerics and students to form a procession. They entered Kiev through the Golden Gate which Grand Duke Yaroslav the Wise had built in the eleventh century in emulation of the Golden Gate of Byzantine Constantinople.

Elizabeth's stay in Kiev was delightful. The entertainments which had been devised pleased her and she derived much satisfaction from the short retreat she was able to take in the Monastery of the Caves. She was touched by the piety of the Kievans and enchanted by their gaiety and friendliness. Shortly before her departure she received a deputation which had come to petition her to restore the hetmanship which Peter the Great had abolished with Moldavia's independence as a punishment for Mazeppa's defection. In 1750 she accordingly conferred it on Kiril Razumovsky, Alexei's brother, as a twenty-first birthday present. When bidding farewell to the city she implored 'God in his heavenly kingdom to love her as she loved the sweet and guileless people of Kiev'. The fortnight she had spent there was one of the happiest in her reign.

Back in Moscow Elizabeth became greatly concerned by Britain's decision to attack France in the Low Countries and the fact that Frederick had seized Prague and was advancing on Bohemia. It was more pleasant to learn that Louis had consented to address her by her imperial title and that Marie Theresa, anxious to bury all memory of the Botta affair, had appointed a new envoy to Russia. He was the bearer of letters couched in the friendliest terms.

Scarcely had the empress finished dealing with the documents which had accumulated in her absence, and the travellers settled back into their customary routine, than Peter fell ill with some kind of malarial fever. It held him for several weeks and left him much weakened. Before he had regained his strength he contracted chicken pox and languished for several weeks more, seemingly unable to throw off the malady. Elizabeth had postponed the court's return to St Petersburg on his account, but she was anxious to be back there for Christmas and at the first signs of an improvement in Peter's health she gave orders for a return to the new capital.

On the morning that the court left Moscow the empress went into the courtyard to watch the grand ducal party set off. Catherine was to travel in the same sledge as her mother, Peter and his equerry to follow in another. The weather was bitterly cold and it occurred to the empress that Catherine was not dressed sufficiently warmly. Taking off her own fur coat she wrapped it round the girl's shoulders, glancing irritably at the Princess of Zerbst as she did so, no doubt silently rebuking her for not taking better care of her daughter. As usual, the empress was the last to leave Moscow. On this occasion it took the grand ducal party longer to reach the half stage of Khotilovo than it did the empress to complete the journey. On reaching Khotilovo Peter, who had complained of feeling ill, fainted as he was descending from his sledge. He was carried to his room and put to bed. The next morning Catherine went to inquire after his health, but was prevented from entering his room by an equerry who told her that the Grand Duke's symptoms resembled those of smallpox. On hearing the disastrous news the Princess of Zerbst was overcome by panic. With no thought for the poor young man she sent for her sledge and insisted on departing immediately for St Petersburg with Catherine.

A messenger had already been sent on the fastest horse available to inform the empress of the misfortune which had occurred. Like the Princess of Zerbst, Elizabeth – the woman who has gone down in history as vain, self-indulgent, selfish and irresolute – sent immediately for her sledge; but in her case it was in order to speed back to Khotilovo. Near

Novgorod she met Catherine and her mother driving in the opposite direction. Pausing only long enough to hear the last report on Peter's health the empress hurried to him heedless of her own health and beauty. On reaching Khotilovo she took charge of the sick room. She nursed her nephew through his nauseating and dangerous illness with courage and serenity, staying at his bedside for over a month. Cut off from the outer world she cared for him so skilfully that he recovered. Meanwhile, in St Petersburg, by order of the empress, the Princess of Zerbst and her daughter had settled in two separate though identical apartments in the Winter Palace. These had been especially prepared for them; each contained two rooms facing on to the street and two on to a court, the front ones hung with pale blue silk, the inner ones with red. Catherine wrote to Peter almost daily. Her letters were drafted for her by Adadurov and she had merely to copy them, an arrangement which she did not think it necessary for the empress to know of. The letters were so cordial in tone and worded in such excellent Russian that the unsuspecting Elizabeth was charmed by their content and delighted by what appeared to be Catherine's mastery of the Russian language.

Peter undoubtedly owed his recovery to his aunt, but although she had saved his life she was unable to erase the ravages which his illness had caused to his face. Never a handsome youth, he emerged from his sick room disfigured and repellent. He was strong enough to travel back to St Petersburg in time for his birthday, but on seeing him Catherine was so horrified by the change in his appearance that she was unable to conceal her distress. Peter could not bring himself to appear in public on his birthday. The empress showed great understanding. She left the young couple free of engagements in the hope that they would soon readjust themselves to Peter's altered appearance. Catherine wondered whether she could indeed bring herself to marry Peter, but felt unable to exchange the splendid future which Elizabeth planned for her for the drab and penurious existence at Zerbst. Peter, possibly acting in self-defence, spent his time playing with toy soldiers, teasing his dogs, tormenting his servants. By March the empress felt that little would be gained by marking time and she settled on 21 August for their wedding day. The necessary arrangements were put in hand without further delay. Though Catherine's father was not to be invited to attend the wedding the Russian nobility and gentry were all instructed to assemble in the capital in good time for it, bringing their richest clothes and finest jewels with them.

Though war raged in Europe, threatening to engulf Russia, Elizabeth was chiefly concerned with the wedding arrangements. She had set her heart on making the wedding the most splendid known to Europe and had sent to Dresden for details of the ceremonial adopted there for the wedding of Augustus III, and to Versailles for that followed at the Dauphin's wedding, asking in each case for sketches and descriptions in addition to details on protocol. The French wedding proving the more magnificent of the two Elizabeth decided to follow its broad outline, but to surpass it in solemnity and brilliance helped by the gorgeous setting and impressive ritual of the Orthodox Church. To make doubly sure of success she ordered all guests belonging to the two top grades in the Table of Ranks to provide at least two heyducks and eight footmen for each of their carriages. To enable officials to appear in magnificent clothes each was given a year's salary in advance, but since it did not seem to occur to anyone to inquire how they were to meet the following year's expenses the concession did not solve their difficulties. Nevertheless all the guests entered into the spirit of the celebrations with real zest, giving free rein to their splendid imaginations and love of extravagance. Sergei Naryshkin spent seven thousand roubles merely on having his carriage refurbished and its wheels inlaid with mirror. On the wedding day he entered it wearing a caftan adorned on the back with a tree, the trunk of which was of gold leaf, the branches, some of which extended along its sleeves, of silver leaf, and its leaves and berries of precious and semi-precious stones.

As soon as the Neva was free of ice the goods ordered personally by the empress started arriving in the capital. They poured in from many parts of Europe and ranged from new carriages to countless bales of fine textiles. Elizabeth had chosen silks of superb quality for the dresses which she and Catherine would need for the occasion, and some magnificent stuffs for wall hangings. She had decided on cloth of silver for Catherine's wedding dress; it was to be made up in the Spanish style, with a wide Velasquez-type skirt and close-fitting bodice pulled in tightly at the waist. Over it Catherine was to wear a cloak of silver lace and the finest of the jewels which Elizabeth had given her. Peter was also to wear silver, and Elizabeth's dress was to be of chestnut-coloured Naples silk, likewise cut on Spanish lines.

Elizabeth was so determined that Catherine should look her best on her wedding day that she helped to dress her. The wedding was the first royal marriage to be celebrated in St Petersburg, and vast crowds had assembled in the capital to watch the bridal procession as it made its way to the Kazan Cathedral, and its return to the palace for the state banquet.

Contrary to Orthodox practice the empress and bridal pair drove to the cathedral seated together in the carriage which Elizabeth had had made for the occasion. Its wheels were covered in gold foil, its side panels were adorned with exquisite paintings and the six splendid horses which drew it were harnessed in bejewelled trappings. The long religious ceremony was exhausting, but Elizabeth was too happy, too buoyed up by hope to notice this. Indeed, she was so obsessed by her longing for an imperial baby that after the wedding banquet she unceremoniously hurried the wedded pair from the ball to their bedchamber.

Elizabeth had had the walls of the bridal chamber hung with scarlet velvet and their bed fitted with silver pillars encircled with carved wooden floral sprays. Their apartments were close to her own in the Winter Palace, their sitting room abutting on to her private dining room where, to ensure her privacy, she had a mechanical table so that servants were unnecessary. Peter soon discovered this and on an evening when, dressed only in a loose-fitting gown, Elizabeth was entertaining Razumovsky, wearing an embroidered dressing gown, and ten intimate friends, Peter made some holes in the partition separating the two rooms. He was amused by what he saw and called his friends to join him in spying on the empress. When Elizabeth learnt of the escapade her face turned scarlet as was usual when she lost her temper; but when Peter apologized, equally characteristically, she readily forgave him.

The grand ducal wedding night was a disappointment to all concerned. According to Catherine Peter did not join her for some hours. When he did so it was in order to go to sleep. Their marriage was never consummated. Two days of almost continuous celebrations followed the wedding day. They served as a prelude to a spectacular, essentially symbolic spectacle devised by the empress for 30 August, St Alexander Nevsky's day. According to custom the sovereign and his court paid homage to the saint on that day at the shrine which had been dedicated to his memory in the monastery which Peter the Great had founded in his honour in the outskirts of St Petersburg. On this particular anniversary the empress chose to attend wearing naval uniform. Her arrival at the monastery was marked in the Petrine manner by salvos of gun fire. A *Te Deum* formed part of the service held in the monastery's cathedral church during which further salvos were fired. Then, at Elizabeth's express orders, the first little boat which Peter the Great had built – the one known to all Russians as the Grandfather of the Russian Navy – was brought from its shed and displayed to the onlookers. The empress stepped into the boat and devoutly kissed a portrait of Peter the Great which had been placed in it. The gesture implied that her nephew's marriage would serve to perpetuate Peter's line.

The little craft was no longer seaworthy. To the sound of gun fire it was therefore carried down to the water's edge and placed on the deck of a barge, where a company of drummers and pipers were lined up. Elizabeth followed and, stepping into Peter's little boat, she stood upright in it for all to see her. Her courtiers grouped themselves round the boat and the barge sailed towards St Petersburg to the sound of music. It was accompanied by numerous small craft. As the armada neared the capital the Admiralty's guns began firing welcoming salvos and the trumpeters and pipers aboard the barges replied with fanfares.

Filled with hope for the future Elizabeth was in a gay mood. The months which followed were remarkable for the number of court balls, masquerades and metamorphoses held both at court and in the houses of the nobility. Though quadrilles and minuets were in fashion at the time, Elizabeth's affection for all things Russian was responsible for the inclusion of the native folk dances which she loved and could perform well. Later in her reign she was also to enjoy taking part in the English country dances which Semeon Naryshkin introduced to Russia. Since most of St Petersburg's private houses were still fairly small in size it was not easy for courtiers to give balls in them in honour of their empress. Many preferred to borrow one of her palaces for the purpose. Even then there were difficulties to overcome. Thus when Prince Tatishchev obtained permission to use her palace of Smolny for the ball which he wished to give for her, he discovered that the central section of the building had been destroyed in a recent fire and that he would have to make do with the side wings. He decided to use one as a ballroom and the other as a supper room, but since the ball was being held in January his guests had to face the bitter winter cold whenever they wanted any refreshments. As a result, Peter caught a severe chill and fell ill again. Catherine and Elizabeth visited him assiduously during his illness, but Peter proved extremely difficult to amuse. It may well be that he came to realize as he lay in bed that although his future prospects were magnificent he had been saddled with a country and a wife neither of which was of his choosing. Though Catherine was growing into an attractive young woman Peter was not drawn to her. Time was to increase his sense of isolation and unsuitability. Catherine was to recall that he often assured her that 'he was not born for Russia; neither did he suit the Russians nor the Russians suit him; that he was certain he would perish in Russia'.[5] As Peter languished Catherine became increasingly bored, puzzled and lonely. Her mother had left Russia soon after her wedding. She had departed disgraced after a stormy love affair with Count Betsky and was thought to be pregnant. Catherine had wept at parting from her for her mother had been her one link with the world of her childhood. She tried to comfort herself with the thought that the empress was devoted to her.

Apart from fortune-seekers comparatively few foreigners visited Russia during Elizabeth's reign. The empress may have been partly responsible for this as she never seemed to need them and therefore made no effort to attract them to Russia. Her thoughts centred on Russia and Russians, and this helped her to revive the nation's pride in itself within a couple of years of her accession. She was dispelling the gloom which had settled over the country at her father's death and was engaged in establishing a cultivated, westernized yet specifically Russian society. Almost nightly she assembled her courtiers either to attend a play, to listen to music, to dance or to play cards. She joined them at ten o'clock accompanied by the grand ducal pair and seldom withdrew before two in the morning. She would lead her guests in to supper and encourage them to enjoy good conversation, food and wine. She remained gay, for Russia was still at peace and her nephew was married to a beautiful and intelligent girl who would surely soon produce a baby. She was still able to dance for hours on end. She continued to hunt as keenly as in years gone by and rode as dashingly as ever.

However, as the weeks slipped by without a sign of the baby so necessary to her and to the nation, Elizabeth began to feel disappointed. Soon her sense of dissatisfaction became tinged with irritation. She felt that she had done everything possible to ensure that Peter and Catherine were happy. Though she must surely have known that their marriage had not followed a normal course it never occurred to her that, whether for psychological or physical reasons, Peter was unable to consummate it. She began to blame Catherine for its failure. Her resentment and concern increased when she learned that Anna Leopoldovna had died in childbirth on 26th February 1746 in distant Kholmogory leaving five young children for her husband to bring up.* Elizabeth's fear of Tsar Ivan quickened,

* Her death did not enable Anton Ulrich and his children to leave Kholmogory. Indeed, the prince was to die there twenty-nine years later. His three daughters survived him. They had spent their entire lives as prisoners in Siberia and they now appealed to the empress for their release. In a rare instance of unforgivingness Elizabeth refused to grant it. In 1780

but she arranged for the Grand Duchess's body to be brought back to St Petersburg for burial. It reached the capital on 7 March and was carried to the Alexander Nevsky Monastery for burial on 21 March. The empress and her court attended her funeral; three thousand roubles were spent on it and it was not lacking in pageantry, but the cause of Anna Leopoldovna's death and the fact that she had left two sons in addition to Tsar Ivan was kept a close secret.

Elizabeth's dissatisfaction with Catherine fanned her deep-rooted dislike of Frederick of Prussia, which had revived in the autumn of 1744 when, in disregard of the peace treaty of Berlin, he once again attacked Austria. His successful capture of Prague shortly afterwards increased Elizabeth's antagonism, and she often petulantly remarked that 'Frederick never went to church and had indeed become the Nadir Shah of Prussia'.[6] Nevertheless, Bestuzhev pressed her to fulfil her moral obligations to Austria by sending her troops. He affirmed that Prussia was rapidly developing into Russia's most dangerous rival. Although his arguments impressed Elizabeth her hatred of war made her hold back. Throughout 1745 she remained hesitant but as she watched Frederick repeatedly scoring over Austria her concern increased. She received the news of Maurice de Saxe's brilliant victory on 11 May 1745 at Fontenoy with mixed feelings. In the autumn, fearing to push Russia into Austria's arms, Frederick declared himself satisfied with his conquests and signed a separate peace treaty with Austria leaving his French allies to continue the fight unaided. The Treaty of Dresden accorded him Silesia and Gratz. True to her principles, Elizabeth expressed her disapproval and declared Mardefeld *persona non grata*. Frederick was obliged to recall him. Mardefeld's departure left Lestocq with no one to confide in and Frederick with no one but Lestocq to rely on and, in May 1746, Marie Theresa's newly appointed ambassador to Russia succeeded with Bestuzhev's aid in persuading the empress to renew the treaty of alliance with Austria entered into twenty years earlier by her mother.

Anton Ulrich's sister, now queen of Denmark, begged Catherine to set them free. Catherine not only agreed to do so, but she gave orders for two thousand roubles to be spent on providing the princesses with clothes, furniture and plate and for each to be given an annuity of eight thousand roubles. She also provided them with a priest and two acolytes, a doctor, several nurses and a number of servants. On 13 October 1780, when they finally set out on their journey to freedom, she presented them with a travelling church. They reached Denmark three and a half months later. By 1787 two had died and the Princess Elizabeth had become stone deaf. Since she knew no languages other than Russian she was driven almost mad by loneliness. In 1803 she begged the Emperor Alexander to allow her to return to Russia, but her petition was refused and she died in Denmark four years later.

In the spring of 1746 Elizabeth's mood became steadily more bad-tempered. She was extremely angry when she discovered that Catherine was spending much of her time in the company of three handsome, young and high-spirited equerries of Peter. They were the two Chernyshev brothers and their slightly older cousin; all three had accompanied the court to Kiev and the elder brother, Andrey, had since then become a close friend of Catherine's. Catherine's faithful valet and friend, Timofei Evreinov, learnt of Elizabeth's disapproval and managed to warn Andrey who feigned illness and hastily retired to his estates in the hope that his departure would allay the empress's suspicions. Elizabeth managed to conceal her displeasure for some weeks and Catherine did not realize that she had vexed the empress. She had always been careful to comply with the empress's wishes, at any rate outwardly, and had never yet dared to disregard the order forbidding her to write direct to her mother, but to send her letters to the College for Foreign Affairs for forwarding to her. With Andrey absent she began to feel so lonely and yet was so sure of the empress's regard that she appealed to the two most devoted members of her household, i.e. Timofei Evreinov and her clever maid Ekaterina Petrovna, to help her to correspond direct with Andrey. She did not realize that she was endangering their future by doing so. She also became friendly with Lestocq, who was now in Sweden's pay as well as Prussia's and Britain's. He encouraged her to use an Italian Knight of Malta, Sacromoso, to get her letters to her mother. Neither Lestocq nor Catherine had any idea that Bestuzhev knew of the arrangement and would later use the knowledge to be rid of Lestocq.

It came as a complete surprise to Catherine when, one May morning in 1746, soon after the court had moved from the Winter Palace to the Summer Palace, the empress angrily entered her room and accused her of seconding the Princess of Zerbst's attempts to betray her to the king of Prussia; of having an affair with one or more members of her husband's household; and of dividing the rest of her time between tears and day-dreams. Elizabeth spoke with considerable bitterness of Catherine's failure to make a success of her marriage. Distressed and frightened Catherine spent the day in bed crying. Her tears would have flowed even faster had she realized that the empress's tirade was only the prelude to a surveillance that at times verged on persecution.

Elizabeth had decided to appoint a lady-in-waiting to watch over Catherine's conduct and a gentleman to act in a similar capacity in Peter's case. She dismissed Brümmer, who was also charged with spying, and a fellow Holsteiner from Peter's service, expelling them from Russia on the grounds that Peter no longer needed to be supervised by them. She replaced Brümmer by Prince Repnin and appointed pretty, twenty-four-year-old Marie Choglokova, Elizabeth's cousin and favourite lady-in-waiting, to keep watch over Catherine while her husband did so over Peter. Marie Choglokova was expected to bring the grand ducal marriage to fruition as much by example as by admonition for Marie had married for love, was already the mother of several children and seemed to be in a permanent state of pregnancy. She was also to ensure that Catherine carried out her religious observances with true sincerity, 'not merely for the sake of appearances', to prevent her from being unfaithful to her husband and to make her realize that she had been raised to her present high station for the purpose of providing an heir to the throne. Marie was also to prevent Catherine from interfering in politics and corresponding directly with her parents. Choglokov's orders with regard to Peter were very similar. These instructions were in each case confirmed in writing. Catherine assumed that they had been drafted by Bestuzhev and held him wholly responsible for them. In fact, Elizabeth was as much of an autocrat as her father had been and nothing could be done in Russia or at court without her knowledge and approval.

Events conspired to make the empress suspicious of every proposal which could be traced back to a foreign source. In 1747, at Prussia's instigation, Lestocq made a fresh attempt to disgrace Bestuzhev, this time enlisting Mikhail Vorontzov's help. But on 8 October Bestuzhev retaliated by informing the empress that Lestocq was in foreign pay and that he was plotting to replace her by Catherine. Elizabeth could hardly bring herself to believe it, but she gave orders for watch to be kept over Lestocq. When he discovered he was being spied on, the doctor rushed to the empress to assure her of his loyalty. She listened to him in silence. Fearing the worst he hurried home and burnt all his papers. Catherine stated in her memoirs that he also warned her of his imminent disgrace. 'Coming one day into Her Majesty's apartments,' she recorded, 'I approached Count Lestocq and spoke to him. He muttered, "Don't come near me." I took this for a joke. "Move away from me." This distressed me and I said: "Are you avoiding me?" He replied, "I tell you, leave me." ' He was arrested on the following day, 18 November. A letter he had received from the Prussian ambassador was found in one of his drawers. It compromised Catherine for a sentence in it read, 'Had the Princess of Zerbst followed your and Brümmer's advice the Grand Duchess would have led the Grand

Duke by the nose.' Though Catherine was wholly innocent on this occasion Elizabeth afterwards always connected her with disloyal intrigues resembling those associated with her mother, Frederick of Prussia, and Lestocq. Convinced even on this occasion that the young woman had meddled in politics she ordered Bestuzhev's spies to intensify their watch on her. Catherine had been greatly depressed by the death in the autumn of 1746 of her father. Now her condition verged on despair.

Lestocq was committed for trial. The hearing opened on 19 November, but made little headway for Lestocq refused to speak even under torture, and went on a hunger strike for eleven days. On 24 November he was told that his possessions had been confiscated. Though he never confessed his guilt the evidence against him seemed irrefutable. Unlike Peter the Great, Elizabeth was seldom shocked by corruption, but she could not endure disloyalty. Though Mikhail Vorontzov was found to have accepted gifts from foreign powers he had never been disloyal to her and Elizabeth did not feel that he had betrayed his country. He therefore escaped punishment. Not so Lestocq; on 29 November he was pronounced guilty. Nevertheless, Elizabeth could not forget his past services. Early in the new year he was informed that he was to be banished to the old city of Uglich. Twelve years later he was pardoned and brought back to St Petersburg by Peter III, to die there in 1767 an embittered old man. He had served nine Russian sovereigns and had helped to alter the course of the country's history, but he was the last foreigner ever to be in a position to do so for none of the rulers who followed Elizabeth to the throne allowed an alien to become as powerful.

Lack of funds prevented Elizabeth from supplying Austria with the military aid specified in the Russo-Austrian treaty of alliance, until Britain and Holland provided the money. Even then there were delays, for Elizabeth refused to infringe Poland's autonomy by sending troops across her territory without having first obtained the necessary permission. It was therefore not until 1747, when Elizabeth was feeling especially disheartened as a result of Lestocq's betrayal, when Austria and Savoy were being defeated in the Alps and when Britain was using all her resources to fight the French in America and India, that Elizabeth at last severed diplomatic relations with Prussia and appointed Prince Repnin to lead ninety thousand Russian soldiers across the Vistula in the direction of Germany. Writing in his memoirs[7] some years later Frederick refused to admit that Lestocq's disloyalty could have influenced Elizabeth's decision; he ascribed her action to intrigue by asserting that the Russian ambassador to Prussia had interpreted the loss of an invitation to the wedding reception held at Charlottenburg on the marriage of his son Henry to the princess of Hesse as an intentional insult. Frederick averred that the ambassador had made use of the incident to convince Elizabeth that he had been plotting to reinstate Tsar Ivan.

Evidence that the empress intended to fulfil her treaty obligations to Austria startled Europe almost as much as did the appearance of a Russian army on the banks of the Rhine. Its presence there was undoubtedly responsible for the hurriedly reached yet unanimous decision of the belligerents to end the war. They also quickly agreed that Russia was to be debarred from the conference to be held at Aix to settle the peace terms. They gave Russia's tardy entry into the war as the reason for her exclusion from the conference, stressing that her troops had done no fighting. With Hanover safe, King George refused to transmit the promised subsidy on the grounds that Prince Repnin's troops were not in Germany as belligerents. Indeed, he now attached so little importance to Russia's friendship that he was more than once heard petulantly to remark that the empress would be well advised to court France's friendship. Mikhail Vorontzov was only too anxious to do so. Elizabeth was outraged by the king's attitude. She felt that she had been personally deceived by him and Russia insulted. Her deep-rooted distrust of Britain and Austria once again burgeoned.

6

An Uneasy Interlude
(1748-56)

Elizabeth's life was increasingly blighted by failing health. Plump in youth she was now grossly overweight. Her first serious illness occurred in February 1749; it was followed by frequent acute and dangerous attacks of colic and constipation. Nevertheless, she could not bring herself to abandon the pleasures of her youth and she continued to organize hunting expeditions and balls as frequently as in the past, only to find that she was obliged to drive herself to take part in them while concealing severe bouts of pain as much from herself as from others. Had the political situation not remained almost as menacing after the peace of Aix-la-Chapelle as it had been during the war which preceded it she might well have preserved the serenity and cheerfulness which were hers by nature. The growing complexity of the political problems she had to deal with and the necessity of providing herself with heirs fostered the melancholy which had entered her soul as a result of the real or imagined conspiracies which had followed upon her coronation. Her depression resulted in a growing inability to sleep at night, in a marked tartness in her dealings with the grand ducal couple and in a stronger reluctance to commit herself on major political issues. As a child she had not been taught to rise, go to bed or to take her meals at set hours. Now no one could predict when she was likely to do any of these things.

Her book learning remained almost as slight as it had been in her youth. She was still unable to grasp facts as elementary as that of Britain being an island. Yet she had acquired a clear understanding of Russia's role as a European power. It was this that enabled her to appreciate Bestuzhev's skill in making Russia's voice heard in European politics. At the start of her reign her hatred of bloodshed – always a powerful emotional force in the pattern of her behaviour – rather than any doubts about the quality of her soldiers, had prevented her from taking part in the war of the Austrian Succession. By 1746 she had, however, come to understand the extent to which her country's honour depended upon her own ability to take a firm stand in cases involving a principle. Though she was relieved that it had not been necessary for Russian blood to flow in Austria's defence she was justifiably furious when the belligerents took advantage of so providential a dispensation to charge her with duplicity in order to debar her from the peace conference table. She did not realize that their decision was caused by fear of Russia, yet she knew that it was due to the presence of Russian soldiers near the Rhine that the war had been brought to an end. That knowledge left her determined to secure a place for Russia alongside Europe's great powers.

At this period in her reign Elizabeth relied on Bestuzhev's help in framing policy yet she often found his ideas displeasing. The conflict within herself was constantly inflamed by the very people she was most attached to, and more especially by the three Shuvalovs, Mikhail Vorontzov, Alexei Razumovsky's brother Kiril, and by Alexei Bestuzhev's brother Mikhail. These six men formed her intimate circle; they all shared her love of France and therefore found themselves opposed to Alexei Bestuzhev's foreign policy.

Following the peace of Aix-la-Chapelle, Sweden and Poland, Russia's traditional enemies in north-western Europe, started to draw closer to Denmark, Prussia and France. Elizabeth's dislike of Frederick was becoming obsessive, yet the memory of Austria's defection in the third year of the Russo-Turkish war of 1736–9 prevented her from relying on Marie Theresa. Her love of France had never wavered and when Ivan Shuvalov became her lover the delight he took in French culture excited her desire for closer contacts with that country. Bestuzhev's dislike of France stood in her way, as did his hope that she would repair the breach in Anglo-Russian relations, a desire which King George came to share in 1750, but one which Elizabeth was extremely reluctant to fall in with. Court life therefore followed its customary course during the two years spent in settling the terms of the Aix-la-Chapelle peace. Though the Choglokovs were endeavouring to carry out their instructions they had not succeeded in bringing the grand ducal couple closer together. Andrey Chernyshev had returned to St Petersburg to find that both he and his two boon companions had been posted each to a different regiment, all in equally

16. Portrait of the Grand Duke Peter and the Grand Duchess Catherine, the future empress Catherine II, at the time of their marriage, by Grooth.

17. Catherine's son the future Emperor Paul, as a boy, by Losenko.

18. A colour wash engraving of the village of Ismailovo in 1727 by I. Zubov, showing the palace in the far left.

19. The Troitse-Sergieva Lavra, the monastery founded by St Sergius of Radonez at what is now known as Zagorsk. The empress often went into retreat there.

remote districts. Shortly afterwards Timofei Evreinov was discharged from Catherine's service by the empress because she thought that Catherine had come to depend on him too greatly. Peter was becoming increasingly difficult to live with. Following Prince Repnin's departure for the front in 1746 Peter's childish amusements had acquired a streak of sadism. He began to spend hours on end in his rooms drilling a pack of dogs, distressing Catherine by the sounds of his whip and loud voice, and the howling and barks of the unfortunate dogs. Peter was also making a point of parading his hatred of Russia, his love of Holstein and Prussia and his adoration of Frederick. He had never recovered from the disappointment he had felt when Elizabeth refused the Swedish throne on his behalf. His hope of obtaining it revived in 1750 when it fell vacant, but when it passed to his uncle, Adolphus Frederick of Holstein, as the result of the earlier agreement, Peter became embittered. He started openly to voice his regret at having come to Russia, and his longing to reign over Sweden and Holstein. In his unhappiness he often turned to Catherine for comfort, and although he also made a point of frequently offending her, both found relief in each other's company, for both were equally lonely, equally jaded and equally young and repressed.

Catherine was bored. She found her enforced intimacy with Peter increasingly distasteful, especially as the bed she was obliged to share with him was covered with his toys which he insisted on playing with till dawn, probably just to prevent her from sleeping. Though they could sympathize with each other's unhappiness they had no common interests. To make matters worse Catherine knew that she was being spied on. Her health became affected and she began to suffer from headaches and sleeplessness. In 1748 she contracted measles and became so ill that her doctors feared for her life. She made no conscious effort to recover, but her strong constitution triumphed over the disease. After several disconsolate months her innate energy also revived and she began to take advantage of the outlets which were available to her. She reappeared at court and was seen to dance at Elizabeth's balls with much the same energy as the empress. When the court moved from the capital to one of Elizabeth's country palaces Catherine would take to riding 'like a madcap'. Elizabeth had encouraged her to learn to ride when she had first arrived in Russia and the empress had never prevented her from pursuing a pastime which she herself delighted in. All she did was to forbid Catherine to copy her in riding astride lest by doing so the young girl should encourage comparison between them. Catherine gave the impression of willingly complying. She would leave the palace sedately seated on a side saddle, but it had been made to her specific instructions and, when out of sight, she would remove its pommel, add a stirrup, swing her leg across her mount's back and break into an exhilarating gallop. On formal occasions, however, Catherine would appear seated side saddle, wearing a pale blue silk habit with crystal buttons and a black hat trimmed with diamonds. She had become exceedingly attractive but the empress had no cause for jealousy for although Catherine was very vivacious she could not overshadow Elizabeth who still looked splendid on horseback.

The empress had given Peter and Catherine Menshikov's former magnificent palace of Oranienbaum as a summer residence. Pulling on a pair of trousers and a man's jacket as she sprang from her bed at three in the morning Catherine would rush out duck shooting; accompanied only by a huntsman and a fisherman she would steer her small boat into the reeds fringing the Gulf of Finland and spend many hours there. She would return to the palace at mid-day and leave again on a horse in the early afternoon, yet in the evenings she was ready to join in the dancing till late into the night. When the weather kept her indoors Catherine turned to books. To begin with she read nothing but novels. Lestocq, Mardefeld and above all the Swedish ambassador Count Gyllenburg tried to persuade her to take an interest in more serious works. The type of book Gyllenburg recommended was not to be easily obtained in Russia, but some of those which came into Catherine's hands made a lasting impression on her. She became fascinated by power politics and started to take a close interest in current affairs.

After Marie Choglokova had acted as Catherine's duenna for five years both women had come to understand each other, even to feel attached to each other. Choglokova had come to recognize Catherine's difficulties and learnt to sympathize with her in her loneliness. Catherine had endeared herself to her by the many kindnesses she had shown to the Choglokovs' children and had won Marie's profound gratitude for the tactful way in which she rebuffed the advances of Marie's adored, though faithless husband. Now she ardently desired to help the Grand Duchess.

In 1751 Peter's household had come to life following the appointment to it of three gay, young and attractive noblemen. Two of them, Peter and Sergei Saltykov, were brothers; the third, Lev Naryshkin, was the most intelligent of the three. The marriage of Peter and Catherine had still not been consummated, and although the empress must have realized that Peter was unable to provide the heir on whom Russia's future depended she would not admit it to herself and became increasingly vexed with them for their failure to beget a child. She noticed the friendship springing up between the grand ducal couple and the three young courtiers and grew angry with the Choglokovs, accusing them of letting themselves be fooled by the young people. Both Choglokovs defended Catherine, Marie daring to tell the empress that it was not the Grand Duchess who was to blame for the absence of a child since nothing had been done to enable her to have one. The empress became angrier still. She was in the dangerous frame of mind when the least trifle could enrage her and it was precisely at that moment that an incident occurred which she considered sinister. It happened to Peter when on a hunting expedition. He had ridden ahead of his companions and was followed by young Lieutenant Yakov Baturin of the Butyrsky regiment who, on catching up with the Grand Duke, rapidly dismounted, flung himself on his knees and swore that 'he considered him his sole master and would carry out all his orders'.[1] Peter was panic stricken. Abandoning the hunt he galloped back to Catherine, to confide in her and to ask her advice. Was there a conspiracy afoot and was Baturin involved in it? Catherine remained convinced that the lieutenant had planned to kill the empress, set fire to the palace and place Peter on the throne.[2] He was arrested and so were the huntsmen. The lieutenant was tried on three charges and found guilty. He was banished to Kamchatka, but succeeded in escaping to Formosa, where he lived out his life. This curious incident confirmed Elizabeth's fears about Peter's aptitude for governing. Her affection for Catherine had waned with the Grand Duchess's failure to provide her with the one thing she desired above all else – an heir to the throne. Moreover, the immense debts incurred by Peter and Catherine served to set her against them.

Nevertheless the winter of 1751/2 was the most pleasant Catherine had experienced since her father's death. Although she did not greatly like Peter Saltykov who, to use her own words, had 'large, protruding eyes, a flat nose and a gaping mouth' which she found distasteful, she thought Sergei 'handsome as the dawn',[3] charming and intelligent. Petersburgian society did not agree with her verdict but considered him vain, foolish and wanting in good taste – an appraisal which was nearer to the truth than Catherine's. Sergei was twenty-six years old and had been married for two years to Matrena Balk. Oblivious of her feelings, disregarding the risks, Sergei and Catherine made no effort to control the attraction each felt for the other. They met daily throughout the spring and summer of 1752, spending hours on end together, Saltykov courting the Grand Duchess so assiduously that the courtiers took notice. Peter was more than once heard to remark that 'Sergei Saltykov and my wife are duping the Choglokovs.'[4] He seemed glad of it rather than otherwise for he believed himself to be in love with a Miss Shafirova, one of Catherine's least attractive ladies. He made no secret of his feelings, frequently describing them to Catherine. As court gossip increased Catherine took fright and persuaded Sergei Saltykov to withdraw for a time to his country estate, and Lev Naryshkin to do likewise.

Sergei Saltykov rejoined her at Oranienbaum at the end of the summer. Early in December the empress ordered the court to transfer to Moscow. As Marie Choglokova was expecting her eighth child she was to follow later. Saltykov and Naryshkin decided to wait for her in the hope of misleading the gossips. When Catherine left St Petersburg on 14 December she was pregnant but travelled so fast over the bad roads that she had a miscarriage. She was very ill on arriving in Moscow but made a rapid recovery and was able to appear at court ten days later. No records exist to reveal her thoughts at the loss of her baby, and there is no evidence that Elizabeth knew what had happened. In the absence of Marie Choglokova and her two favourite courtiers Catherine felt very lonely but this time she did not give way to her feelings. Instead she spent her time reading and studying the political situation. She had grown up in the course of the last two or three years; she had learnt to think for herself and was able to examine her mother's allegiance to Prussia with detachment. She now found that her own views often corresponded with those of the grand chancellor's and that like him she favoured an alliance with Austria rather than France. Had she, however, more personal reasons for seeing Bestuzhev in a new light? She was deeply in love with Sergei Saltykov and desperately anxious to continue meeting him. Did the thought of a second pregnancy occur to her? Even if this was not the case she must have known that her relationship with Saltykov could all too easily place her in a position where she would need the help of a powerful protector. Though Alexei Bestuzhev was a solitary figure no one wielded more power in Russia at that time than the grand chancellor.

Elizabeth's failing health was causing anxiety in court circles. Catherine must have been conscious of this and she must have considered some of the problems which would arise when her husband inherited the throne. She alone knew the full extent of his emotional instability, his intellectual limitations, his unreasoning and blind adoration of Frederick. Although she had so far generally managed to persuade him to accept her advice in all matters of importance she realized that she could not always expect to do so. She knew that he was unfit to reign and had no illusions about her own position should he become tsar.

Catherine and Bestuzhev had not been attracted to each other when they met for the first time. This may have been partly due to Frederick's success in setting the young girl against the minister, partly too to Bestuzhev's opposition to her on grounds of nationality. The princess of Zerbst's political activities had increased his dislike of Catherine just as Catherine's belief that Bestuzhev was responsible for the harsh instructions issued to the Choglokovs on their appointment to her household had turned her distrust of him into aversion. Nevertheless, early in 1753 Catherine sent Bestuzhev a note asking him to call on her. Her request surprised the chancellor, but he could neither ignore nor refuse it. Elizabeth's failing health also made it advisable for him to be on better terms with the empress's heirs. Even so, Bestuzhev made his way to the Grand Duchess's residence reluctantly. She received him in private. After a somewhat stilted exchange of trivialities their talk suddenly took a more serious turn. Unconsciously both became animated. Surprised by the ease and liveliness of their conversation they discovered to their mutual satisfaction that they were intellectual equals. Their sudden cordiality quickly became a friendship which made them into political allies. Yet wholly against Catherine's wishes and intentions that friendship was to be the cause of Bestuzhev's downfall.

The Choglokovs, Sergei Saltykov and Lev Naryshkin arrived in Moscow soon after Catherine's first interview with Bestuzhev. Catherine told her lover how successful their meeting had been and soon Saltykov was acting as their messenger. According to Catherine's Memoirs it was then that Marie Choglokova came to her and asked to speak to her in private and with complete frankness. She began by referring to the sanctity of marriage and conjugal fidelity, but she proceeded to qualify these remarks by saying that there were certain very exceptional cases in which these principles did not apply. Astonished, perturbed, fearing a trap, Catherine listened carefully and in complete silence. 'Take note of the quality of my love for my country no less than the extent of my frankness,' she heard her duenna say; 'I feel sure that in your heart of hearts you prefer one man to all others; I leave it to you to choose between Sergei Saltykov and Lev Naryshkin, though I think you prefer the latter.' Pretending not to understand, Catherine hotly denied this. 'Well, if it is not Naryshkin,' remarked Marie Choglokova, 'then it must be the other one. You will find that I won't put any obstacles in your way.'[5] Catherine feigned incomprehension and no more was said. Catherine never discovered whether Marie Choglokova had acted on her own initiative or under orders. The secret was so well kept that it must remain unanswered, but from that day Catherine was able freely to meet Saltykov. By May she was pregnant again. Long walks and rides led to another miscarriage. This time she needed longer to recover; her life was in danger for a fortnight, and a couple of months elapsed before she was able to leave her bed.

After her recovery Catherine continued to see as much of Saltykov as in the past. Though Peter made frequent references to their relationship, commenting on it in a semi-humorous, semi-censorious manner, nothing was done to end the association. Saltykov even started showing signs of tiring of Catherine, but her love for him remained as ardent as in the past and their romance continued. In February 1754 Catherine was pregnant again. This time she was not to be permitted to lose her child. She was made to take care of herself and to rest frequently. She found these measures very irksome. They became more so in April when the sudden death of Choglokov resulted in the empress appointing Alexander Shuvalov, the dreaded head of the Secret Chancery, Marshal of Peter's household. Catherine found him personally repulsive, but it was the knowledge that the appointment indicated that she and Peter were to be watched more closely than ever that made her dread him.

In May the court returned to St Petersburg. Catherine was ordered to travel very slowly, attended by a midwife who had been instructed never to leave her. The spring and summer months passed pleasantly enough for Catherine, for both in the capital and at Peterhof she was able to spend most of her time with Saltykov. In August she moved back to her own apartments in the Summer Palace but learnt with dismay that she was not to be confined in them since the empress had arranged for her to have her baby in rooms specially prepared for the purpose; they were situated close to the empress's apartments and at a distance from Peter's. Catherine dreaded the prospect and the inevitable lack of privacy.

A rumour had been circulating for some time in St Petersburg that a minor operation had recently been successfully performed on the Grand Duke. On 20 September Catherine's child was born after a long and painful labour. To Elizabeth's immense joy and relief the child proved to be a boy. Forgetting Catherine and her need for attention Elizabeth's thoughts centred on the baby. She gave orders for him to be swaddled. Then, in much the same way as Anna Ivanovna had taken possession of

Anna Leopoldovna's first child, Tsar Ivan, Elizabeth took Catherine's boy in her arms and carried him off to the nurseries which had been fitted out for him in a set of rooms adjoining her own. It was she and not Catherine who took charge of the baby. During the first three days of his life Catherine was forgotten. She lay alone and neglected but for a short call from Peter, who had recently fallen in love with one of Catherine's ladies, Elizabeth Vorontzova, the almost deformed niece of Mikhail Vorontzov.

The empress decided that the baby was to be called Paul, arranged for him to be baptized on the sixth day after his birth and asked the empress of Austria and her husband to be his godparents. Although it has been said that they refused, a despatch of Guy Dickens, the British Ambassador to Russia, shows that this was not so.[6] He informed his government that the child had been baptized in the Summer Palace with Elizabeth representing his Austrian godparents and also standing as one herself. After the ceremony Elizabeth gave Catherine a hundred thousand roubles and what Catherine petulantly described as several small pieces of jewellery, as a reward for the birth of an heir to the throne. As Catherine was heavily in debt the money was welcome, but her future seemed bleak to her for she had been told that Saltykov was to leave for Stockholm to inform the king of Sweden of Paul's birth. She dreaded being left alone, especially since she had not been allowed to see her baby since his birth nor even to hear how he was. Secretly she had been told that he had almost died of ulcers of the mouth and that the empress insisted on his room being kept at so high a temperature that he was covered in perspiration as he lay in his cot beneath countless blankets. Though Catherine had not got strong maternal instincts she greatly minded being deprived of her child. She was allowed to hold him in her arms for a while on the fortieth day of his life when tradition obliged her to receive the formal congratulations of the court. She was too miserable and unwell to respond to them with warmth. She took no part in the celebrations, held daily until mid-November, to mark her son's birth. She longed for Saltykov's company and tried to kill time by reading. Her lover returned early in the new year, only to discover that he had been appointed Minister to Hamburg. He was able to see Catherine several times before leaving and tried to reconcile her to his departure. It was on his advice that she re-entered court life on 10 February, her husband's birthday.

Catherine and Bestuzhev had continued to meet during her pregnancy. Dickens commented in his despatches on the frequency of their meetings and the cordiality of their relationship. Like most men holding high positions at Elizabeth's court Bestuzhev was disliked. He was extravagant and lived above his means. Though his possessions and estates were of great value his salary of seven thousand roubles a year, lavishly supplemented by what he regarded as monetary gifts, but which had all the appearance of bribes, did not provide him with nearly as much ready money as he required.* In 1746 Elizabeth had acknowledged the services he had rendered by the gift of land on Kamenny Ostrov (Stone Island) a district of St Petersburg and had given orders for a summer residence to be built for him there on a peninsula facing the Neva's south bank. The house was completed in 1750. It consisted of two large, two-storied blocks linked by a pedimented colonnade and flanked by curved, single storied wings. Bestuzhev's high position and great influence would of themselves have sufficed to turn those who were jealous of him into active enemies, but his intense arrogance had considerably increased their number. They watched his debts pile up and, noting the pleasure with which Elizabeth listened to the francophile sympathies of Ivan Shuvalov and Mikhail Vorontzov, they spread the rumour that Bestuzhev was in Britain's pay. The chancellor gave no sign of knowing of the rumour, but waited patiently for the chance to retaliate. He thought that the opportunity had come when the empress presented him with his new house. She had failed to provide him with either the furniture or the money with which to equip it. Asserting that he could not use the house until it was furnished but that he could not afford to furnish it for himself, he appealed to the empress to do so. When she failed to respond he hit on a Machiavellian plan for furnishing the house and striking at his enemies. He asked Dickens to raise a mortgage of fifty thousand roubles on the house in England on his behalf. Dickens and his government interpreted the move as a request for a bribe and readily agreed. However, when the British loan became available Bestuzhev insisted on complying with the Russian law on mortgages which obliged borrowers to furnish certificates of indebtedness for every thousand roubles raised, each bearing a third party's guarantee of repayment. He accordingly applied to fifty of his worst enemies for these certificates. None dared to refuse him. It was an astute move for it enabled him to flaunt his poverty not only before his sovereign and countrymen but also in the face of Europe's diplomats. Thus he scotched the rumour that he was corrupt and a paid British agent whilst demon-

---

* All historians agree that Bestuzhev refused all foreign bribes at any rate until 1752 (Waliszewski, *op. cit.*, p. 116) and most think that he consistently did so.

strating his faith in Britain and his intention of pursuing a pro-Austrian policy. Nevertheless, the incident did not help to endear him to his fellow courtiers.

The war of nerves and diplomacy had been steadily gaining momentum. The struggle between Marie Theresa and Frederick for Russia's support continued to be waged with duplicity and passion. King George of Britain, regretting having offended Elizabeth and disrupting the Anglo-Russian alliance, sent Dickens to Russia as ambassador for the purpose of renewing it. Versailles was casting its net ever wider in its simultaneous attempts both to win Russia's friendship and to weaken her by surrounding her with a belt of antagonistic states, encouraging Sweden, Prussia and Bourbon Italy to fear and distrust Elizabeth. Louis strove to gain a foothold in the Crimea by making use of Russia's age-old rivalry with the Crimean Tartars, now ruled by Khan Giray. He appointed a Hungarian officer, the Baron Tott, ostensibly to act as military adviser to the khan, but in reality to serve as a spy. Nor did he overlook the restless Zaporozhie Kozaks, sending agents in their midst to ferment anti-Russian feeling. In 1751 Dresden, where Augustus, Elector of Saxony and King of Poland, had established his court, became the point from which France and Britain conducted their offensives.

The French manoeuvres were directed from France by the Duke de Broglie, the British were handled on the spot by the new British ambassador, Sir Charles Hanbury Williams. He was to play an important, dangerous and inglorious role in Russia, where he became sentimentally and emotionally involved and, as a result, lost first his health, then his sanity and finally his life. Born in Winchester in 1709 Charles Hanbury Williams grew up admiring Horace Walpole. Though an ardent Whig he was more successful socially than in the field of politics. His good looks, wit and ability to write amusing satirical verses were enhanced by his courtesy and worldliness. His interest in foreign affairs developed slowly, but in 1747 he was appointed envoy to Dresden. Three years later he was promoted to ambassador and posted to Berlin, but his caustic tongue offended Frederick. The king took a dislike to the ambassador and although he thought him dangerous he nevertheless asked for his recall. Hanbury Williams was reappointed to the Saxon court. In Warsaw his efforts were to be mainly directed at countering Frederick's attempts to win the Elector's allegiance and at persuading the Elector to break with France. Hanbury Williams was obliged to visit Warsaw regularly. He made many friends there. His relationship with the Chartoryzhkis was particularly cordial, and it was probably through them that he became acquainted with Count Augustus Poniatowski and his attractive young son, Stanislas.

A foolish quarrel in public in London between the French and Russian ambassadors led to one between King Louis and Elizabeth, with the result that diplomatic relations between the two were intermittently broken off. By 1754 Louis was in great need of a representative in Russia capable of keeping him informed of developments there, but he was too proud to be the first to ask for the resumption of diplomatic relations. Instead he hit on what seemed an ingenious solution to his difficulty. His plan consisted in sending a Monsieur de Valcroissant to St Petersburg under an assumed name, in the guise of a merchant. His task was to act as a secret agent.

Monsieur de Valcroissant reached St Petersburg in 1755, at the very time when Louis' policy had succeeded in enclosing Russia within a belt of potential enemies. To the watching world Russia seemed to be in Louis' grasp. Appreciative of the danger, Bestuzhev instructed his spies to exercise the utmost vigilance. They lost no time in reporting Monsieur de Valcroissant's arrival. Bestuzhev sensed from the start that the merchant was a spy and had him detained in the fortress of Schlüsselburg and then expelled from Russia.

The British Government was displeased with Dickens for his failure to persuade Elizabeth to renew the alliance first suggested to her as far back as 1750 and decided to replace him by an envoy more likely to charm and influence the empress. Thus Sir Charles Hanbury Williams became ambassador. On the face of it there was much to commend the decision. Sir Charles was a professional diplomat of considerable experience whose duties in Saxony had involved him in complex problems concerning Russia. His temperament, appearance and cultivated tastes were likely to charm the empress. Indeed, at their first meeting he made a very favourable impression on her and Bestuzhev.

Sir Charles travelled to Russia via Warsaw. In Poland he engaged the twenty-one-year-old Stanislas Poniatowski as his secretary, and the young man accompanied him to St Petersburg. Early in September 1755 the empress invited Sir Charles to Tsarskoe Selo. He got on well with her courtiers, especially with those who, like Ivan Shuvalov and Mikhail Vorontzov, formed part of her intimate circle, but he established especially good relations with Bestuzhev. The ambassador and the chancellor were soon carefully examining the treaty proposals which Sir Charles had brought to Russia. This time the discussions went well and on 16 September Elizabeth at last expressed herself willing to agree to the renewal of the treaty. She ratified it a few months later. According to its terms Russia undertook to keep fifty thousand men on the Livonian frontier, ready to defend Hanover if it were attacked by Prussia; in return she was to receive a subsidy of £100,000 a year to help towards their upkeep and an additional £500,000 if their services were required.

Elizabeth's health was far less good than most people realized. She had begun to suffer from acute attacks of asthma and dropsy. Sir Charles took note of this and, with an eye to the future, began to pay court to the grand ducal couple. Catherine's relations with Peter had deteriorated sharply after Paul's birth. Peter was now twenty-five years old and had recently had an association with a certain Mrs Groot. It had been contrived for him by Marie Choglokova and his self-confidence had benefited from the knowledge that he was not impotent, for although it seems probable that he was sterile he cannot have known it. He took no interest in Paul, but Elizabeth may be chiefly to blame for this for she seldom let him – or even Catherine – see the child. Husband and wife went their own ways, Catherine showing more assurance and wilfulness than before.

Early in 1755 a visitor from Holstein, named Brockdorf, arrived in St Petersburg. Elizabeth had done everything possible to curb Peter's passionate love of his duchy, but her efforts seem to have had the contrary effect. As a Holsteiner Brockdorf had no difficulty in gaining admittance to Peter's presence; indeed, he obtained an appointment as chamberlain. His influence over Peter was disastrous. At Easter, when the household moved to Oranienbaum, Catherine was shocked and upset to find a detachment of Holsteinian troops, wearing the duchy's uniform, installed in the palace. Peter was even more infatuated than formerly with all military things. He turned the palace into a camp and, dressed in his duchy's uniform, he spent the entire summer drilling the Holsteiners. He openly admitted that he preferred them to Russians, but Princess Dashkova averred that most were work apprentices who had escaped from their masters, while some of them were soldiers or warrant officers who had deserted from the armies of various German princelings.[7] The men in the Preobrazhensky regiment were deeply affronted by their presence, for the Grand Duke was their lieutenant colonel; their feelings were shared by all Russians who knew what was happening. The empress ignored the situation. She spent most of her time with the infant Grand Duke, whom she adored. She had now lost all confidence in Peter and was greatly troubled by the knowledge that he was unfit to govern Russia and Paul too young to be proclaimed her heir. Experience had taught her to fear having a minor occupying the throne. She must have known that her health was failing and that time was no longer on her side. Was she seeking a solution to her difficulties in Tsar Ivan? In 1756, she arranged for him to be secretly transferred from Siberia to the fortress of Schlüsselburg. Her misgivings must have communicated themselves to Catherine who became conscious of the increasing uncertainty of her own future. The uneasy calm persisted. In the autumn the court returned to St Petersburg and Peter's detachment of Holsteiners were sent home. Peter consoled himself by playing with his toy soldiers; he now had many thousands of them and was so fascinated by military ceremonial that he never tired of setting them out in parade formation.

It was Sir Charles's first winter in Russia. Delighted by his success in negotiating the alliance, confident that the agreement would be duly ratified, he entered into the capital's social life with zest and quickly made his mark in society. One glance at the Grand Duke must have sufficed to convince him that there was little chance of curbing his passionate devotion to Prussia. Sir Charles was equally quick in forming a high opinion of Catherine. The pleasure he took in her company was matched by that which she derived from conversing with so witty, courteous, worldly and accomplished a person. The more the ambassador saw of the Grand Duchess the more did he admire her. He found 'in her all the qualities of a great sovereign'.[8]

Sir Charles's young Polish secretary, Count Stanislas Poniatowski, fell in love with Catherine at their first meeting. Though she found him attractive and was diverted by his conversation it seems unlikely that she would have returned his sentiments had not Sir Charles encouraged their romance. Sir Charles and Catherine had started writing to each other and the ambassador began to use young Poniatowski as his messenger. Peter flaunted his devotion to Elizabeth Vorontzova and Catherine took a keen interest in the young Pole.

The letters which Sir Charles and Catherine wrote to each other were of a political nature, but they were lavishly interwoven with flattery. During the winter of 1755–6 they corresponded almost daily, sometimes even twice or several times a day. Catherine kept the ambassador as fully informed as possible about what was being said at court and what was happening there, speculating about future developments and suggesting possible courses of action. She even asked Sir Charles to sound out the king of Denmark on her behalf on the possibility of exchanging Peter's Duchy of Holstein for Oldenburg. She went further, and more than once asked him to obtain considerable sums of money for her from England to enable her to settle her more pressing debts.

Frederick of Prussia was greatly perturbed by Sir Charles's popularity in Russia; so too was Louis of France. With de Valcroissant still in prison Louis could not obtain secret information from Russia. Though persistent reports continued to reach him about the warmth of Elizabeth's feelings for France he dared not rely on them.

Eighteenth-century Europe was not lacking in adventurers, more particularly in Scottish ones, anxious to win fame and fortune. While Louis was wondering how best to renew relations with Russia the Prince de Conti suggested that he should send a Scot, named Mackenzie Douglas, to see what could be done. The idea appealed to the king as well as to the Scotsman. Mackenzie Douglas agreed to go to Russia as a French spy. He was to try to win Hanbury Williams's confidence and so discover Britain's intentions more especially with regard to Sweden and Turkey, and to send all information back to Versailles. He was also to try to obtain free access to the empress in order to encourage her to accept as genuine France's protestations of friendship. Versailles decided that Douglas should go to Russia as a furrier, anticipating that Elizabeth's love of finery would suffice to enable Douglas to see her in private. The code he was to use in his despatches was based on the fur trade, Hanbury Williams being designated as a black fox, Bestuzhev as a lynx and Russia's soldiers as little grey skins. Having concealed his instructions in a snuff box fitted with a false bottom Douglas set out for St Petersburg in the late summer of 1755.

It was not generally known that soon after his arrival Sir Charles had persuaded Bestuzhev to agree to his request that no British subject arriving in St Petersburg should be received at court unless Sir Charles were willing personally to present the visitor to the empress. Even so, had not chance intervened there was no real reason why the French plan should have miscarried. It so happened that when ambassador in Dresden Sir Charles had met Lord Pulteney who was touring Europe with a tutor named Douglas. Like many another tutor this one proved of questionable character and over-fond of the bottle. Sir Charles had disapproved of him. On hearing Douglas's name mentioned his suspicions were aroused; it did not take him long to discover that the drunken tutor and the new arrival were brothers. That knowledge strengthened his instinctive distrust of Douglas and he refused to present him to the empress, who was recovering from another bout of serious illness. Douglas kicked his heels in St Petersburg for some weeks. According to gossip he was often to be seen

in the company of a beautiful young woman calling herself Lia de Beaumont, whom he introduced as his niece. Eventually, recognizing that he
would not be received at court and that he could make no headway with
the British ambassador, Douglas decided to leave Russia. That, however,
was not to be the end of the affair.

Meanwhile Elizabeth, regretting her agreement to a British alliance,
showed no desire to ratify the document. Worn out by the long and
difficult negotiations Bestuzhev lost his temper. In a memorandum drafted
in anger he pressed her to sign the treaty. His tone was irritable and
trenchant; the empress was accustomed to greater deference and felt
offended. Nevertheless, on 1 February 1756, she complied.

Bestuzhev and Sir Charles were delighted that the alliance had come into
force. Twenty-three days were needed on average for a courier to travel
between St Petersburg and London. Hanbury Williams despatched one
to London never doubting that his sovereign would be satisfied on reading
his letter. But while his messenger was hurrying towards England western
Europe learnt with astonishment that, in mid-January (allowing for the
difference in calendars), a mere fortnight before Elizabeth had ratified her
alliance with Britain, King George II had entered into a semi-secret alliance
with Prussia, upseting the pattern of alliances which had been carefully
built up in Europe over the centuries. The treaty, known both as that of
Westminster and as the German Neutrality Convention, was designed to
prevent foreign troops from entering Prussia; should any do so Britain
pledged herself to come to Prussia's assistance in return for a guarantee
of the retention of Hanover.

Sir Charles had been kept in complete ignorance of the Anglo-Prussian
negotiations. It nonetheless fell to him to inform Bestuzhev of Britain's
agreement with Prussia. The news came as a profound shock to both men.
Bestuzhev realized from the start that the Treaty of Westminster struck
at the spirit, meaning and purpose of the Anglo-Russian agreement.
Dismayed and shaken he went to inform the empress. Elizabeth was
furious. She was convinced that she had been tricked and deceived. The
possibility that a clause in the treaty might involve her in a war against
France profoundly distressed her. It was an unimaginable predicament in
which to find herself – one which she neither could nor would accept.
She acted without hesitation, announcing for all to hear that she considered
herself no longer bound by the British alliance.

Prussia and Britain attempted to present their agreement to the world
as one of minor importance. They maintained that it did not invalidate

the Anglo-Russian treaty, but the world knew better. Russia, Austria and France were united in thinking that the Treaty of Westminster marked the start of a new phase in Europe's history. Even they failed to realize that it was to rank with the most fateful in Europe, ending as it did the supremacy of the houses of Hapsburg and Bourbon and marking the rise of Russia and Prussia.

Bestuzhev sensed that the Treaty of Westminster would prove disastrous to him personally. He had no illusions about his future; he knew that he had never possessed the empress's friendship, that he had now forfeited her trust and that the treaty destroyed all chances of success for the policy he had pursued as Minister of Foreign Affairs. The hateful Shuvalovs would now be able to introduce their pro-French policy in place of his plan for Russia's alignment with Britain and Austria. Britain had not only misled him, she had probably destroyed him. Yet he could not change his beliefs and he was too much of a politician to give up without fighting. Incited by Sir Charles he foolishly tried to salvage the little that remained of the treaty, unrealistically asserting that even though Britain could not be accepted as an ally there was no reason why the two countries should not adopt a neutral attitude with regard to each other. In Elizabeth's eyes the suggestion served only to confirm her belief that Britain had treated her with cynical disdain. On 19 February, only four days after learning of the existence of the Treaty of Westminster, the empress formed a committee for dealing with Russia's foreign relations; it consisted of Bestuzhev, Mikhail Vorontzov, the three Shuvalovs, Prince Nikita Yukieirch Trubetskoy and Count Apraxin. They were to meet under her presidency. By including Bestuzhev Elizabeth was generously attempting to protect him, but although he retained an appearance of authority he must have known that the empress had formed the committee largely in order to control his activities and to limit his powers. The empress herself provided the committee with the five principles on which Russia's foreign policy was in future to be based. The first expressed her determination to ensure the return of Silesia to Austria and the re-establishment of Prussia's original boundaries. Elizabeth also announced that she intended to send an army of eighty thousand men to assist Austria and that she hoped to persuade France to take no part in the war which seemed imminent.

Elizabeth informed Austria that she would wait to despatch the army she was sending to assist her until she had obtained Poland's permission*

---

* It was largely dependent on France's attitude which had, until then, laid down Russia's exclusion from Poland.

for her men to cross its territory but suggested that, in return for that concession, the Poles should receive certain areas of Courland from Russia in exchange for some districts in eastern Prussia which would fall to Russia at Prussia's defeat. At a secret session of her Committee for Foreign Affairs Elizabeth stated that she had signed the British alliance only because it provided her with the opportunity of striking at Prussia. Sir Charles managed to hear of this (possibly through Bestuzhev) and hurried to notify the British ambassador in Berlin, who promptly told Frederick.

Although Sir Charles's position was a less dangerous one than Bestuzhev's it was scarcely less embarrassing and difficult. He had been sent to Russia largely to set Elizabeth against Frederick. Even though the king of Prussia was now an ally of his own sovereign he could hardly be expected to go back on all that he had so recently said to the empress. His government thought of recalling him, but Frederick was finding him so valuable an informer that he dissuaded his new allies from doing so. The ambassador set himself two objectives. One was to second Bestuzhev's efforts to avoid their countries going to war with each other; the second was to strengthen his friendship with Catherine who, it seemed, might well soon be empress.

The intensity of Elizabeth's anger with Britain disturbed Catherine. She hastened to inform Bestuzhev of her correspondence with Sir Charles, giving him some indications as to its nature. She confessed that she would have liked to see Sir Charles recalled, but begged the chancellor not to let the ambassador discover this and also asked him to help her maintain her correspondence with Sir Charles. When he discovered how deeply Catherine had committed herself Bestuzhev felt afraid for her; he knew that he would not be able to protect her if the empress heard of the correspondence. He tried to obtain the ambassador's recall and, acting against his better judgement, he also agreed to arrange for Catherine's letters to continue to reach Sir Charles. He had no sooner done so than he took fright and refused to act as a go-between; then he relented and again agreed to do so. When replying to Catherine Sir Charles often made use of Swallow, the man who was soon to be appointed British Consul in St Petersburg. Swallow had more than once assisted Peter to obtain a loan from the banker Baron Wulff, who also acted as British consul, and he could therefore enter Peter's apartments as he wished. Sir Charles persuaded him to pass the letters to Peter's valet, Bresson, who in turn gave them to Catherine. Sometimes she was able to hand Swallow her replies, but since she did not want either him or Bestuzhev to discover how frequently she and Sir Charles wrote to each other she also often used Alexander Narysh-kin and her French jeweller, Bernardi, as messengers. Suspecting this Bestuzhev questioned Sir Charles, but learnt nothing by doing so.

Sir Charles tried to retain Catherine's friendship, both by helping her to meet Poniatowski and by obtaining monetary gifts for her from the British authorities. The first payment amounted to forty thousand roubles and was transmitted to Catherine by Baron Wulff on 21 July 1756. Further sums of much the same size reached her on one, possibly even on two, further occasions, one being conveyed to her by Bernardi. Regarded as bribes by the British they need not have seemed so to Catherine who may well have thought of them as presents due to her in return for her pro-British sympathies. Hanbury Williams's despatches reveal him to have been a wishful thinker of the type capable of misleading himself as well as others, for they give the impression that Catherine was able to supply him with valuable secret information. Yet, at the time, Catherine knew no state secrets. She had for some time been steadily losing Elizabeth's favour. The empress was in addition so convinced of Peter's incapacity that she seldom permitted him to attend the meetings of her Cabinet; even when she did so it was unusual for Peter to tell Catherine what had taken place there.

Though Elizabeth knew nothing of Catherine's correspondence with Sir Charles, by the spring of 1756 she had decided no longer to countenance Catherine's affair with Poniatowski. She forbade the count to visit Catherine at Oranienbaum, but, greatly daring and with Peter's con-nivance, the lovers continued to meet, Poniatowski visiting Catherine disguised. But Elizabeth had also complained to Augustus III about the young man's conduct and the Elector recalled him to Poland. In June Elizabeth had a stroke and was so ill that all thought she would die. Poniatowski took advantage of her condition to postpone his departure till August.

Catherine found life unbearable without him and persuaded Bestuzhev to write to the Saxon court to obtain permission for Poniatowski to return. Elizabeth seemed on the point of death and the possibility of a change of sovereign led even the Shuvalovs and Mikhail Vorontzov to treat the grand ducal couple with great courtesy. Bestuzhev felt unable to refuse Catherine's request and on 3 December Poniatowski arrived in St Peters-burg as Saxon ambassador. His meetings with Catherine were resumed.

Louis had been almost as much upset by the Treaty of Westminster as Elizabeth. His relations with Britain were at their worst, for the two countries were at war in America and India. It seemed to him that the treaty was mainly directed against France and he therefore informed Frederick that he would be unable to renew their treaty of alliance, due to expire in the following year. Instead he determined to win Russia to his side and decided to do so by sending Mackenzie Douglas back to St Petersburg, this time as his envoy.

Douglas reached St Petersburg in April 1756. A certain 'marchand de gallanterie' named Michel was popular in court circles. His father had come to Russia from France in 1717 at the invitation of Peter the Great to develop trade between the two countries. Michel was known to the Russians as Rodrigue. He settled in St Petersburg but went to Paris in the spring of each year, returning to Russia in the autumn with fresh supplies of bonnets and other Parisian creations. His lively chatter amused Elizabeth and he was always sure of admittance to her private apartments where he showed her the new creations designed by Parisians and informed her of much of the town's gossip. When Douglas reached St Petersburg for the second time he installed himself in Michel's house, where he gave his study the appearance of an embassy's chancery. It was almost certainly Michel who, on 7 May, presented Douglas to the empress. The envoy assured Elizabeth of King Louis' sincerity and of his desire to enter into diplomatic relations with Russia.

Meanwhile Louis had secretly taken the most effective step at his disposal for strengthening his position. On 1 May 1756 he had put his name to a treaty of alliance – that of Versailles – with Austria. Although Cardinal de Fleury and Kaunitz had in the past advocated such an agreement Louis' decision represented so great a break with tradition that Europe was as surprised by it as it had been by the Treaty of Westminster. The historian Vandal described Louis' action as revolutionary.[9] Louis had in fact acted in self-defence having at last grasped the measure of Prussia's ambitions. Douglas was not told of the new treaty but he was instructed to redouble his efforts to persuade Elizabeth to side with France since her support should enable the new allies to conquer Prussia. At Louis' insistence, the treaty contained a secret clause debarring Russia from sharing in the partition of Prussia planned by the two allies.

Versailles decided to provide Mackenzie Douglas with a secretary and chose the exquisite Chevalier d'Eon de Beaumont for the post. He arrived in St Petersburg early in June, startling the court by his astonishing resemblance to Lia de Beaumont. The young woman had stayed on in St Petersburg when Douglas had left Russia. She had often been seen in the company of Mikhail Vorontzov, and the latter apparently amused the empress by his stories about Lia and her Jacobite companion. Lia left St Petersburg shortly before Mackenzie Douglas's return to the city, but the surprising degree to which the Chevalier d'Eon resembled her led many courtiers to conclude that they were both one and the same person. The impression gained ground when it was rumoured that the Chevalier had visited Russia some years earlier disguised as a woman in order to become the empress's favourite reader and much else besides. These ridiculous surmises came to be widely believed largely because, while serving as Douglas's secretary, the Chevalier was said to have been seen travelling to France on at least one occasion dressed as a woman, having borrowed Madame de Caravaque's passport for the purpose.

While the gossips had been spreading these rumours the empress had fought her way back to health. In September she resumed her normal routine. The political situation had worsened. Frederick had invaded Saxony, thus launching the Seven Years War. He had already captured Dresden, defeated an Austrian army at Lobositz, driven it into Bohemia, and destroyed a Saxon army of fifteen thousand in the battle of Pirna. Peter's delight at his hero's achievements was almost unbearably painful to Elizabeth. It may well have been responsible for her decision, reached at about this time, to see Tsar Ivan. She arranged for him to be brought in great secrecy from his prison in Schlüsselburg to the Winter Palace, a measure which was taken more than once in the months to come. There is reason for thinking that on some of these visits she talked to him disguised as a man, but that usually she watched him being interviewed concealed from his sight. She may well have been trying to decide whether she should make Ivan her heir but the idea of disinheriting her nephew was one which she could hardly bring herself to contemplate and she delayed coming to a decision. In September she received Mackenzie Douglas for the second time. She spoke to him of her sympathy for France, but said that if anything were to come of it, it would be necessary for her and King Louis to enter into a personal correspondence, and that if they did so it would be essential for the King to be frank and sincere in his dealings with her.

7

Living Conditions in Elizabeth's Russia

Court life was of wider importance in eighteenth-century Russia than in western Europe because it was not confined to courtiers. Virtually all the well to do inhabitants of both capitals were received at court. When the court was in Moscow the impact which it made on the inhabitants was transmitted, if in an attenuated form, to the regional capitals, whence its effect gradually penetrated to the houses of the larger landowners. The tone of the court's life was defined by the sovereign and since three of Russia's rulers in the eighteenth century – Peter the Great, Elizabeth and Catherine II – were people of exceptional ability and strongly marked individuality it varied sharply with each of them.

Elizabeth has gone down in history as perhaps the laziest, most extravagant and most amorous of sovereigns. The verdict is a grossly exaggerated one yet her laziness and extravagance, if not her laxity, led her courtiers to excuse their own indolence and their inability to live within their incomes by regarding these failings as pale reflections of their sovereign's character. Many of them could have controlled these tendencies and there is every reason to assume that Elizabeth could also have mastered them had she been taught to do so when young. When writing her memoirs late in her life Catherine rather priggishly remarked that 'laziness had prevented [Elizabeth] from applying herself to the cultivation of her mind';[1] she also stated that 'flatterers and gossip-mongers succeeded in surrounding this princess with such an atmosphere of pettiness that her daily occupations consisted of a tissue of caprices, religious observances, indulgence; lacking all discipline, never occupying her mind intelligently with any serious or constructive matters, she became bored during the last years of her life and the only escape open to her from depression consisted in spending as much time as possible in sleeping'.[2] She also felt that Elizabeth 'was endowed with great intelligence; she was gay and loved pleasure to excess. I believe that, basically, she was kind at heart; there was distinction in her and great vanity; she wished to excel in all things and wanted to be admired; I think that her physical beauty and innate laziness greatly harmed her character. Her beauty should have preserved her from envy and the feeling of rivalry aroused in her by all women who were not hideous yet, in reality, it was concern lest that beauty be overshadowed by another that aroused her extreme jealousy, often reducing her to a condition unbefitting to Her Majesty.'[1]

Elizabeth in fact possessed quite outstanding abilities and her range of interests was wide. Lord Hyndford admired her intellect. According to Field Marshal Münnich[3] she had a penetrating intelligence allied to great physical courage. When he first met her she was only twelve years old yet even then she was greatly interested in architecture and a few years later she was actively encouraging the construction of churches and palaces. She hated cruelty and bloodshed. She wrote a good hand, was well mannered, danced well and was always keenly interested in military affairs. Until immobilized by ill-health the vivacity of her mind was reflected in the speed with which she moved, a trait which greatly taxed her ladies. It was unfortunate that she had no one who could train her mind or set her a good example, for the lack of such a person probably accounts for the careful attention with which Elizabeth studied the conduct of the two Annas, and the extent to which she modelled her own on Anna Ivanovna's. The spying to which she was subjected in her youth left a permanent mark on her character, making her suspicious and vindictive.

Mackenzie Douglas described Elizabeth's court as 'one of the most scheming, most deceitful and most difficult to classify in Europe'. The foreigners who were attached to it were in no small part to blame, for even though Elizabeth was unable to curb the courtiers' love of gossip, she did succeed in ending their political dissensions and the habit they had acquired of interfering in the succession to the throne.[4]

Elizabeth frankly admitted that she was only wholly contented when in love. Nevertheless her known romances do not exceed seven in number. Though it would perhaps be unfair to hold Anna Ivanovna responsible for her amorousness Elizabeth's extravagance can legitimately – if only in part – be traced to that empress. No Russian ruler had ever been as prodigal as Anna Ivanovna nor lived as splendidly in so continuous a sequence of entertainments, nor displayed such ostentation. At her banquets guests were expected to eat standing whilst she sat beneath a canopy with Anna Leopoldovna and Elizabeth at her sides. Elizabeth quickly gave up the practice, preferring to seat her guests at E-shaped tables.

Elizabeth, gay yet passionately jealous by temperament and permanently in need of money, must have watched Anna Ivanovna indulging her whims with feelings of profound longing. When she in her turn became empress there was no one to advise her to control her fondness for lovely clothes and lavish receptions. At that decisive moment of her life de la Chétardie was still beside her, still influencing her, and his own way of life was so extravagant and spectacular that it must have been used by Elizabeth as a yardstick. In a short time her expenses had outstripped those of Anna Ivanovna. She had an instinctive appreciation of quality and her dresses were extraordinarily elaborate. She especially liked hand-embroidered silks and silver lace trimmings, a taste pandered to by Lord Hyndford when ambassador. Nevertheless Catherine was to prove even more extravagant then Elizabeth, and the courtiers of both empresses kept in step with their sovereigns. They excelled over the west's more sophisticated courtiers in at least one respect – they took regular baths and saw to it that their clothes were clean.

The extravagance of Elizabeth's court made it seem natural for Alexei Razumovsky's buckles, buttons and epaulettes to be set with diamonds and for the carriage which Michael Vorontzov obtained for him from Maille of Paris to have cost three thousand roubles; natural for Field Marshal Apraxin to have thought nothing of commandeering five hundred horses in the opening phase of the Seven Years' War for the purpose of transporting his luggage, which included 360 snuff boxes; natural for Shuvalov to order his suits in tens rather than singly and to dress his pages and footmen in cloth of gold. Although his income exceeded a hundred thousand roubles, and even though he was thought to double it by accepting bribes, at his death his debts exceeded a million roubles. Frederick of Prussia could not forgive Kiril Razumovsky for having persuaded the empress to cede her famous chef Baridian to him for his town house and for paying him a yearly salary of five hundred roubles whilst employing the scarcely less distinguished Duval at his Ukrainian residence of Baturino. In order to re-stock his cellar Kiril Razumovsky on one occasion ordered a hundred thousand bottles of wine, six thousand of which were of the best champagne. Elizabeth had first employed Fournay as her head chef, but had then replaced him by Baridian; at his departure she placed her kitchens in the charge of the Alsatian Fuchs. She used Tokay as a toasting drink but was especially fond of Margaux and encouraged her courtiers to drink French wines, more especially burgundies. Champagne and pineapples were served at her receptions.

Until she was forty Elizabeth's amorous adventures and the enjoyment she derived from folk songs and dances contented her, but when life brought its disappointments she started taking an inordinate interest in the table. She was an excellent cook and even as empress she continued to enjoy preparing some of her favourite Russian dishes for Alexei Razumovsky and other close friends. Continental dishes were, however, served at her official receptions and banquets. These were so lavish that, in 1758, Catherine found herself spending between ten and fifteen thousand roubles on the entertainment she gave in an effort to effect a reconciliation with her husband. Yet at the time her annual allowance was fixed at thirty thousand roubles, a sum which was greatly exceeded by her debts. She held her reception in the park at Oranienbaum on 17 July. She relived it when describing it in her Memoirs, noting that,

in a concealed glade the architect Antonio Rinaldi, whom I employed at the time, made a great float, one large enough to hold an orchestra of sixty. I had had verses especially written by the court's Italian poet and music by the choir master Araja. I had arranged for elaborate illuminations to be erected in the main alley and for a curtain to be hung at its far end; the supper tables had been erected at its opposite end. When the first part of the supper had been served and eaten the curtain was raised and the guests saw the float advancing towards them pulled by twenty or so begarlanded oxen, surrounded by all the male and female dancers I could find.

The moon appeared at exactly the right moment. After enjoying the spectacle for a time the curtain was lowered and the guests resumed their supper. When the second set of dishes had been removed 'fanfares and clarions sounded and a hunter appeared shouting "Ladies and Gentlemen, come to my stall; there you will find free lottery tickets." As he spoke two smaller side curtains parted to disclose two booths.'[5] The lottery tickets and the prizes consisting of pieces of delicate porcelain were handed out from one booth, the other prizes, consisting of flowers, ribbons, fans, combs, purses, gloves, sword trimmings and the like, from the other. When all the prizes had been distributed the guests resumed their seats for more food. Dancing continued till six in the morning.

Elizabeth held a court on Thursdays and Sundays. There were concerts on two evenings of the week, a French comedy was performed on one and court balls were held twice a week. One of the balls was limited to two hundred guests drawn from the court's officials and the empress's personal friends; the other was for eight hundred guests and all the officers serving in the Guards regiments stationed in the capital were invited to it together with officers from the rank of colonel upwards from other regiments, as well as members of the lesser nobility and the leading merchants. The guests invited to the smaller ball came masked, but after 1744 these evenings often took the form of a metamorphosis. Elizabeth would appear at the latter dressed either as a cossack, a French carpenter or a Dutch sailor and would call herseif Mikhailova in memory of her father who had been called Mikhailov when he worked as a shipwright at Saardam.

In the country there were fewer diversoins; cards, dancing and occasional amateur theatricals providing the only distractions. As Elizabeth grew older and her health deteriorated she became difficult to amuse and the evenings grew so dull that the time spent in the country came to be dreaded. Catherine has left a lugubrious impression of it:

The empress would take all the gentlemen of the court and a quantity of ladies, those whom she especially liked. The ladies were four to a room in addition to their maids and chattels. There was much disagreement among them which did not help in making the empress's visit enjoyable. You probably think that they were there to wait on the empress or to contribute to her pleasure in staying in that palace; far from it, for they seldom saw Her Imperial Majesty; sometimes two or three weeks would pass without the empress emerging from her apartments or sending for any of them. None dared to go to town, and their town relations would send to ask after them very secretly for the empress disliked anyone coming to the palace uninvited; even a liveried servant not from her own household only dared to set foot there in secrecy. Furthermore, no one from the empress's suite was permitted to enter the garden at the back of the palace, whether the terrace or the walks below it, because the empress's apartments faced in that direction. Although the palace [Tsarskoe Selo] was already in its present state Her Majesty nevertheless continued to live in the ground floor apartments; she entered the piano nobile no more than ten times after its completion. To add to the strangeness of it all no one knew the time at which it would please Her Majesty to dine or sup; it was not therefore unusual for this court, after playing cards (its one diversion) till two in the morning having retired to bed and fallen asleep, to find itself roused to attend her Majesty's supper. All would foregather and she would spend a long time at table so that everyone was tired out and half asleep, not a word would be said, the empress would get very angry and say 'they only enjoy being among themselves; I seldom send for them and even then they do nothing but yawn and won't divert me'. These suppers often ended with the empress throwing her napkin on the table in anger and with-drawing. It should be stated here that it was as difficult to converse in Her Majesty's presence as to guess the time of her meals. There were quantities of subjects she disapproved of. Thus, she disliked talk concerning the king of Prussia, Voltaire, illness, death, beautiful women, French behaviour, the sciences; all these displeased her. In addition, she also had aversions for certain people and when that happened she was very apt to take exception to anything they said, and since those who were with her intentionally encouraged her to think ill of others, none was certain that she had not turned against him and that made conversation very sticky.[6]

Foreigners received a different, and probably fairer, impression. Even those who met Elizabeth at the close of her life and were most infuriated by her dilatoriness, were invariably charmed by her. In 1745 Lord Hynd-ford had considered her 'worthy of the admiration of all the world'.[7] Two years later Catherine herself thought her 'still lovely in men's clothes, her eyes like those of a merry bird, her hair beautiful in colour, but her face needing, and indeed, being made up'. Diplomats soon realized that although the empress inherited her beauty from her mother her character resembled her father's. Like him she was quick-tempered and restless, fond of physical activities, able to outwalk most of her courtiers and, when in town, riding almost daily in Biron's riding school. She was as calm as Peter in the face of danger. In November 1753 Dickens wrote with admiration of the empress: she had gone to spend the evening in the palace which Rastrelli had built for her in 1742 on the Pokrovka in Moscow, near the church and vicarage where some authorities believe that she was married to Alexei Razumovsky, when a fire broke out in the palace in which she was living. When told of it the empress hurried to the scene and spent three hours 'showing great concern and giving her instructions with all the coolness of mind imaginable'.[8] Many foreigners remarked on Elizabeth's warm-heartedness and kindness – characteristics which Peter had lacked. She delighted in seeing people happy. She was gentle and affable, and her gaiety was devoid of malice. She also possessed great dignity. Unlike Catherine II Elizabeth was never calculating and her generosity was always disinterested. When she learnt of the devastation caused to Lisbon by a severe earthquake she was so distressed by the plight of the city's inhabitants that, even though Russia had not established diplo-matic relations with Portugal and was not considering doing so, she offered to rebuild the town at her personal expense. This typically Russian reaction was one of her most endearing characteristics. Another lay in her love of children. Childless herself, Elizabeth adored the young and they responded by loving her. She made a habit of giving children's parties, generally inviting some eighty young guests who sat down to supper at miniature tables whilst the empress led their parents, tutors and governesses to a different dining room. The children ate miniature food off miniature plates – a type of party which continued to be given in certain Petersburgian circles until the outbreak of the revolution.

Elizabeth's personal household was a large one. It consisted of six Gentlemen of the Chamber, eight chamberlains, Count François de Santi, a nobleman from Piedmont and her Chief Master of Ceremonies, her ladies and numerous servants. The ladies belonged to the two top grades in the Table of Ranks, and were thus entitled to the same privileges as a field marshal, but they were divided into two categories. Those ranking as ladies-in-waiting received an annual salary of six hundred roubles from the empress with, in addition, free food and lodging in the palace; when they married Elizabeth gave each a dowry of six hundred roubles and the right to retain their rank and order of precedence if married to a commoner. The maids of honour received no salary but, as *dames à portrait*, they wore a bejewelled miniature of the empress pinned to their dresses and often received expensive presents from her. She treated them and her young courtiers like beloved godchildren, helping their romances to end happily, assisting those in financial straits. When any of her ladies married she personally dressed the bride for her wedding, lending her her finest jewels for the occasion. On the eve of the wedding day, whilst the groom dined with his men friends, the bride supped in the empress's bedroom, Elizabeth supervising the meal to ensure that she did not overeat. On the following evening the empress gave a ball in honour of the bridal pair. The warmth with which she congratulated Princess Dashkova on her marriage reduced that emotional young woman to tears in the presence of the entire court. 'Come, come, child,' murmured the empress, 'compose yourself or all your friends will think I have been scolding you.'

Forgiveness followed an apology almost automatically, however grievous the offence. Nevertheless, like her father, Elizabeth was passionate and demanding; she was unimaginative and self-centred. Though extremely religious she was also extremely superstitious; should a fly settle on her pen or paper when she was on the point of signing a document she would postpone doing so.[9]

Elizabeth's intimate circle consisted of a small number of men differing considerably in background, character and interests. Some, like Mikhail

Vorontzov, had been her devoted friends during the most difficult years of her life. They had had no administrative experience when she rewarded them for their loyalty by assigning them to positions of high office. Only one of her senior ministers, Alexei Bestuzhev, belonged to the Petrine age; he was the only minister whom she never really liked. Of her intimates, gentle, unassuming, music-loving Alexei Razumovsky must have known from the start that he would never be able completely to satisfy Elizabeth's restless and turbulent spirit. Her relationship with the brothers Alexander and Peter Shuvalov was different again. Both had helped her to the throne. She had for a time been attracted to Alexander, the man who became the dreaded chief of her Secret Chancery, but it was his brother Peter whom she came to rely on most as an administrator, and to their remarkably handsome and intelligent cousin Ivan that she was to give her heart. As well as playing important parts in Elizabeth's personal life, all three Shuvalovs were of great help to her in the task of steering Russia along its turbulent course; Peter being mainly responsible for the country's economic development, Ivan for its cultural growth.

On her accession Elizabeth announced that she intended to adopt three political aims. The first to revive her father's basic policies; the second was to strive to avoid warfare; and the third was to restore to the Church the independence and autonomous powers which her father had curtailed and to ensure her own strict observance of the canons of orthodoxy. Theoretically these principles should have enabled her to improve living conditions in Russia, but neither the empress nor her ministers were able clearly to understand Peter the Great's policies. Peter's aim had been to transform Russia from a retarded, inefficient medieval power into a mighty military nation, and although little had been done after his death to complete the change Elizabeth in fact found herself mistress of just such a state. Yet the country she had taken charge of was still precariously poised on the tightrope connecting the stagnant, outdated yet characterful world of medieval Muscovy to the tumultuous, perplexing scientific Petersburgian age. Even a man as intelligent and determined as Peter had been unable to dissociate the new Russia from the old or to eradicate the worst of the country's evils – serfdom. Elizabeth likewise did not know how to solve the difficulties created by serfdom and turned a blind eye on them. Her task of governing had been made unnecessarily difficult by Peter's decision, taken late in his reign, to remodel the Russian administrative machine on the lines of Sweden's collegiate system. Alone of all her ministers Alexei Bestuzhev realized this and calmly ignored the College for Foreign

Affairs, dealing personally with all matters affecting Russia's foreign relations.

In order to govern Russia as she thought Peter had done Elizabeth hastened to abolish the Cabinet or Council of State which Anna Ivanovna had established and to restore all its former powers to the Senate.* To stress the new Senate's importance Elizabeth convened it on the second day of her reign, making a point of attending its first session. Indeed, during the first half of her reign she was often present at its meetings. She made the Senate responsible for the affairs which had formerly been dealt with by eight of the Colleges founded by her father; but she gave full autonomy to the college which dealt with religious affairs, and placed the three which retained their original names – those for Foreign Affairs, the Army and Navy – under the sovereign's direct control. And although the Senate did not introduce any major reforms during Elizabeth's reign it dealt with all administrative matters, and in doing so it passed much necessary, if unspectacular, legislation.

Elizabeth was determined to end the political controversies which had for so long divided the nobility into factions, for she wished to secure for the sovereign the loyalty of all its members. Though the nobility numbered only seven per cent of the population it included the greater part of the country's gentry and therefore exercised great influence in the rural districts. By exempting noblemen from the duty imposed on them by Peter the Great of serving the state Elizabeth was to make them all-powerful in the countryside. Many landowning officers took advantage of the concession to retire from the army; some undertook various duties in the country districts which had until then been carried out by the voivodes whilst others received crown lands as gifts from the empress. Many proved efficient administrators and, whereas French nobles thought it a penance to live on their estates, Russians started to enjoy it. Many took great pride and interest in their lands. The more they became involved in rural affairs the less, to Elizabeth's satisfaction, were they inclined to figure in court intrigues. By Catherine's reign the country districts possessed a resident upper class. Another change had also been unnoticeably accomplished by then; whereas Peter had divided his subjects into fourteen clearly divided categories Elizabeth had transformed them into a series of inter-

---

* In February 1711 Peter established a senate composed of nine senators and a clerk. It was to govern the country during his absences from St Petersburg. In addition it was to act as the country's supreme judicial authority, to be responsible for regional administration and when necessary to undertake certain special additional duties.

locking cogs. Nevertheless, many of her noblemen continued to send their sons to serve in the army, entering their names at birth on a regiment's list, with the result that a boy attained officer rank when still in his teens. This was not to the army's advantage.

At the beginning of the eighteenth century Russia had been a wholly agricultural country, and it remained largely so throughout the century. Although its population had dropped by twenty per cent between 1678 and 1710,[10] it had risen to fourteen million by 1743 and to seventeen million by 1761, the year of Elizabeth's death, ninety per cent of the people lived in the country. By the middle of the century the improvement in their living conditions and their relative security from Tartar raids had begun to attract not only Russian settlers but also Slavs emigrating from the Turkish and Austrian occupied areas of central Europe. The latter settled in the region bordered by the Dnieper and Bug rivers which Anna Ivanovna had joined to Russia, forming a community known as New Serbia. It was soon so well populated that it provided Russia with four regiments of light cavalry. According to Princess Dashkova, however, the money advanced by Elizabeth to would-be immigrants was misappropriated and the number of settlers declined.[11] Nevertheless others came to Russia to settle in the central as well as the western areas which were becoming underpopulated as a result of the migration to the south and east.

Two-thirds of the country people were serfs living for the most part in central Russia, i.e. the districts which had constituted the Grand Duchy of Muscovy. Excluding the Ukraine, the privately owned serfs formed fifty-three per cent of the total serf population, thirty-nine per cent were monastic serfs, 6.9 per cent belonged to the crown and the remainder were employed in industry. Thus forty-three per cent of the total number of serfs belonged to seven per cent of the population; until Elizabeth's reign eighty per cent of these serf owners possessed at least twenty-five serfs and rather less than a hundred; richer landowners had about a hundred serfs, and those owning a thousand or more were considered to be immensely prosperous. The situation altered sharply when Elizabeth rewarded those who had helped her to the throne so lavishly. Catherine was to carry the system of excessive rewards even further. Peter the Great had provided them with a precedent when he rewarded Field Marshal Sheremetiev for the part he had played in winning the battle of Poltava by presenting him with an entire province, enabling him to bequeath sixty thousand serfs to his son. Acting on the same principle Peter II had given Prince Alexei

Dolgoruky, his future father-in-law, forty thousand serfs. The two Annas had behaved in a similar manner, the first when manifesting her love for Biron, the second her sense of indebtedness to Münnich. Elizabeth was therefore doing no more than follow in their steps when she gave Alexei Razumovsky, the two Shuvalovs and Mikhail Vorontzov fifty thousand serfs each for helping her to the throne, although with her such gifts became habitual, and Kiril Razumovsky ended by acquiring 120,000 serfs. Landowners had full powers over these unfortunate people, whether they were men, women or children. They could fine, arrest, punish, torture, sell, confine them to prison or send them into exile. Many grossly abused these powers, but few quite so outrageously as Countess Darya Saltykova who, in 1756, inherited six hundred serfs from her husband. During the next seven years she treated them so barbarously and sadistically, often for entirely imaginary offences, that many died. The number is put as high as 138. Gradually her neighbours realized what was happening and brought so much pressure on the local authorities that the latter instituted a public inquiry. Darya Saltykova was pronounced guilty; she was deprived of her rank, exposed for an hour in Moscow's public pillory and banished to a convent, but the final episode in this ghastly affair was the least forgivable of all, for the authorities ordered the unfortunate serfs who had carried out Darya Saltykova's orders to be flogged and banished to Siberia as a punishment for having done so.

Elizabeth had not intended to place the peasants so completely within the powers of the landowners; all she had had in mind was to give the latter the necessary authority to maintain law and order in their new role of rural administrators. Since serfdom had by then become a recognized and firmly established institution it had seemed to her no more than logical to employ the serf owners as magistrates, even though the decision helped to enforce the serf's lack of civic rights.

About half the total number of serfs were obliged to work for their masters three to four days a week. They were not paid for doing so; indeed, in some districts they were expected to pay their owners between one and three roubles a year even though in summer they often worked a sixteen hour day. A bad landowner could exact more than the half-week's work to which the law entitled him. Crop yields averaged from three to five times the amount sown and no landlord ever thought of selling his surplus produce; he aimed at growing only sufficient for his needs less the deliveries in kind due to him from his serfs. The peasants were always expected to make payments in kind to their masters, delivering to their doors, if necessary to their town houses, such produce as hay, wood, meat, poultry, lengths of home-woven linen and so on. Bad harvests averaged one in ten; at such times landowners were expected to provide their serfs with food and seed corn. Domestic serfs, and these included tutors, actors and artists, received a small wage; it varied from fifty kopeks to six roubles a year with board, food and clothes in addition.

Living and working conditions were almost equally bad for all serfs. They had greatly worsened under Peter the Great, with the result that many serfs had tried to escape from their masters by fleeing to the Urals, to Siberia, the Caucasus, the Baltic States, even to Poland. Within two years of Peter's death peasant risings had broken out. Between 1727 and 1744 the number of runaway serfs exceeded three thousand; others refused to pay their taxes and started setting fire to their masters' houses, even murdering them. Many, including some monastic serfs, formed themselves into bands and roamed the country side attacking members of the land-owning class. Once it had even proved necessary to call troops to deal with them. In 1752 three thousand serfs from the Demidovs' Kaluga estates managed to obtain some firearms, rioted and routed a regiment of dragoons; six regiments were needed to quell them. In the same year a thousand of Alexander Shuvalov's serfs working in the mines also mutinied. In 1754 new, considerably harsher measures were adopted for dealing with escaped serfs.[12]

The average monastery possessed only a score or so of serfs, and these were generally the least unfortunate of all, but large monasteries had acquired much land and a great many serfs. By 1740 the Troitse-Sergievan Monastery owned land in fifteen districts and 106,000 serfs. The Monastery of St Cyril Belosersk owned twenty thousand serfs.

The peasants who found that they had been transferred to industry met with worse treatment and conditions than the agriculturalists and showed themselves more ready to riot. In 1740 those employed in Moscow's state-owned factories mutinied. In 1758 those working in the silk-weaving factories which had recently been established on the Volga found that rioting was of little use and proceeded to escape in a steady trickle, often finding work in Siberia. The state-owned peasants were few in number; together with the very few free peasants they were better off than the rest. The majority of the freemen lived in north-eastern Russia and the Volga basin, and consisted largely of minority groups such as Tartars or Bashkirs. It fell to them to maintain the roads and to supply travellers with fresh relays of horses.

To begin with Elizabeth had been anxious to improve the peasants' conditions. She introduced a poll tax in 1740. To compensate for the loss of revenue caused by the change in taxation and also to help finance the war against Sweden she reduced the salaries of civil servants and officers serving in the army and navy. Peter Shuvalov had by then come to dominate the Senate. He was proving an able financier. To strengthen the nation's economy he imposed drastic cuts on the state's spending, reducing the sums available for state functions and forbidding courtiers to wear gold or silver trimmings or imported lace more than three fingers wide. In 1752 he reduced the poll tax, adjusting the cost to the treasury by retaining the sums produced by the taxes imposed in the previous year on salt and vodka, and by turning the salt industry into a crown monopoly.

Until well into the eighteenth century money lenders provided the only source of credit available to landowners; often they exploited their monopoly, charging interest rates as high as two hundred per cent. In 1729 a Monetary Counter had been established to help those overburdened with debts; there the rate of interest was fixed at eight per cent and loans could be raised by providing jewellery as a security. Unfortunately the Counter closed down in 1736. In 1752 Peter Shuvalov decided to use the money raised by the tax on vodka to establish a fund for providing mortgages at six per cent for landowners wishing to improve their estates. These transactions were to be handled by Banks of the Nobility, the first two of which opened in 1754, one in St Petersburg and one in Moscow. Shuvalov was also responsible for measures taken that year for delineating estate boundaries in the districts of Moscow and Novgorod. The absence of agreed boundaries had until then frequently led to pitched battles between neighbours. Shuvalov was also able to found peasants' savings banks and took steps towards revaluing the currency.

Though the bonds of serfdom tightened during Elizabeth's reign agriculture greatly expanded. Its growth was partly due to the rise in the population which enabled much fresh land to be brought into cultivation in the Black Earth region, in south-eastern Russia and in Siberia, but it also resulted from deeper ploughing of the soil. The potato was introduced to Russia in about 1760 and first cultivated in the district of Novgorod, though, with poor results, but the export of rhubarb to England was still bringing in considerable sums. As late as 1737 the British Resident Claudius Rondeau[13] was deploring his failure to obtain any rhubarb seeds for despatch to England though he had offered two hundred ducats for them. It was Elizabeth's Scottish physician, Dr Mouncey,[14] who managed to

20. Makhaev's drawing of the Summer Palace which Rastrelli built of wood for the empress.

21. Central section of the park front of the Catherine Palace at Tsarskoe Selo, the work of Rastrelli the Younger.

22. The Smolny Cathedral at St Petersburg, by Rastrelli the Younger.

23. The silver shrine which was made in the mint, St Petersburg, between 1750 and 1753 to contain the remains of St Alexander Nevsky.

procure a root; by smuggling it out of the country and keeping it in good condition he was responsible for its introduction to Britain.

Elizabeth's policy of winning the nobility's loyalty was greatly helped by the introduction of four laws which carried considerable economic and social benefits – achieved at the peasants' expense. The first annulled a law passed by Peter the Great which entitled peasants volunteering for military service to acquire the status of freemen. The law had lapsed under Peter's successors, but when it became known that Elizabeth had ascended the throne and that she intended to revive her father's policies the peasants assumed that it would come into force again and therefore hurried to enlist. Elizabeth refused to revive the concession for fear of alienating the nobility; moreover, she punished those peasants who had enlisted, at the very time when she was trying to make life easier for them by introducing the poll tax. This tax made a census necessary. To simplify and speed the count the landowners were instructed to conduct it, but they were not asked to furnish any details about those involved. Hence there was no opportunity for the free peasants to record their status, and they were recorded together with the serfs, as agricultural labourers instead of small-holders.

The third edict was issued in 1754. It limited the ownership of villages to the hereditary nobility. Many of the gentry found that it dispossessed them of their property whilst peasants who had been fairly well treated by the gentry learnt that they had become the property of landowners living for the most part in the capital. The bitterest law of all came into force in 1760, when Elizabeth was broken in health and spirit. It was introduced for the purpose of populating Siberia, but the method resorted to was diabolical. The law entitled a landlord to punish a serf aged under forty for a major offence by banishing him to Siberia and obtaining in return a certificate of conscription made out in the man's name. The serf's family could, if it wished, accompany him to Siberia, and in that case the Government compensated the landlord for the loss by paying him ten roubles for each of the man's sons aged under five, twenty roubles and a recruitment certificate for one aged between five and twenty-five and half these amounts for girls of similar ages. Many a frail and innocent serf suffered deportation under this law in place of a strong and healthy delinquent.

The policy of opening up Siberia was adopted at the start of Elizabeth's reign. As part of the process landlords were encouraged to settle along the banks of the Volga and monastic foundations to establish outposts in that area from which to send missionaries further eastward. Gifts of clothes, money and three years of tax exemption were offered as additional inducements. Although the number of emigrants fell short of what had been hoped for, a whole new town – Orenburg – was founded; seven hundred houses, four churches, seventy-five shops and forty bazaars were erected on its site between 1744 and 1746. It was not only in the east that Russia's boundaries expanded during Elizabeth's reign. In the west Esthonia and Latvia became incorporated in Russia, but they retained their own administrators who, though directed by a Russian governor-general, were elected by the native German nobility. In the south the Khan of Kazakstan decided, in the face of a renewed Djungarian threat, to place himself under her protection.

The treasury was permanently short of funds under both Elizabeth and Catherine II; much of this was due to the empress' personal extravagance though the peasants' habit of burying their money, thereby withdrawing it from circulation, as well as the refusal of a large section of the population to pay its taxes, were contributory factors. On Elizabeth's accession unpaid taxes amounted to five million roubles; they were annulled by a manifesto of 1752 yet by 1766 they had again reached the figure of eight hundred thousand roubles. Nevertheless, the economy was buoyant. Even though, by 1750, the yearly deficit to the budget was in the region of half a million roubles, industry and commerce were expanding rapidly. Their growth was largely due to Peter Shuvalov. Even though he made an immense personal fortune by acquiring for himself and his brother what should rightly have been state monopolies – such as the fat extracting refineries and the Gorodetsky mines in the Urals – he nevertheless contributed more than any one else to Russia's industrial development. It was no more unusual for a Russian nobleman of the period to acquire industrial assets than it had been in the sixteenth and seventeenth centuries for English ones to be involved in trade. In Peter Shuvalov's hands the Siberian metal mining industry developed in a spectacular manner. By 1755 iron ore was being mined at forty-two points in the Urals, the annual output exceeding that of Britain by topping the two million pud* mark. Half the mined iron was exported. The mining of silver expanded with the same speed so that whereas only ten puds of silver were delivered annually to the mint in Peter the Great's day, by 1760 the amount exceeded ten thousand. These achievements were made possible by the increase to Siberia's population.

The peopling of Siberia was also responsible for the increase in the

* A pud equalled 36 lb.

number of factories founded there and resulted in a similar expansion in western Russia. Peter the Great had been able to found only ninety-eight factories in the course of his reign, but by 1768 the number had increased ten fold. The majority were concerned with the production of textiles and although the first of these was not established till 1740 others sprang up rapidly, mostly in and around Moscow and Vladimir – areas where the production of textiles had been concentrated from early times in the hands of cottagers. The manufacture of silks and tapestry were new ventures and for these St Petersburg became the main centre of production.

To encourage the development of industries Peter Shuvalov created administrative assessors and secretaries; he also appointed a councillor whose duties it was to provide technical advice concerning the manufacture of silk, cotton and linen. The empress was especially interested in the new silk factories and in 1746 personally chose the Russian velvet which was to be used for court dress; it had a red ground with darker red stripes on it. By 1752 silk worms were being raised in the district of Astrakhan, the raw silk being reserved for the making of velvets and taffetas. The finest were woven with designs similar to those fashionable at the time in western Europe. Throughout the remainder of the century the silk industry was both state sponsored and state protected yet, in sharp contrast to food, which was cheap, silk and other home-produced luxuries remained very expensive. The selling price was fixed by the state and only merchants belonging to the five top grades of the Table of Ranks were entitled to trade in silks of the highest quality.

Peter Shuvalov was keenly interested in the army and did much both to improve conditions for the men and to modernize their equipment. He invented a new type of howitzer which, when brought into use in the Seven Years' War, proved extremely effective. Although the army had been allowed to stagnate in the reign of Catherine I and her successors, at Elizabeth's death, as a result of Shuvalov's exertions, it was as efficient and large as it had been at the end of Peter's reign. Shuvalov raised a force of thirty thousand men and equipped it at his own expense, but took little interest in the navy. Although he kept the shipyards at Archangel working their output was much smaller than in Peter's reign, and the navy was so ineffective that it could play no part in the Seven Years' War.

Peter Shuvalov was as interested in economics and finance as he was in the army and industry. In 1753 he introduced economic measures of far reaching effect. They embodied the results of much careful work under-taken for the purpose of abolishing internal tolls. When these were lifted trade within the country began to flourish even though pirates continued to operate on the Volga and highwaymen rendered road travel dangerous. The appalling condition of most roads also seriously hindered the expansion of internal trade at the very time when the increase in population and economic reforms were encouraging its growth. Hence throughout the century canals were constructed. Even then most goods continued as in earlier times to be carried on sledges during the winter months, though merchants gradually began making more use of the waterways in the warmer weather. When travelling upstream barges were dragged by burlaks; the strain on the men was such that, even though they worked in large gangs, one in sixty is believed to have died every summer. Their suffering is commemorated in the Song of the Volga Boatmen.

Until 1726 all Russia's trade, whether external or internal, had been handled by merchants, but the passing in that year of a law entitling landowners to sell their surplus agricultural produce and permitting peasants to trade in the small wares which they made for themselves led to drastic changes. Neither the landowners nor the peasants paid any further attention to the few remaining restrictions on free trade and in 1745 Elizabeth abolished them altogether. She also encouraged the commercial class by sending some merchants to western Europe to study trading methods. Her love of anything exotic, rare or lovely helped to stimulate foreign trade and sometimes resulted in useful developments. Thus her desire to be kept supplied with fresh peaches and grapes made it necessary for a postal road to be built to link Moscow to Astrakhan; a section passed through Tsarytsin and Kiev. When finished the road was 1,144 kilometres long and, in 1756, when still in good condition, a traveller could count on covering an average of fifty kilometres a day on it.

Elizabeth warmly supported Peter Shuvalov's efforts to develop Russia's foreign trade. Nevertheless she had to agree when he felt obliged to impose a thirteen per cent tax on imports to compensate for the loss in revenue resulting from the abolition of the internal tolls. In order to encourage foreigners to use St Petersburg as a port the new tax was not applied in full there. Imports, however, lagged behind exports because Elizabeth could not raise loans in western Europe. Much of Russia's foreign trade therefore turned eastward, to China, Persia, Turkestan and Central Asia, and came to consist largely of fruit, tea and cattle with only a small number of luxuries. Trade with China was a state monopoly. Nevertheless, by 1754, Russia's trade with Britain was proving very profitable and held the promise of becoming still more so.

The growth of industry stimulated inventors. A man called Priadinov, a member of the sect of Old Believers, discovered petrol in 1749, but the use to be made of it led to such fierce disagreement between the College of Mines and the Medical Chancery that although petrol was soon being used for lighting purposes the unfortunate discoverer was sent to prison and there is no evidence that he did not end his days there. Two years later another prisoner, one Lev Chamchurenkov, when in detention in a Moscow jail, in petitioning to be released, described himself as the inventor of a vehicle which foreshadowed the modern motor car. It needed two men to keep it in motion, but it could travel over a considerable distance and even ascend hills. Chamchurenkov reminded the authorities that in 1736 he had already invented a machine for moving earth and raising church bells into position, but that it had been destroyed by fire. He was given permission to construct another of his vehicles;[15] it worked and he was paid a rouble for it. Greatly encouraged he produced a more advanced version, mounting it on runners instead of wheels and fitting it with a device for measuring the distance travelled to a maximum of a thousand versts.*

Elizabeth was more concerned over spiritual matters than were any of her ministers. Her superstitious attributes did not prevent her from being profoundly religious and her devotion to the Church expressed itself as soon as she became empress. Of all the anti-clerical measures introduced by Peter the Great that which transferred the administration of the Church's property from the clerical hierarchy to the recently established Monastic Bureau was among those most fiercely resented. The Monastic Bureau had been abolished in 1726 when its duties were entrusted to an Administrative Agency forming part of the Economics College. Elizabeth promptly closed down the Agency and made the Holy Synod once again solely responsible for the administration of Church lands, but it carried out its duties so badly that mutinies among the monastic serfs became frequent. Yet it was not so much because of the unrest among the monastic serfs that the empress reversed her decision in 1756 and entrusted laymen with the task of administering the Church's property as her need for funds with which to finance Russia's military commitments. The Church learnt that it was to receive only part of the revenue obtained from its estates, the remainder passing to the crown mainly to establish homes for maimed soldiers. The first of these institutions was situated in Kazan and was ready to receive its inmates in 1760; others were in use soon after. Often, more

* A verst equalled ·66 miles or 1·067 km.

especially in the districts of Voronezh and Nizhni Novgorod, retired officers were used to collect this tax; they proved honest and efficient, but the ecclesiastical authorities were never reconciled to the measure and continued fiercely to resent it.

Elizabeth's accession sparked off a spontaneous religious revival through-out Russia. The activities of missionaries multiplied and extended to the remaining pockets of paganism in an effort to convert Muslim and other minority groups such as the Chuvash, the inhabitants of the Mordva and so on. This fervour was not expressed in the form of intense and devout piety, but proceeded to prompt outbursts of savage fanaticism. The Holy Synod was largely to blame for these excesses and must be held wholly responsible for the closure of the Armenian churches in St Petersburg and Moscow and for the proposal to abolish the dissident churches. In the regions where Tartars and Orthodox lived side by side the mosques were closed and the construction of new ones forbidden. Similar prohibitions were applied to Jews who were also expelled from Russia proper. Devotion to Orthodoxy reached such proportions that at Ustyug fifty-three Old Believers tied themselves together and set themselves alight, inspiring other members of the sect to follow their example.

Elizabeth's government made considerable efforts to provide educational instruction for members of the lower clergy in an effort to improve the standard of their personal conduct. At the beginning of Elizabeth's reign the number of scholars in Moscow's Ecclesiastical Academy had fallen to five and even they spent most of their time debating such unprofitable themes as whether angels thought by analysis or synthesis. Now appeals were sent to abbots asking them to select their more promising monks and to despatch them to the Academy to receive a higher education.

The legal code of 1649 was already thoroughly out of date in Peter the Great's reign. The tsar had intended to have it revised, but had never had time to see that it was done. Elizabeth's decision to abolish capital punish-ment made the revision of the code essential. All the empress's ministers were opposed to the abolition of the death penalty, but the empress was determined to put an end to capital punishment in all cases other than those of heresy which, she felt, should be dealt with by the Church since it was not for her to interfere in doctrinal matters. Although political prisoners continued to be sentenced to death, Elizabeth personally com-muted their sentences. However, in 1753, there were still 3,579 prisoners waiting for this act of clemency. In order to catch up with these cases the Senate obtained the empress's permission to commute their sentences on her behalf to flogging followed by banishment to Siberia, the measure to be applied alike to rich and poor, nobleman and man of humble origin.

Although those who endangered the stability of the throne were savagely punished, Elizabeth's sense of compassion led her to insist on the introduction of a more humane attitude to prisoners. In 1742 she made it illegal for youths aged under seventeen to be tortured and in 1757 she put an end to the custom of punishing women offenders by cutting off their noses, though facial mutilations remained in force in the case of men. Whereas under Tsar Mikhail forty-seven venial types of offences, even those involving priests, were punishable by torture or by severe corporal chastisement, Elizabeth reduced the number to a dozen or so. Seen in conjunction with the abolition of the death penalty these measures constituted a major advance. Elizabeth made no attempt to dissolve or even to curb the activities of the secret police. Indeed, under Alexander Shuvalov's direction, the Secret Chancery became the most dreaded of the security departments.

Elizabeth was constantly being reminded that the legal code had become so confused as hardly to be useable. 'Even angels would not be able to make sense of it',[16] she was often heard murmuring in distress. In 1754 the Shuvalovs undertook to revise both the criminal code and court procedure. Elizabeth asked them to bear in mind the need for the code 'to be clearly worded and to be made up of intelligible laws suited to present day conditions whilst taking into account past customs and conventions'.[17] Within a year two sections of the country's common law had been revised, but many of the punishments advocated seemed to Elizabeth so cruel that she cried out in horror and refused to ratify the document, asserting that it was 'written not with ink but with blood'.[18] After that setback little more was done till 1760 when Roman Vorontzov, by religion a freemason, by temperament an ambitious politician, by inclination an enlightened and cultivated man, persuaded the Senate to appoint a committee to provide a new legal code under the joint presidency of three elected noblemen and three elected merchants. The work was halted by Elizabeth's death.

Peter Shuvalov's efforts to provide the judiciary with workable laws revealed the harm that was being done to the country by officials whom he scathingly referred to as 'non-able administrators'.[19] In 1755 he laid before the Senate proposals for 'training people to administer counties, provinces and towns by using the provinces as training grounds for young men destined to apply the laws and for teaching young noblemen the art of governing, thus fitting both groups for service in the central administration'. The historian Kluchevsky saw in these proposals an elaboration of Peter the Great's plans for the training of administrators, with the one difference that whereas the tsar wanted to see the country controlled by men of ability Shuvalov reserved such roles for noblemen. If that was indeed his purpose Elizabeth failed to appreciate it, but the results were not those he had intended, for his measures, taken in conjunction with economic developments, helped to create a middle class consisting of men of urban, small town and village origins.

The aims which Elizabeth had set herself on her accession were not perhaps outstandingly ambitious, but they enabled her to give Russia eleven years of external peace and twenty without a palace revolution. The laws for which she was responsible were less harsh than those introduced by any of her predecessors and they became more humane with each passing year. The improvements which she carried out, though limited in range, were introduced without fuss or ostentation and her major legislative measures, regardless of their degree of enlightenment, often provided a basis for those which Catherine II was to introduce. Thus it was Elizabeth who inaugurated the series of social and economic benefits which Catherine II conferred on the nobility; it was Elizabeth who made the first attempt to divest the central administration of some of its powers in order to transfer them to the country gentry; it was Elizabeth who first endeavoured to revise and humanize the legal code. Although lawlessness persisted in Russia's vast rural expanses during Elizabeth's reign the urban police forces achieved some success in curbing thieving in Moscow and other large towns and in enforcing some measure of decent behaviour and order. In St Petersburg, Moscow and certain other large towns steps were taken to end such practices as the simultaneous use of the public baths by men and women, of semi-tame bears roaming the streets unattended to scrounge for food, terrifying the inhabitants. Some such improvements were not without importance; their introduction invariably required great effort and determination, and many a sovereign might have been satisfied with less.

8

Learning, Literature and the Minor Arts

Although the facility with which Elizabeth spent her own and the nation's money caused the treasury considerable difficulties, the impetus she brought to industry and commerce, together with her efforts to humanize the country's customs, mark the first notable advances attained in these spheres since the death of Peter the Great. These achievements, however, are overshadowed by those which she accomplished in the cultural field. Lomonosov spoke no more than the truth when, as he looked back over the past, he described Elizabeth's rise to power as the dawn of a golden age. Notwithstanding her own scanty education she created a climate in which the spirit was at ease and the mind stimulated.

Elizabeth's admiration for France proved as beneficial to Russia as her immediate predecessors' admiration for Germany had been harmful to it. Vauban's theories on the construction of fortifications were adapted to Russia's needs and the works of writers such as Corneille, Racine, Mollière, La Fontaine, Fenelon and Voltaire sparked off the national genius. Regardless of the difference in background, outlook and religion, educated Russians were able effortlessly to appreciate their achievements. So many students went to complete their education in Paris that the embassy was obliged to provide a Russian church for them. Had Elizabeth needed encouragement to establish links between the two countries Kyril Razumovsky, Mikhail Vorontzov and Ivan Shuvalov would readily have supplied it. When Vorontsov saw Versailles for the first time he sent Elizabeth a vivid and enthusiastic description of its glories; his admiration for everything French led him to furnish the mansion which Rastrelli designed for him in St Petersburg in the French style. On hearing this

King Louis presented him with a large consignment of furniture. Vorontzov was delighted with it although according to Catherine the king had given him nothing 'but old furniture which no longer pleased Madame de Pompadour, his mistress, and which she had sold at a profit to the king, her lover'.[1] Her accusation is untrue. Louis ordered 'all that was finest [for Vorontzov] allotting £30,000 for wall tapestries, £6,000 for chairs, a maximum of £84,140 to be spent in all'. Unfortunately the ship transporting these objects was lost at sea but the tapestries were replaced by a new set illustrating scenes from Don Quixote costing £31,810. Vorontzov also received from the king a fine series of engravings in the royal binding as well as other books and a handsome cabinet containing a collection of medals, a hundred and fifty of which were of gold and valued at £30,000. In addition Vorontzov himself acquired much valuable French furniture for the house. Ivan Shuvalov shared his delight in French objects. According to Catherine 'he loved France and everything that came from France almost to madness'.[2] He too bought furniture and objects in Paris and had them sent back to Russia and the king sent Elizabeth chiffonières, gilt chairs and a writing table with many drawers, all in the styles admired by Vorontzov and Shuvalov.[3]

Many of Peter the Great's fledglings, as the youths whom he sent to train in the west were called, returned to Russia when Elizabeth was still a girl. They may well have played some part in forming and influencing her taste. Yet much though Elizabeth admired things French she remained an ardent patriot. Whenever a vacancy occurred in any government department she invariably tried to fill it with a Russian; if the name of a foreigner were pressed she would anxiously ask: 'Are you quite sure that we have no Russian who could carry out these duties equally well?'[4] Her attitude was a reflection of her father's. His policy was designed to make it possible for Russians to take over and whereas the first generation of Russia's academicians were men of foreign birth, by 1740 there were enough Russians who had been educated in the Academy to succeed them. They included scholars such as V. K. Trediakovsky, poet and translator of Fenelon, S. P. Krashenninikov, the ethnographer, explorer and author of a pioneer work on Kamchatka, or the mathematician Adadurov. Krashenninikov was very much a man of the new stamp. Born into a poor soldier's family living in Moscow in either 1711 or 1713 he nevertheless entered Moscow's Slavo-Graeco-Latin Academy in 1724, moving to St Petersburg in 1732 to spend a year as a student in the Academy of Sciences. In 1733 he was chosen to take part in the second Kamchatka

Exploration Expedition. He spent the next ten years of his life in the east, devoting himself to the study of Siberia's geography and inhabitants and to the exploration of Kamchatka. His book remained a standard work for decades to come, but when he returned to St Petersburg his love of exploration was still so strong that he transferred his attention to the Petersburgian region, publishing his botanical discoveries in 1749 under the title of *Flora of Ingria*.

Elizabeth was fortunate in possessing one man of remarkable genius in this talented generation. The peasant boy Mikhail Lomonosov was to outstrip all his contemporaries and to tower over them, setting a standard which several generations of Russians strove to sustain. The son of an Archangel fisherman he was born in a small village near Kholmogory. As a child he experienced hardships and privations, yet his passion for knowledge was so keen that a neighbouring literate peasant taught him to read and write. The only books available were religious ones, but one day another peasant gave the boy a Slavonic grammar and a psalter written in verse by Semeon of Polotsk, saint and tutor to Tsar Alexei's children. Lomonosov soon knew both books by heart and longed for others. Because he could not obtain them he ran away from home and made his way to Moscow in the hope of getting some schooling there. He reached Moscow by 1730. On arrival he went to its great cathedrals to pray to God for help and guidance. As if in answer to his prayers he met a fellow townsman, a prosperous merchant, as he strolled past the fish-market. The merchant took Lomonosov to his house and eventually arranged for him to become a student in the Slavo-Graeco-Latin Academy. The boy's time there was spent in abject poverty. The state allowance for penniless pupils amounted to three kopeks a day. Lomonosov would only allow himself one glass of kvass and a loaf of bread for his daily food. He endured loneliness as well as hunger and, at first, he was mercilessly teased for his ignorance. Another boy would have given in or become a delinquent, but Lomonosov saved farthings from his pitiful allowance and bought books. In a very short time his brilliant gifts, his analytical brain, retentive memory and astonishing powers of concentration won him the admiration of his tutors, and his immense size and strength impressed his fellow students quite as much. He went from success to success, moving from Moscow a few years later to study science at the Academy of Sciences in St Petersburg. Within a year he had won a coveted travelling scholarship. It took him to Germany in 1736 and then to Frieburg. He studied metallurgy there and went to Marburg to do science under the famous J. C. Wolf, but his scholarship money reached him so irregularly that he was often penniless. He contracted debts, worried and sought consolation in drink. Drink made him violent and, eventually, he was arrested and sentenced to prison for disorderly conduct. He managed to abscond, but fell into the arms of a recruiting officer. Once again he contrived to escape. In Marburg he had fallen in love with a tailor's daughter. He married her and decided to return to Russia. Throughout all these adventures he had never stopped reading or studying. Nothing was beyond his grasp. He became a master of grammar and rhetoric, a notable poet and a physicist much in advance of his time.

Lomonosov was back in St Petersburg by 1741. Three years later he was elected to the Academy, but it was not until 1748 that he acquired a small laboratory of his own in which to pursue his work in physics, chemistry and geology. He staunchly maintained that Russians could make as good scientists as Germans, insisting that the country would in due course produce her own Platos.

There was much for Lomonosov to do in Russia and he did not spare himself. As a civil servant he composed odes celebrating the great events of Elizabeth's reign which are still known to every educated Russian. As a naturalist he found much to record, yet it was as a philologist and grammarian that he made his greatest contribution to Russian scholarship. The clarity of his mind, the breadth of his outlook and the range of his knowledge enabled him to revitalize the language and to eliminate many linguistic archaisms and outdated mannerisms. By modernizing the language and freeing it from the antiquated Slavonic he made the adoption of the technical terms needed in industry possible. He rendered the language flexible and had it not been for his reforms Pushkin's genius could not have expressed itself with the limpid purity which is one of its chief beauties. Pushkin was not exaggerating when he described the great man as Russia's first university. Lomonosov's faith in his country and people served constantly to inspire him. It was for them that he translated the works of many of the foremost foreign writers of his day; for them that he compiled up-to-date text books, including one on metallurgy and the first history of early Russia; for them that he constructed a telescope and that he qualified as an artist in order to revive the glass mosaic industry which had remained dormant since Kievan times.

Elizabeth appreciated the importance of education. In the religious sphere she therefore sponsored the revision of religious texts and the provision of more and better run seminaries. In 1747 a school was founded under the auspices of the Academy of Sciences for the purpose of fitting boys for the Academy's advanced courses. In 1752 the two schools which Peter the Great had established for training engineers and artillery officers were merged into a single college of science; a school was also founded for the sons of soldiers, and another was attached to Moscow's main hospital. A law was passed obliging every factory to establish a school for the children of its workers.

It was in 1754, when the court was once again in Moscow, that Ivan Shuvalov spoke to the empress of his and Lomonosov's desire to establish a university there. Elizabeth welcomed the idea and the proposals which Shuvalov laid before the Senate were dealt with so rapidly that the university was in existence within a year. It contained three faculties, those of law, philosophy and medicine, the latter including departments of physics, chemistry and mineralogy, but no faculty of divinity. Indeed, it was the only university in eighteenth-century Europe which did not possess a theological faculty. At Lomonosov's insistence the University was open to students of all races, religions, and social classes, other than serfs, but Ivan Shuvalov's dream of seeing students, regardless of birth, automatically promoted to the tenth grade in the Table of Ranks and all doctors to the eighth with the right for both to carry a sword, was not realized. He was also disappointed in his desire to see universities established in his lifetime in St Petersburg and at Baturino, the capital of the hetman of the Zaporozhie Cossacks, and schools in every provincial town. However, he was able to found schools along Russia's southern borders for the children of soldiers stationed there as well as one at Orenburg for the children of men serving prison sentences in Siberia. Finally two schools were created as dependencies for Moscow's university, the one for preparing noblemen's sons, the other sons of freemen for a higher education. As a result, the Decembrist Nicholas Turgenev was still able to maintain in his *La Russie et les Russes*, which he published in France in 1847, when he was living there as a refugee, that 'in no country has an institution proved more useful and more instrumental in producing such admirable results [as Moscow University]. Still today it is rare to find a man able to write his native tongue correctly, or to find an enlightened and upright official or a firm and honest magistrate other than one formed in Moscow's university.'[5]

In St Petersburg Elizabeth created the sort of intellectual and cultural life which her father had dreamt of establishing throughout Russia. Books of greatly varying types and content were coming off the presses which

Peter had set up. Magazines, journals and newspapers were appearing regularly and being widely read. A new occupation – journalism – had come into being for the purpose. Between 1750 and 1760 magazines such as *Monthly Contributions* (*Ezhemesiatchnyja Sochinenia*) or *The Busy Bee* published poetry and literary works as well as articles of a scientific, historical or geographical nature and, more importantly, criticisms of prevailing social ills. As a result, at any rate in St Petersburg, the deep distrust of the west which had taken root in Russia at the time of the Mongol occupation began to fade among the better educated. The culture which was taking shape in the capital was neither eclectic nor superficial and, while retaining a native stamp, was acquiring a distinctive western-ized character. This was to some extent due to Lomonosov whose determination to preserve the nation's essentially Russian character is reflected in his opposition to the so-called Varangian theory propounded by the Academician G. F. Miller.

Miller had come to Russia from Germany in about 1735 to work as a scientist in Siberia and the Urals. On returning to St Petersburg in 1743 he was made an academician. Working in conjunction with the academicians G. A. Bayer and A. I. Schlessinger he evolved the theory which, six years later, was to anger Lomonosov and his friends, and especially Krashenninikov. Broadly speaking the German academicians maintained that Russians were incapable of creating any kind of culture or of advancing science by their own efforts and that everything of note existing in Russia stemmed from men of Varangian birth who, they asserted, had governed Kievan Russia as overlords and had never fused with the native Slavs. Lomonosov and his friends set out to disprove this theory. Their arguments acted as a spur to native patriotism and creativity, gaining additional impetus from the empress's determination to sponsor everything Russian. She invariably encouraged Russians to excel and, at court, never permitted the Russian language to be subordinated to French, as was to happen under Catherine. Elizabeth reaped her reward in 1746 when the Comte de l'Isle informed her of Voltaire's desire to be elected a corresponding member of the Russian Academy of Sciences. She was neither surprised nor flattered by the news, considering it a fitting tribute to Russia's genius. Her attitude was the same when, some twelve months later, Kiril Razumovsky and d'Allion hoped to please her by persuading Voltaire to write the History of Russia under Peter the Great. She simply asked Ivan Shuvalov to give Voltaire all possible assistance in his work.

The Academy sponsored such ambitious projects as the detailed geographical survey of Russia which led to the publication in 1745 of the first atlas of the country. Under the influence of men such as V. N. Tatishchev, a one-time Governor of Astrakhan, and of Prince Antioch Kantemir, poet and diplomat, but above all, of Lomonosov, the Academy rapidly extended the range of its activities. No one could have been more fully conscious of the difference in climate between the age of Anna Ivanovna and that of Elizabeth than the scholar and minor poet V. K. Trediakovsky. Although Anna Ivanovna considered scholars and artists useful court appendages, she treated them as creatures of an inferior kind. It was probably fortunate that Trediakovsky's gifts were slight for she might have destroyed a greater talent by the treatment which she meted out to him. Like Lomonosov, Trediakovsky came from the north, where his father was a priest. Born in Astrakhan in 1703 he gained admittance at the age of twenty to Moscow's Slavo-Graeco-Latin Academy. Four years later he won a travelling scholarship which eventually took him to the Sorbonne where he became a passionate admirer of Fenelon. He returned to Russia in 1730 and it fell to him to supply Anna Ivanovna with rhymes for the masques performed at her court to settings devised by her cabinet minister Volynsky. In 1732 Trediakovsky was also appointed official translator to the Academy of Sciences. Nevertheless Anna Ivanovna continued to treat him in the same manner as her jesters and dwarfs, hitting and beating him when she felt so inclined. Somehow, even in such conditions, Trediakovsky succeeded in 1735 in publishing a treatise on the technique of Russian poetry – *A New Short Method for Russian Versification*. It was the first work of the kind to be written in a form of Russian which was closer to the spoken language than to the written Slavonic. Lomonosov did not entirely agree with some of Trediakovsky's conclusions, but after long drawn out discussions the author revised the contested passages to conform with Lomonosov's linguistic reforms. Trediakovsky fared better under Elizabeth for she employed him to write tragedies for her theatre as well as to translate the works of Fenelon and books such as Rollin's *Ancient History* and Boileau's *Art Poetique*.

Turns devised by actors, dancers, jugglers, jesters and mimes had been popular in Russia from very early times. In the Kievan period their entertainments had become more professional and sophisticated, influenced by the performances enacted in the hippodrome in Constantinople for the emperor and inhabitants of Constantinople. The Mongol occupation and the numerous problems which it created in Russia arrested the development of the theatrical arts as it did of so many other cultural activities, and there was no revival in the years of Muscovy's expansion. The situation altered with the advent of the Romanovs. Tsar Alexei took great interest in the theatre and encouraged its growth. Peter the Great's half-sister, Sophia, was so fascinated by the stage that she wrote plays for her actors to perform. In her youth Elizabeth had enjoyed producing ballets and masques, and she never ceased taking an interest in the theatre. Although she had never seen any western productions her appreciation of the theatrical arts was developed by her involvement in amateur productions. She took advantage of her coronation to provide Moscow with a public theatre with a seating capacity of three thousand. On the first night the entertainment included a curtain raiser which had been composed for the occasion by the violinist Domenico Dalloglio (also spelt d'Ologlio), the Italian leader of the court orchestra. Entitled *Oppressed Russia Consoled*, a translation of Stählin's German text by Lomonosov. The principal parts were sung by Marigi, Rosina Bon (whose husband was responsible for the settings), the Giorgi and the buffo Crichi. Johan Hasse's opera *La Clemenza Di Titto* followed; it had been performed in Dresden for the first time four years earlier. The evening concluded with two ballets, one called *The Golden Age*, the other *Astree appears on the Horizon to Delight the People*. The Muscovites were enchanted by these spectacles and flocked nightly to the theatre.

Illuminations and fireworks had first been frequently used by Peter the Great and they continued to be used by Elizabeth. In St Petersburg the large Theatre of Illuminations, situated on the Strelka, the tip of land jutting out into the Neva from the Vassilievsky Ostrov, was a large wooden building which drew capacity audiences. Grimmel was responsible for the finest of the sets, records of which survive in engravings by Makhaev and Vinogradov. Lower down the river, near the site Catherine was to choose for the Tauride Palace, the Workshops for the Manufacture of Fireworks employed a large number of people. Meanwhile, doubtless in order to please Alexei Razumovsky, Elizabeth was transforming her court into the country's leading musical centre. The Italian and Russian singers engaged on her behalf were expected to perform in unison in the choir of the imperial chapel and to appear as well in the operas which Giovanni Battista Locatelli produced for her at court. With Dalloglio often supplying the music, they included such famous French singers as Caristina, Saletti and Compassi.[6]

Locatelli came to St Petersburg in 1757 bringing a company of Italian *opera-bouffe* with him. It met with such success that he took a long lease of the old wooden opera house attached to the Summer Palace, and let his boxes to courtiers for as much as thirty roubles a year. Here they heard such distinguished singers as Maria Comati, known as La Farinella, the castrato Massi, the tenor Buini and his wife, also an accomplished singer, the baritone Barozzi and the bass Dol. Locatelli employed Francesco Zoppi as both conductor and composer while the latter's wife, Giovanna, appeared on the stage under the name of La Stella. But his popularity declined and his attempts to revive it by engaging in 1759 the famous Mantovanina and the castrato Manfacchini did not save him from bankruptcy. Anna Ivanovna's small company of dancers had become a ballet school under the direction of Laudé and the ballets they performed proved more popular than the operas. Yet Elizabeth still enjoyed most the plays which her Russian and French companies of actors produced at court twice weekly throughout the winter months. The French company was directed by Sérigny who received an annual salary of twenty-five thousand roubles. Although her courtiers preferred the Russian plays, the empress stipulated that they should attend Sérigny's performances throughout the 1750s and was extremely vexed if they arrived late.

Elizabeth encouraged amateur actors as warmly as professionals. Soon after her accession Prince Yusupov persuaded her to take an interest in the plays staged by the youths training to be officers in the Corps des Pages school of which he was a director. In 1744 Sumarokov was a pupil there. He was to become the foremost dramatist of his age, the author of twenty-six major plays and the translator of Shakespeare as well as of France's leading writers. He was also to edit the journal *The Busy Bee*. Elizabeth delighted in the plays which the boys produced and encouraged them to make them a regular event. Sumarokov probably owed his interest in drama to these school productions.

Elizabeth was charmed by the youthfulness and gaiety of the boy actors. In 1749, while becoming attracted by cadets Beketov and Kachenovski, she was also on the point of falling in love with Ivan Shuvalov. Her infatuation for Shuvalov dismayed Bestuzhev partly because he disapproved of the young man's love of France and all things French, but chiefly because he feared for Alexei Razumovsky's interests. It has been suggested that Bestuzhev, knowing how easily Elizabeth was captivated by a handsome face and pleasing personality, decided to use young Nikita Afanasievich Beketov to strike at Ivan Shuvalov's interests and further Alexei Razumovsky's, never thinking that the empress could be married to Razumovsky. Beketov was so attractive that he was often cast for a leading part in the school's plays. Matters were so arranged that at one performance the empress's attention was drawn to the youth. After that the situation developed in the direction intended by the chancellor and for a time Beketov and Ivan Shuvalov shared the empress's favours. By the end of the year Beketov appeared to be meeting with greater success than his rival. His triumph was more than Shuvalov could bear and he decided to rid himself of the cadet. He planned his counter move with care and cunning. Early in 1752 he gave Beketov an ointment which, he assured the youth, would vastly improve his somewhat spotty complexion; instead it brought Beketov out in a repulsive rash. His appearance became a subject of conversation at court. Shuvalov casually remarked in the empress's hearing that Beketov's loose morals and his fondness for members of his own sex were the cause of the rash. There was not a word of truth in the allegations, but Ivan Shuvalov knew that his words would disturb the empress. In fact, they shocked and terrified her. She fled to Tsarskoe Selo in a panic and forbade Beketov to follow her, indeed, ever again to appear before her, and ordered him to withdraw to his estates. Sympathy for his predicament soon led her to relent to the extent of appointing Beketov governor of Astrakhan, but she maintained her original decision never to see him again. Shuvalov's plan had worked. With Beketov's removal he became the sole possessor of Elizabeth's heart. Bestuzhev's fears for Alexei Razumovsky proved groundless. Shuvalov became a friend of Razumovsky's and made no effort to undermine his position.

Although Elizabeth helped to create a theatre-loving public in St Petersburg and Moscow, Feodor Volkov (1729–63), a native of Yaroslavl, was chiefly responsible for its lasting popularity. When still a young man he visited St Petersburg. One day he was taken to see a play produced by the officer cadets. It transported him into a new world. On returning to Yaroslavl he set himself up in a theatre of his own. He became its actor-manager, decorator and stage-hand. He charged his audiences from one to five kopeks for a seat and his productions drew such large houses that his reputation spread beyond the borders of his home town. The local voivoda, Prince Mussin-Pushkin, soon became his patron. In 1752 Volkov was asked to bring his company to St Petersburg to give a performance at court. He employed both men and women as actors; they all were such a success in the capital that the empress decided to retain them there to enable Volkov to found a national theatre in St Petersburg. Although he died before completing his task he was able to lay the foundations of a national school of acting by training such distinguished actors as I. A. Dmitrievsky and Y. D. Shumsky. Shumsky, at Volkov's death, became the theatre's director.

Amusing objects were as necessary to Elizabeth as theatrical and musical diversions. She encouraged Russians in their production, especially those making use of glass and precious and semi-precious metals and stones. Russians had excelled at working metals from an early date and Muscovy had rapidly developed into a great centre of craftsmanship. In 1725 Moscow's guild of metal workers was far larger than St Petersburg's. It contained 283 registered silversmiths and 30 goldsmiths as compared with 20 and 16 respectively in the new capital, with a similar division probably existing among the unregistered workers. Twenty-five years later the numbers had evened out, 61 registered silversmiths and 15 gold-smiths being registered in Moscow as compared to St Petersburg's 51 and 13, the latter now ranking as the more highly skilled of the two groups. Until about 1740 metal workers in both towns had produced small objects in the styles in favour during the final period of Muscovy's greatness. With Elizabeth a clear break was made with the past, Henceforth a new, exuberant, asymmetric, flamboyant rococo style was in fashion. Only at the Mint did the Petrine style remain in force both for the coinage and the medals which Peter had made indispensable to the sovereign.

Though jewellers continued to use all the old techniques, chasing became especially fashionable during Elizabeth's reign, tending almost to supplant the popular engraved and niello decorations. The great advance which had been made in mining and metallurgy enabled craftsmen to produce for the first time in Russian history very large objects such as great bowls, dishes and bulbous jugs. The great silver shrine made at Elizabeth's order to commemorate St Alexander Nevsky expresses this love of the immense and embodies the spirit of the age. Destined for the monastery which Peter the Great had founded on the outskirts of his new capital the silver shrine weighed ninety pud (3,240 pounds). Made in sections by workers of the Kolykhvansk Foundry in St Petersburg to form an immense funerary casket, with a pyramid shaped lid surrounded by an array of spectacularly disposed trophies, it was allegorical, with emblems executed in low relief and then finished off with chasing. An inscription dedicates the shrine jointly to Alexander Nevsky and Elizabeth.

Elizabeth possessed a Fabergé of her own in the person of Jeremy Pauzié, who was brought to Russia from Switzerland by his father in

1729, ostensibly to visit a relation working as a surgeon in Moscow, in reality that his father might find employment there. The father died in Moscow two years later and in 1733 Jeremy was sent to St Petersburg to be apprenticed to the jeweller Gravelot. He stayed with his master for nine years and then opened a shop of his own in the capital. He was commissioned to make the crown for Elizabeth's coronation. Throughout Elizabeth's reign Pauzié worked almost exclusively for the empress and her favourite courtiers, decorating the objects he made for them with exquisite, asymetric motifs of restrained rococo style. Few of them survive, but those that do are as remarkable for their fine workmanship as for their inventive designs. However, it was Sampsoie, who came to Russia as a French spy, who made some of the finest snuff boxes of the century for the empress. He adorned the one which she commissioned for Alexei Razumovsky with a splendid portrait of Elizabeth whilst embellishing her's with an exquisite view of Tsarskoe Selo.

The great dinner service which Simon Pantin and Paul Crespin made for Elizabeth ranks with the most impressive objects associated with her reign. It contained thirty-six silver-gilt plates and 329 white silver plates and dishes. Paul Lamerie made a most splendid chandelier for her. Ballin supplied her with a magnificent *surtout de table* and François Thomas Germain was responsible for the enormous service and *surtout de table* which are as astonishing in their elaborations as in their display of boisterous grotesques. Elizabeth paid a million livres* for them, but she was never to use the service for the last pieces were being delivered to her as she lay dying. At the revolution it was sold by the Soviet authorities to Gulbekian. Germain also made the frames of three mirrors intended for the empress's personal use; the two smaller ones are elegant and beautiful: they cost 1,200 livres; the third, measuring six feet in height, cost five hundred écus.

The silver and gold objects which were made in Russia during Elizabeth's reign are important not only for aesthetic reasons but also because of their number. Never before had so much tableware of intrinsic value been produced in as great a variety nor so much sumptuous jewellery created. It is particularly interesting to learn that the copper objects coated with either pale or dark blue, white or, very occasionally, delicate

---

* N. Mitford, *Voltaire in Love*; Penguin edn, p. 16 says that the purchasing power of the livre was the same as that of the US dollar in 1956. She adds that there were twenty-four livres to a louis and that the latter was the equivalent of an English guinea. The écu was usually the equivalent of three, occasionally of six livres.

pale green enamel, and decorated with silver appliqué motifs were produced first in Anna Ivanovna's and Elizabeth's reigns and not, as has been supposed, in that of Catherine II.[7] It has now been established that these enamels were first made at Ustuig, then at Solvychegodsk. The earliest known examples, both goblets in dark blue enamel, bear the respective hall marks of 3/1732/4 and of 2/1743/25. The first goblet is not as accomplished as the Elizabethan example for its decorations are executed in silver paint instead of in metal; in the later goblet the silver plaques were attached to the glazed enamel ground covering the copper frame before the enamel had fully hardened, and the whole was then subjected to a final firing. To make the enamel retain the silver plaques, the object was made of very thin copper which was covered by several coats of enamel, each fired individually. The style was probably inspired by the painted enamels being produced at Augsburg, but the technique is quite distinct from the one followed in Germany.

Glass had been made in Russia in Kievan times but its production ceased with the Mongol invasion and did not revive till late in the seventeenth century. Peter the Great wished to see the industry concentrated in and around St Petersburg. The factory which he established at Yamburg made both blown and moulded glass, decorating the finer pieces with enamel glazes and also producing glass toys and animals. From 1740 many factories had mastered the technique of *fonde d'oro*. With the finest objects the gold was generally applied over a red glaze, but quite often silver foil replaced gold leaf. Engraved inscriptions, monograms, cyphers, crests and decorative devices such as trophies and pastoral scenes enclosed in rococo frames decorated the less expensive articles, and the cheapest were adorned with traditional motifs.

Elizabeth loved everything colourful and it was to please her that Lomonosov revived the manufacture of colour glass mosaic cubes, founding for the purpose glass works at Ust Ruditsky, some sixty-five verst from St Petersburg. In addition to the cubes the lovely turquoise coloured glass which came to be preferred for sconces, chandeliers and certain luxury wares was also made there. Lomonosov did not want his mosaic panels to resemble paintings; he wished them to form a distinct type of art and, disregarding the criticisms of his fellow academicians, he therefore insisted on using large cubes in the panels depicting scenes from the life of Peter the Great which he had designed for the Cathedral of SS Peter and Paul. He hoped to decorate the Neva's bridges and the capital's public buildings with similar panels, but only one panel of the Petrine cycle – that of the Battle of Poltava – was completed. Most of the work was done by Lomonosov's best pupil, Petr Druzhynin, who had acted as Lomonosov's assistant when that remarkable man made his mosaic portrait of Peter the Great. Lomonosov's heirs took no interest in the factory and refused to maintain it; the number of mosaic panels is therefore very small.

Pottery was never a highly developed craft in Russia, but in 1742 Afanasy Grebenshchikov founded a factory for the manufacture of glazed tiles and good quality table ware. He tried to produce china in it, but the cup which he submitted to the St Petersburg authorities in 1747 on the assumption that it was of china failed to pass as such. Meanwhile, largely as a result of trial and error, Dimitri Vinogradov, a trained scientist, had succeeded in the previous year in making a china cup. It was the first china to be made in Russia and, in 1747, Vinogradov was instructed to establish a porcelain works in the capital, and appointed its first director.

The earliest piece of china to bear Vinogradov's mark is dated 1748. The clay used at the time came from regions as widely separated as Siberia and the Ukraine, for Vinogradov was anxious to discover which clay was best suited for the purpose. The paste he finally chose was a whitish-grey in colour. In 1750 he fitted out a workshop to make dinner and tea services for the empress. Within a year he was also making exquisite china snuff boxes, giving some the shape of an envelope, decorating others with views of Tsarskoe Selo or portraits of the empress and Alexei Razumovsky; all are of the highest quality. Within another year Vinogradov had begun to produce exquisitely modelled figurines of the type which Meissen had made fashionable. He built his first large kiln in 1750 and used it for firing the large china service decorated with flowers and basket fret which was to remain Elizabeth's favourite. In 1758 his workshop became the Imperial Porcelain Factory. Vinogradov died several months later without knowing that his factory was soon to rank as sixth in importance in Europe. He had marked his earlier pieces with a blue W and the date of their manufacture, placing both inscriptions beneath the glaze, but at the founding of the Imperial Porcelain Factory it was replaced by a double eagle stamped on the object after glazing.

The tapestry works which Peter established in 1717 by bringing French weavers to St Petersburg was the least successful of his ventures even though the tsar appointed the great architect Leblond to direct it. At Leblond's death two years later the College of Mines was obliged to assume control of the workshop, but its output remained so small that the tapestry works were withdrawn from the College's supervision in

1732 and placed under that of the court. By that time most of the weavers were Russians, the Frenchmen having been largely replaced by 1724. Ivan Kolybiakov and Mikhail Atmanov were considered the most skilled of the weavers and Dimitri Soloviev the best among the dyers. Elizabeth's failure to take any interest in their output almost brought the work to a standstill and reduced the workers to such poverty that they had to beg for their living. In 1755 the Senate felt compelled to take charge of the workshops. Output rose slightly for a time, then dropped again, and a couple of years later the workshops were closed down. In Petrine times the tapestries intended as wall hangings had generally been of a historical or allegorical character, while the chair and sofa covers displayed flower or bird motifs, but during Elizabeth's reign they either took the form of portraits or displayed exotic scenes or baskets of fruit. In all of them the colours tended to be dull, with browns and greens predominating.

Wallpapers made their appearance in Elizabeth's reign. To judge from a despatch of Guy Dickens dated 19 January 1753 they must have been introduced into the country by Englishmen, for the ambassador wrote to inform Whitehall that

a Mr Thompson, formerly book and warehouse keeper to the Charitable Corporation . . . set up in Moscow a Manufactory of Paper Hangings. . . . The business was conducted in the name of Martin Butler who was one of the manufacturers of this kind of hanging in England, and besides this Thompson, one Thomas Nesbitt attempted to set up a like manufacture here at St Petersburg upon which a dispute having arisen between him and Martin Butler, who then appealed for Thompson to the Senate in September 1752, the Senate renewed Butler's patent and forbade Hewitt to set up in St Petersburg because Martin Butler engaged to take Russian subjects and to learn them the art and mystery of painting and stamping paper engravings to as much perfection as they do abroad.[8]

To encourage the Russians to make their own wallpaper the Senate thereupon imposed a tax on wallpaper imported from abroad.

9

The Fine Arts

Russia's first school of secular painting was established in the Palace of Arms in Moscow, late in the seventeenth century under the directorship of Mikhail Petrovich Avramov, a man highly respected by Peter the Great. In 1711 Peter transferred the school with its best pupils to St Petersburg attaching it to the Office of Works and housing it in the Printing House. Greater attention was paid to art studies there than had been the case in Moscow. Students were taught to draw not only from casts and by copying engravings but also from nature, and lessons in painting were included in the curriculum. The students in the Naval Academy were also obliged to learn to draw and to acquire some knowledge of architecture. No portraiture was taught, even though it was the first form of western art which had appealed to the Russians and the one which remained permanently popular. The omission obliged Russians either to turn to foreign artists living in Russia for paintings of quality or to make do with the portraits produced by serfs, for the most part self-taught. Caravaque was the most admired of the foreigners. He came to Russia in 1716 and had, by Elizabeth's day, come to rank as the foremost portraitist working in St Petersburg. On her accession the empress turned to him for the twelve portraits of herself which she needed for Russia's twelve embassies; they cost her twelve thousand roubles.

By Elizabeth's reign there were quite a number of both foreign and Russian artists working in St Petersburg. Among portraitists few were as skilled as Caravaque, but of the many Germans the brothers G. H. and L. F. Grooth were the most admired. Their father was court painter at Stuttgart, but both sons went to Dresden in 1741 to complete their artistic training. They were living in St Petersburg two years later, and soon after George Grooth was given the task of painting thirty-seven icons for the church which Rastrelli was building for the Palace of Tsarskoe Selo. He probably realized that he was not well suited to work of that type and he proceeded to set himself up as a portrait painter, finding many clients among Elizabeth's courtiers. His appointment as court painter followed quickly, encouraging him to produce somewhat flattering paintings of his sitters. The tendency can be discerned in the portrait which he painted in 1743 of the Grand Duke Peter. The young man appears on it as better looking than contemporary records might lead one to expect. George Grooth's fully developed court style is seen at its best in the portrait which he painted of the empress at much the same time. She appears in it wearing the uniform of the Preobrazhensky Guards, astride a spirited horse and holding a field marshal's baton. It shows her as she liked to picture herself and in the manner in which she is represented in a Meissen statuette. In the picture her young Arab groom stands beside her. The painting is executed in the silver and pastel shades Elizabeth was fond of; it strikes a regal rather than a decorative note and lacks the intimacy which characterizes Russian art. George's brother also became a court painter, Elizabeth turning to him for pictures of her favourite animals – these included her ducks, peacocks, swans, and especially her horses and dogs.

Count Pietro Rotari was also a master of the decorative, elegant and rococo in portraiture. He trained in Rome and Naples and had been court painter both in Vienna and Dresden before coming to Russia in 1756 to become court painter there. His sitters included the empress and her architect Rastrelli as well as many of her courtiers, but it was peasant girls who really attracted and enchanted him. He spent much of his spare time painting them and put his whole heart into it. His choice of subject surprised the Russians but they quickly came to admire these paintings and a number of them found a place on the walls of the palatial residences belonging to the girls' owners. Rotari's interest in this genre influenced a number of Russian artists of the next generation.

These eminent foreigners were to find themselves outmatched by the Frenchman François Tocqué. A pupil of Bertin and Nattier he was so greatly admired in France that the three emissaries whom Louis XV chose to represent France in Russia – the Marquis de l'Hôpital, Mackenzie Douglas and the Chevalier d'Eon – thought that by persuading Tocqué to visit Russia in order to paint the empress's portrait they might persuade her to enter into an alliance with France. After much persuasion Tocqué agreed to do so. He reached St Petersburg in 1754 and installed himself in Mr Michel's house, where he stayed for two years. He was vexed to learn soon after he arrived that a few days earlier Rotari had finished a portrait of the empress showing her wearing two million roubles' worth of diamonds, but the affability with which the empress welcomed him and her decision to accord him a salary of forty thousand roubles a year soon restored his good humour. At the end of his visit he declined Elizabeth's invitation to stay on in Russia for he had taken note of the sharp deterioration in her health. He returned to France a rich man. The portraits he left in Russia are elegant and accomplished examples of French court art. His portrait of Elizabeth has the additional merit of having been painted from life. That painted by Vanloo almost certainly cannot have been since there is no evidence that he visited Russia.

True to her policy of employing Russians whenever possible Elizabeth commissioned as many works from them as from foreign painters. Ivan Jakovlevish Vishniakov was a painter of ability; he had not studied in the west but had trained under Caravaque when he entered the Office of Works in 1721. Ten years later he was to make his mark as a painter of children. His best portraits, such as those of Sarah and James Fermor, the children of Count Fermor, director of the Office of Works, dating from 1745, foreshadow Levitsky's admirable paintings in a similar vein. Two years earlier the empress had expressed her appreciation of Vishniakov's abilities by sitting for her portrait and paying him two hundred roubles for it. It is a far more accomplished work than the portrait which he painted of Anna Leopoldovna in 1741. By 1748 Vishniakov was working almost entirely for the empress at a yearly salary of five hundred roubles, providing her with some of the sets needed for her theatre and decorating the ceilings and walls of certain rooms in the Winter, Anichkov and Peterhof palaces.

A portrait-painter who took a marked interest in the personalities of his sitters was Alexei Petrovich Antropov, and some of his portraits are among the more interesting of those dating from Elizabeth's reign. The son of a soldier stationed in St Petersburg, Antropov became a pupil of the Office of Works school in 1732. He studied first under Matveev, then under M. Zakharov and Vishniakov, and also occasionally under Caravaque. Although Elizabeth encouraged artists to become portrait-painters she tried to extend their range by commissioning them to paint panels for room decorations. In 1749 she turned to Antropov for some. Under Matveev's influence he produced works which, though not pure landscapes, mark an advance over the topographical paintings of Peter the Great's reign.

Ivan Petrovich Argunov also distinguished himself as a painter. By birth

a serf of Prince Chevakinsky he passed into the ownership of the Sheremetievs in 1749 as part of the dowry of a daughter of his first master. The
Sheremetievs soon realized that Argunov was exceptionally gifted and
they sent him to study painting under Matveev and George Grooth.
Two years later he provided some of the icons needed for the chapel of
the Large or Catherine Palace at Tsarskoe Selo, but in 1750 he was already
painting the series of portraits of members of the Sheremetiev family which
established his reputation. In 1753 Elizabeth turned to him for the portraits
of her three favourite court singers; later still, she appointed him a court
painter.

One of Peter the Great's policies was greatly to increase the number of
books published yearly. He used engravings to publicize his military
victories and social reforms and so provided artists with the opportunity
of expressing their skill in design. This resulted in the establishment of
a rich and varied school of graphic art. Artists of the first half of the eighteenth century, such as Ivan Sokolov, produced engravings of a military
nature; they recorded various court festivities, including elaborate firework
displays, and evolved intricate, exceedingly decorative devices, cartouches
and the like to serve as chapter headings, tail pieces and so on. Nor were
woodcuts allowed to lose their earlier importance. They continued to be
used as illustrations for books intended for children and the working
classes and to serve as pictures in poorer households; the single sheets or
'lubki' depicted scenes drawn from fairy tales and byliny (sagas) of peasant
life, but some poked fun at the new middle class while others were as
gallant and ribald as many a contemporary French engraving. Some took
the form of political satires and made their influence felt in the more
sophisticated and accomplished caricatures produced at the start of the
next century.

Both mezzotints and decorative panel paintings owed their popularity
to Elizabeth. The subject matter of the paintings was, to a large extent,
dictated by the type of palace architecture which she herself helped to
evolve. Since there were at first no Russians capable of supplying the
decorative panels she desired, Elizabeth commissioned B. Tarsia, an artist
who had worked for her father, for one of the earliest of her painted
ceilings, but the range of her patronage was quickly extended. Eventually
the artists who worked for her as decorators came to include the Venetian
Guiseppi Valeriani, Antonio Peresinotti of Bologna, Pietro Gradizzi and
his son Francesco as well as several Russians. She employed them simultaneously to provide the painted ceilings, over-door panels and wall

decorations required by Rastrelli. These works were generally executed on canvas rather than on the surfaces of the walls and ceilings. Rastrelli liked to place the great tiled stoves used for heating rooms in the centre of a wall, hanging a painting on either side. The subjects considered most suitable for these decorative compositions were those in which gods and goddesses of the classical world were shown in scenes such as the Triumph of Apollo, for these could be regarded as expressions of homage to the empress.

Valeriani came to Russia in 1745 and, with Peresinotti acting as his assistant during much of the time, he worked for the empress till her death in 1761. He expressed her taste in decorative painting quite as clearly and as faithfully as did Rastrelli in architecture, and his fellow artists took their cue from him. Serafino Barozzi, Stefano Torelli, Vishniakov, I. Firsov, P. Sukhodolsky, the brothers Efim, Ivan and Alexei Belsky, as well as the Muscovites Roman Nikitin and Ivan Adolsky the younger, were among those who were also wholly occupied in providing the empress with decorative panels, designs for firework displays and illuminations, novel ideas for the decoration of the E-shaped dining tables used at her banquets and with stage settings. Very little survives of their immense output and most of that which has come down to us is to be assigned to Valeriani and the Belsky brothers.

Valeriani was undoubtedly the most talented and accomplished of these artists. He was marvellously inventive, and his eye for colour and decorative effects exceptionally keen. Although he provided the designs for the ceilings which are ascribed to him most of them were probably executed by his assistants, and more especially by Peresinotti. The fine ceiling in the first ante-room in the Catherine Palace at Tsarskoe Selo is known to have been painted by Peresinotti in 1754 with Ivan Belsky assisting him. Ivan Belsky was especially admired for the bird and flower paintings which Elizabeth liked using as over-door panels, but Firsov also provided her with some enchanting ones based on scenes selected from the works of Lancret and his followers. Ivan Belsky, the eldest and most gifted of the three brothers, trained under Vishniakov and Girolamo Bono. From 1747 much of his time was spent, first as assistant to Valeriani, then providing independently the wall and ceiling decorations of certain rooms in Petersburg's Winter and Summer Palaces, in the Palace of Peterhof and in the Catherine Palace and Hermitage at Tsarskoe Selo. He also found time to paint a number of traditional icons but, like many icon-painters of the period, his style was so much affected by western naturalism that the panels are of hybrid character and, as such, of minor artistic importance.

Painting was raised to the rank of a fine art in 1758. Acting on Ivan Shuvalov's advice, the empress obtained the Senate's consent for transforming Peter the Great's unpretentious School of Painting into an Academy of Art. Its first president, Ivan Shuvalov, invited Joseph Le Lorrain to become vice-president. Le Lorrain accepted the invitation and went to Russia with the seventeen-year-old Moreau le Jeune. However, he died there the following year. Although his visit was cut short Moreau was able to execute an excellent chalk drawing of the empress, a series of drawings for J. B. LePrince's book, *Voyage en Siberie*, and a portrait of Peter for Voltaire to use as a frontispiece in his *Histoire de la Russie sous Pierre le Grand*. Jean Louis de Veilly took charge of the Academy pending the arrival of J. F. Lagrenée the elder, who had agreed to succeed Le Lorrain as its director, but after only two years in Russia he resigned his post and returned to France. His place was taken by Nicholas Gillet who for twenty years was the Academy's director.

The sculptures which were produced during Elizabeth's reign contrast sharply both in character and subject matter with those of the Petrine era. They are less narrative in content, less static in conception, and their styles and subject matter are more diversified. Nevertheless, they conformed closely with the demands of architecture. Thus, much of the work was still in the form of plaques, with varying degrees of relief work depending on the nature of the building they were to adorn; there were also many carved and gilt panels or devices which were mounted on white walls. The façades of many of the palaces were enlivened by sculptures designed by the architect Rastrelli to stress the building's horizontal or vertical lines. He was fond of aligning gilt statues along the outer edges of the roofs of his buildings and adorning their façades with others in high relief, using cherubs, masks, cartouches, elaborate garlands, scrolls and other devices to fill the areas left empty by capitols and architraves.

At Tsarskoe Selo there were a great many sculptured and carved decorations both within the palace and outside it. Much of the work was done between 1746 and 1766 by the Viennese sculptor, I. Dunken. He was also responsible for the sprightly cupids which adorned the façade of the Tsarskoe Selo Hermitage, but Rastrelli also often applied to Giraudon, Rolland and Schtallmeyer for the sculptures he required. Of the Russians, Anton Yakov, with the help of thirty-six Russian assistants, produced the sculptures for the Chinese Hall in the Catherine Palace at Tsarskoe Selo, and the iconostasis for its chapel was carved by Grigory Kurytzin. In

Moscow the architect Ukhtomsky employed Petr Valekhin to execute the sculptures he had designed for the city's Red Gates, Vassili Zimin made those in the empress's private apartments in the Troitse-Sergieva Lavra. It was in the ante-room there that Peter and Catherine had chatted so pleasantly while the princess of Zerbst was being searchingly questioned by the empress. The room contained no less than thirty-four of Zimin's low relief motifs.

Largely as a result of Rastrelli the elder's work, Petersburgians learnt to admire sculptures of the type which he produced. He paved the way for Falconet and their joint achievements must have proved helpful to Fedot Shubin, the White Sea fisherman's son who, under Catherine, became one of Europe's great eighteenth-century sculptors. Although Falconet had come to be admired in France, he had not won world wide recognition for himself nor amassed there the fortune he desired. Yet Voltaire and Diderot thought so well of him that they persuaded the empress to tempt the sculptor to visit Russia and later in St Petersburg he produced for Catherine the great equestrian statue of Peter the Great on which his reputation now rests.

Elizabeth must have acquired her passion for building from her father. It was so strong in her that she felt compelled to indulge it even when she was still a poor and scorned princess, contriving during those years to build at least one church and to carry out alterations or extensions to the various residences which she occupied after her mother's death. Her life span coincides with that of an age which witnessed the resurgence of architecture on a scale unknown in Russia since the Mongol invasion. Even in her girlhood its revival had not been confined, as it was in Peter's day, to St Petersburg, nor had it been limited to Moscow and its neighbourhood, as had happened in Muscovite times, but had begun to make itself felt in a number of provincial capitals, in both domestic and church building. Under Elizabeth the revival was to become more exuberant, the dissemination far greater than ever before. Whereas under Peter people had engaged in building in response to the tsar's orders, under Elizabeth they did so for their own delight.

Peter the Great's decision to concentrate all building material and his entire labour force on the banks of the Neva for the purpose of building his new capital there seriously affected living conditions in Moscow. Yet owing to these measures by 1716 the foundations of St Petersburg had been laid, its outlines and form had been determined and so many buildings of architectural merit had already been completed that there was no longer any justification for forbidding building activities elsewhere in Russia.

Peter had always regarded his need for foreign technicians, craftsmen and artists as harmful to Russia in the long run. Though temporarily essential to him he was anxious to dispense with their services as soon as they could be replaced by equally well qualified Russians. In 1717, just before the start of his second European tour, Peter decided to send another group of scholars, none aged under seventeen, to complete their education abroad. He helped to select them and it was probably at his wish that, of the seven who were to specialize in architecture, four were to train in Italy and only three in his beloved Holland. The decision may perhaps indicate that Peter had come to realize that the grandiose in architecture was more likely to impress his neighbours than the more modest, and to him far more pleasing, domestic architecture of Holland. So much fine building had been done in Moscow during the latter part of the seventeenth century that Russia was not lacking in competent architects in the eighteenth century. Ivan Feodorovich Michurin was among the most accomplished. He was chief architect to Moscow at the time of Anna Ivanovna's coronation. Her decision to stay on in Moscow after the ceremony created a need for housing which provided the town's architects with their first opportunity to build there for twenty-seven years.

Michurin came to Moscow from St Petersburg some time before 1733. He found the city's oldest and most cherished churches and monasteries in a state of great disrepair. The town's bridges had become unsafe; some were on the verge of collapse and a great many houses were derelict. There had been talk in the past of making a survey of Moscow, but nothing had come of it. For lack of a city plan Michurin scarcely knew which repairs to begin with and so in 1734 he decided to embark on the survey. In 1737 the outbreak of a fire which devastated large areas of Moscow increased his difficulties, yet he managed to carry out the most urgent repairs and to complete the survey by 1739 only to find that, because of the housing shortage, many workers had fled the town and he was faced with a labour shortage. To cope with the more urgent repairs Michurin established what he called an Architectural Counter, or the equivalent of an Office of Works. Those whom he employed there included such excellent architects as Peter's 'fledglings', Evlashev and Ivan Korobov, as well as some promising architectural students. Michurin entrusted the upkeep of Moscow's bridges and streets to Korobov and was as a result able to devote some of his time to teaching the students the methods to be followed when restoring or preserving ancient buildings. He stressed the need to ensure that extensions which were to be added to the oldest and finest monasteries should harmonize with the existing structures without reproducing the latter's archaic and outdated forms. Such fine mid to late eighteenth-century architects as Ukhtomsky and Bazhenov received much of their training from Michurin, learning from him to love and admire Russia's native architecture and also to recognize and use those of its elements which could be adapted to the taste of their day.

Records survive to show that Elizabeth admired Michurin as an artist and respected him as a man. She must have followed his career with considerable interest during Anna Ivanovna's reign for he later designed many buildings for her, including Moscow's new Cloth Hall (1745/6). In 1747 she instructed him to rebuild the bell tower of the Novodevichy Convent in Moscow which had collapsed in 1723, but even when Michurin had completed his designs the undertaking was postponed for Elizabeth had decided to send Michurin to Kiev to supervise the construction of the Cathedral of St Andrew in accordance with Rastrelli's designs. At the same time the empress asked Rastrelli to check Michurin's designs for the tower; when Rastrelli pronounced them excellent there were no further delays. The new tower met with universal approval and in 1750 Michurin was asked to provide another in place of that destroyed by fire in the Troitse-Sergieva Lavra. Once again there were delays and the tower was unfinished at the time of Michurin's death; the task of completing it fell to I. Schumacher and Ukhtomsky.

The architectural revival encouraged Moscow's merchants to sponsor the construction of several parish churches. Many chose Michurin as their architect. The Church of Paraskevi-Piatnitza (1739–44) with its fine bell tower and that of SS Peter and Paul (1740–44) are ascribed to him and are the only ones to have survived to our day. Private commissions of this type ended in 1747 when Michurin was sent to Kiev to build Rastrelli's cathedral there as well as a replica of the palace which Rastrelli was engaged in building for Elizabeth at Perovo, near Moscow. Michurin stayed in Kiev till 1754. During his stay he trained a number of young architects and influenced some older ones, and was thus able to introduce to the region the Rastrelli style in architecture together with other trends considered fashionable at the time in the country's two capitals. He also built a new and impressive church for the monks of the Svensk Monastery, situated near Briansky though a dependency of Kiev's Monastery of the Caves.

Michurin had been succeeded in Moscow as architect-in-chief by Dimitri

24. An over-door panel painting by A. I. Belsky, a leading interior decorator, 1759.

25. A sofa designed by Rastrelli the Younger for use in the Catherine Palace at Tsarskoe Selo and made by Russian craftsmen.

26. Some examples of the
coins minted in the reigns of
the Empress Elizabeth and the
prohibited coins of Tsar
Ivan III/VI.

27. Losenko's portrait of Volkov,
actor and founder of the Russian
theatre.

28. A dandy and a lady of
fashion as they appear in a
'lubok' or peasant
woodcut, by P. N.
Tchuvaev. Second half of
the eighteenth century.

29. A stage set of a throne
room with baroque
features by Guiseppe
Valeriani. Colour wash
drawing.

30. The Swedish frigates which Peter the Great captured in 1720 sail into St Petersb
amidst great celebrations. Engraving by Alexei Zubor.

31. A detail from the mosaic panel of the battle of Poltava produced in Lomonc
workshop under his supervision c. 1760.

Vassilievich Ukhtomsky. He was to prove one of the most sensitive, original and versatile of the Russian architects of Elizabeth's reign. Born into an impoverished princely family he was given a good though traditional education, first in Moscow's School of Mathematics, and, from the age of sixteen, at the Slavo-Graeco-Latin Academy. However, within a year he had left the Academy to study under Michurin. On graduating he became assistant to Korobov. Fortune smiled on him in 1742. When Korobov had gone to Nizhny Novgorod to build a new town hall there Ukhtomsky had been left in charge of the architect's Moscow office and, as such, received an order from St Petersburg instructing Korobov to design four wooden triumphal arches or gates for Elizabeth's forthcoming coronation. Ukhtomsky saw no reason for not providing the designs; when he submitted them they were considered so successful that Korobov's office obtained the coveted commission. The designs combined the Muscovite love for exuberant ornamentation with the light, gay yet ordered style of the eighteenth century. The best of the gates was erected on the Tverskaya, but all four were so much admired that they were recorded in the volume of engravings, accompanied by a Russian and German text, published in 1744 to commemorate the event.

In 1747 Ukhtomsky founded a school of architecture of his own. He had twenty-eight pupils, some of whom were to distinguish themselves during Catherine's reign. Though he did most of the teaching himself he continued to design palaces, hospitals, churches and private houses. All bear the imprint of his genius, but, with the notable exception of Moscow's Senate House (1753) few ever got beyond the drawing board. Of those he was able to build many have disappeared, and the small number that survive have suffered disfigurement and serious alterations so that, today, Ukhtomsky must be judged by his designs rather than by his buildings.

The excellent work carried out by architects such as Michurin and Ukhtomsky is, however, eclipsed by the genius of Bartolomeo Francesco Rastrelli. He was the greatest architect of Elizabeth's reign, the one who epitomized all that was best in her tastes, whose influence was to penetrate to many parts of Russia and who ranks today with Europe's foremost geniuses. His parents were Italian, but the boy was born in Paris and lived there till the age of sixteen when his father's skill as a sculptor took the family to Russia. Bartolomeo must have given early indications of his genius for, in 1721, Prince Kantemir, Hospodar of Moldavia – father of the distinguished poet and diplomat – employed the twenty-one-year-old untried youth to build a stone palace for him fronting on to the Neva.

Eight years later his son, Antioch Kantemir, commented, 'Count Rastrelli, by birth an Italian, within Russia a dexterous architect, is not so proficient in practice as he is inventive in his drawings. His designs are marvellously decorative and that which he has built gladdens the eye.'[1] To judge from surviving designs of the house Russian influence already prevailed in the young architect's work, but the Russian element is that which Peter the Great embodied in his adaptation of the Dutch style. The varying roof levels are also a Russian heritage and so too are the contrasts achieved in the façade by the light and shade effects derived through changes in the building's alignment – a feature which Rastrelli was to exploit in his later and far more important works.

The Kantemir palace cannot have been the only building which young Rastrelli designed at this date, but no documents have so far been discovered to throw light on his early activities. His father was probably the first to realize that the young architect needed to see the world. Soon after Peter's death he obtained Catherine I's permission for his son to visit western Europe. Bartolomeo had, however, returned to Russia from his travels by 1730; some scholars suggest that he may even have done so by 1727. Commissions poured in from 1730 onwards. Anna Ivanovna employed him simultaneously in both Moscow and St Petersburg. She appointed him court architect with an annual salary of eight hundred roubles and instructed him to build a Summer Palace for her in St Petersburg on a site fronting onto the Summer Gardens, with a boathouse on the river. Rastrelli designed it in the form of a very long straight building the ends of which jutted out to form a *cour d'honneur*; he surrounded it with park-like grounds and provided it with a boat house and landing stage, completing the work by 1732, in time for the empress's return to St Petersburg. While supervising work there Rastrelli was also engaged in building two palaces for Anna Ivanovna in Moscow. Both were called Annenhof after the new empress; both were built of wood. The first Annenhof was situated in the Kremlin enclosure, on the site of a palace dating from the fifteenth century. Work there started at Anna Ivanovna's arrival in Moscow, for although comfortable apartments had been perpared for her in the Kremlin's main palace she wanted to live in a house which had been built especially for her. It was constructed with characteristic speed yet she was obliged to spend her first summer at Ismailovo, sharing it with Elizabeth. The Kremlin's Annenhof Palace was ready to receive her in October 1730, but almost at once Anna Ivanovna found that she preferred living outside the town and that she wished to reside in the neighbourhood of the Golovin Palace. She therefore instructed Rastrelli to transport and rebuild the Annenhof Palace on a site at Lefortovo, lying to the south-west of Moscow, close to the Yauza river. With Schädel assisting him, work was begun at the start of the next building season and although the new structure contained three hundred rooms and was proclaimed the finest wooden building in the country, it had been completed by the autumn and was comfortable and fit for Elizabeth to live in when Anna Ivanovna forbade her to stay on at Ismailovo. Anna Ivanovna spent the autumn of 1731 at Annenhof; by then the grounds had been laid out and the main garden provided with lakes and fountains. The small residence which Peter had built for his Swiss favourite, François Lefort, stood within the new palace's park. It was known as the Lefortovo Palace. Rastrelli had carried out some alterations there to enable Anna Ivanovna to live in it while the Annenhof Palace was being rebuilt. Lefortovo was burnt out in December 1753, when three thousand of Elizabeth's courtiers were living in it. Elizabeth was staying at the time in the Golovin Palace, which had had to be enlarged for the purpose, but the work was done so hurriedly and so carelessly that Catherine's apartments were neither windproof nor watertight. The Grand Duchess hated them, but did not have to put up with them for long since soon after Elizabeth had moved into the Golovin Palace it had caught fire and three hours later nothing but a heap of cinders remained to mark its site. Elizabeth was obliged to install herself in the small palace on the Pokrovka which Rastrelli had built for her in 1742 for Annenhof had too many unpleasant associations for her to wish to live in it. The Pokrovka Palace could not house her clothes and plate, and these had therefore been sent to Lefortovo, where it was their turn to be destroyed by fire. Meanwhile five hundred carpenters were engaged to rebuild the Golovin Palace for a daily wage of thirty kopeks. The building was ready for the empress to move into six weeks later, on 10 December 1755; it had sixty rooms, but could not accommodate the courtiers who were rendered homeless when Lefortovo was destroyed.

When Anna Ivanovna transferred her court back to St Petersburg Rastrelli became extremely busy. Biron and Münnich had been among the first to appreciate his talent. Now that Münnich was responsible for all building work in St Petersburg he could express his admiration for the architect in a tangible form. As early as 1731 he turned to him for designs for an opera house in St Petersburg and for a new Winter Palace there for the empress. The opera house was built in two months; it contained three tiers of seats. While work was in progress there Rastrelli was also building a riding school in the capital for Biron; it was exceptionally large and both its façade and interior were much decorated, for the site chosen for it was situated close to the Summer Palace. The new Winter Palace was the third structure to be called so. It was to take the place of the second Winter Palace which Matarnovi had started to build for Peter the Great in 1715 to replace the first Winter Palace, completed in 1711. The new or third Winter Palace was to be built near the Admiralty and eventually to incorporate the house belonging to Count Apraxin in which Anna Ivanovna intended to live while her new palace was being built. The site was later to be occupied by the fourth and last Winter Palace, the one which still survives.

Rastrelli intended the third Winter Palace to be the most regal and impressive palace of western style built in Russia. He designed it as a three-storied building with cellars below ground, situating its reception rooms in the mezzanine floor. It was completed in 1738 and although the alterations which Elizabeth insisted on were not completed till 1749 the building was her principal residence during the whole of her life. She never lived in the fourth and last Winter Palace which Rastrelli was building for her while altering the third to suit her wishes.

Rastrelli owed his appointment as court architect to Biron, who, on becoming Duke of Courland, turned to Rastrelli in 1734 for the palace he wished to build at Rundal, near his capital, Mittau. It was to contain thirty reception rooms and therefore provided Rastrelli with ample scope in which to display his talent as a decorator. He made good use of the opportunity and the palace ranks as one of his first masterpieces. In 1738, after Rastrelli had completed the empress's third Winter Palace, Biron persuaded the architect to go to Courland to build a new, stone, grand ducal palace at Mittau and also a house on his estate of Tzipperhof, situated conveniently close to Mittau. The exterior of the Mittau Palace is fairly severe; in plan it follows the shape of a Russian P, that is to say it consists of a central block with side wings set at right angles to it, П. Two thousand serfs were sent to Courland from Russia to speed the work and, as a result, it was practically finished when Biron learnt that he was to live the life of an exile at Pelim in Siberia.

As she watched these buildings grow Elizabeth cannot have failed to realize that Rastrelli was not only the most gifted architect working in Russia but also the one whose taste and genius corresponded most closely to her own standards of excellence. On becoming empress she hastened to confirm him in his post of court architect-in-chief to the sovereign and, in the winter of 1741/2, she sent him to Moscow to supervise the decorations to be used at her coronation and to enlarge the Annenhof Palace, and make it ready to receive some of the visitors who were to attend. On her arrival in Moscow she instructed him to study closely the Cathedral of the Dormition, which she thought the loveliest church in Russia and wished him to regard as a source of inspiration. Rastrelli took advantage of his time in Moscow to inspect the restorations and work of preservation which Michurin and Korobov were carrying out on the city's oldest buildings, thereby developing his understanding and appreciation of the country's medieval architecture. He also met Ukhtomsky, Evlashev and Zherebtzov, and all four must have benefited from the encounter. Rastrelli must surely have noted the skill with which the local architects handled great masses and volumes as well as their ability to enliven immense buildings by a clever use of light and shade effects. He did as much sightseeing as possible and is reported to have greatly admired the Church of the Archangel Michael, better known as the Menshikov Tower, because it had been built for Menshikov in 1705–7 by Zarudny. Rastrelli was also interested in the church which Prince Galitzine, tutor to Peter the Great, had built at Dubrovitzy between 1690–1704, as well as in two churches recently completed by Evlashev. Rastrelli's interest in churches may have been stimulated by his visit to Moscow, but it was Elizabeth's passionate devotion to them that kept it alight. The Cathedral of St Andrew at Kiev was the first large church which Rastrelli designed; his drawings for it date from 1747 and accord with Elizabeth's conception of the ideal church as one having five domes. However, Rastrelli elongated the four corner domes till they came to resemble turrets and struck a note of ornateness new to Russian church architecture. The building is characteristic of the most splendid phase in Rastrelli's development, one which had begun with the Summer Palace which he built for Elizabeth in St Petersburg between 1741–4. Made entirely of wood, the palace had a ballroom which though narrower than that at Versailles, was longer and could hold more people. The grounds in which Rastrelli set the palace were magnificent by any standards. The improvement in his work was appreciated by the empress and, in 1749, at her wish Rastrelli's salary was raised from 1,200 to 2,500 roubles a year.

In 1740 Rastrelli was put in charge of the alterations which were being carried out to the palace of Tsarskoe Selo. Elizabeth preferred that residence to all her other country palaces because her mother had given the estate of Sarskoe to her father. The site had always been enchanting, but when

Catherine I acquired it for Peter it contained no house suitable for the tsar to live in. In 1718 Peter had therefore commissioned Braunstein to build a small palace there for his private use. Elizabeth had inherited the estate from her mother and had become so attached to it that when she eventually obtained possession of it she commissioned Ivan Bruni to build a small church – Znamenskoe – on it. Work progressed so slowly that it fell to Zemtsov to finish the church in 1738.

After her accession Elizabeth renamed Sarskoe Tsarskoe, meaning tsarist, and asked Zemtsov to enlarge and alter the palace. The work was to cost 16,743 roubles 12 kopeks, but Zemtsov died before it could be put in hand. Kvassov and Chevakinsky took over. They gutted the original building, transforming the ground floor into a vast central hall and adding a gallery to each side of it, flanking each of the latter with a side wing. These wings were one storey high and curved slightly inward to form a *cour d'honneur*; one contained a chapel, the other a conservatory with, in addition, in each case, eight large rooms as well as servants' quarters, offices and store rooms. Work continued on these lines under Rastrelli's direction till 1752, when the empress suddenly decided that Rastrelli was to scrap all that had been done and rebuild and redesign the entire structure. He completed it in 1756.

Rastrelli decided to retain the section of the palace which had been built for Peter the Great and to make it the centre of his building; it was to be called the Catherine Palace in memory of Elizabeth's mother though the name is often mistakenly associated with Catherine II. Rastrelli gave it a new façade, encasing the original front in a four columned portico surmounted by a pediment, making it the chief feature of the new palace's main front. He adopted Braunstein's idea for the rest of the building, extending the palace on either side of the portico in a straight line, breaking its monotony by dividing it into sections, those on either side of the Catherine block together with a section at each of the building's extremities standing slightly back from the rest; he aligned the chapel, which he placed at one extremity, with the central section. He kept the wings one storey high, but curved them to converge at the centre at three superb wrought iron gates, giving the palace a magnificent courtyard. The central portion forming the palace proper is three storeys high and measures 326 feet in length. It is vast even by Russian standards. The general effect is one of a splendid multiplicity of columns, windows and pilasters which serve to create a variety of light and shade effects and to endow the building with a life of its own. Nothing in Europe quite equals it for elegance and magnificence. The entire structure was built in four years when Rastrelli set the seal on its beauty by painting its exterior walls pale blue, its columns white, and gilding many of the sculptures which adorned it and the statues poised on the parapet of its roof. Their presence on so severely symmetrical a building together with the numerous sculptured features of the façade helped to produce the gay, lively atmosphere Elizabeth adored. The windows facing the park were unusually large; they were framed in gilt caryatids and when struck by the rays of the setting sun they seem ablaze. On more than one occasion the empress's firemen rushed to the palace thinking that it was on fire.

Within this basically severe framework Rastrelli disposed rooms which were seldom more than two deep, though, in the central section, each occupied the entire width of the building since these were intended to serve as the main reception rooms. All the rooms opened into each other to form vistas or perspectives evoking those which Peter the Great had mapped out for the main streets of St Petersburg. Each room was superbly embellished with decorations carried out in the baroque style. In the main reception rooms the windows on the outer walls were counterbalanced by mirrors on the inner ones, but in the Hall of Mirrors windows were set along both outer walls and the spaces between them filled with mirrors. All the rooms were provided with gilt fittings. At night 696 candles were lit in them, the shimmering light and nebulous reflections which they produced creating a sumptuous yet delicate effect. The Amber Hall was particularly splendid. Rastrelli had found some exquisite amber slabs lying in one of the old palace's store rooms; he used them to panel the room's walls. The slabs were made in 1707 by Gofrin Tusso for Frederick I of Prussia. Peter the Great happened to see them when on his second European tour and was so enthralled by them that he begged the king to let him have them. He promised to send the king fifty-five of his tallest soldiers in exchange. Frederick agreed and fifty exceptionally tall Russians were conscripted, drilled, inspected and passed by the tsar before being despatched to Prussia. The panels were sent to Peter as promised, but on arrival they were put into an attic and forgotten. Rastrelli was as impressed by their splendour as Peter had been. He designed a room especially to hold them. Although it was small it was admirably proportioned and became one of Elizabeth's favourites. She used it for birthday parties and intimate, though important, receptions. Elizabeth and Rastrelli were both also attracted by chinoiserie. Rastrelli created some exquisite decorations in that style for her; he used them in conjunction with watered silk and lacquer in the room in which the empress displayed her collections of china and lacquer objects and Elizabeth even asked Rastrelli to build pavilions, follies and a village in the Chinese style for her in her park.

Rastrelli and the empress devoted as much attention to the siting of their buildings as they did over the buildings themselves. The grounds which surrounded Elizabeth's palaces were landscaped, transformed into parks, enlivened by sculptures which took the form both of urns and statues of deities, but for his main effects Rastrelli relied on the placing and design of the pavilions, temples, bridges, seats and fountains with which he embellished them. Sometimes he turned to Kvassov or Chevakinsky for these designs, but the loveliest, gayest and most apt were his own creations.

Though the Hermitage is most characteristic of Rastrelli's taste and genius the first design for it was produced by Kvassov and Chevakinsky was later associated with its construction; yet it was Rastrelli who in fact designed and built it. The Hermitage stands in a hollow in the park at Tsarskoe Selo. Elizabeth intended using it both for fairly large receptions requiring an orchestra and also for the very small and intimate gatherings from which even servants were to be excluded. Rastrelli was able to invest the pavilion with the elegance and ornateness of a miniature palace. He placed a large octagonal hall beneath its dome, fitting a square study in at each of its four corners; these led to three diminutive wings of dissimilar sizes set at angles to them. All the rooms were lit by large windows, those at ground-floor level having French windows opening on to the park. Elizabeth's dining room was situated on the first floor. A round table which could seat twelve people almost filled it; the table was fixed to the floor for it was fitted with a mechanism which enabled both its central section and each of the twelve plate rests to function like lifts. When the empress had finished a course she had only to press a button for these sections to be lowered into the kitchen below, whence they reappeared shortly afterwards with the next course elaborately laid out on them. The invention followed that of a lift which had been installed for the empress' personal use. The Marquis de l'Hôpital admitted that he had never seen anything like them before and felt that the table savoured of magic. Western kings were quick to copy the table, the last to do so being Ferdinand, king of the two Sicilies, and his wife Maria Carolina who, when obliged to abandon Naples to Napoleon's troops, established themselves in Palermo and built the Palazzina Cinesi for use there in summer. In Elizabeth's Hermitage the ceilings and over-door panels of all the rooms were adorned with paintings, their walls hung with gilt mirrors and adorned with gilt fittings. Rastrelli painted its exterior pale blue and in order to set off its dome he had the caryatids on its façade and the statues on the parapet of its roof gilt.

Rastrelli devised a grotto for Elizabeth as fine as the best in Italy. The Toboggan Hills which he erected for her were enchanting and exceedingly steep. They were situated midway between St Petersburg and Tsarskoe Selo, and Elizabeth never tired of using them. Elizabeth, third wife of the first Baron Dimsdale, went to Russia in 1781 and learnt from John Bush, Catherine II's head gardener, who hailed from Hackney, that there had been three hills. She noted in her diary that

The highest reached thirty feet perpendicular, the next mountain five or six feet lower to allow friction and resistance; the slides were of wood, about a furlong and a half long. It is used in winter and summer, the carriage on castors, the more people in it, the quicker it went. The horses worked a machine to take the company up again. Upon the mount two very high swings are placed and a chaise to hold one person and two or three wooden horses so constructed anyone can ride round the mount. The wheels underneath are worked by a horse with great swiftness. The Empress Elizabeth had these mountains made, she was fond of it. The Empress (Catherine) often amused herself, she went in one car and her car got off the groove. It might have entailed a nasty accident, they go with such speed. Prince Orloff is strong. He guided it with his leg. He was lame for some time after. Mr Bush said after this they were destroyed.*

Though Elizabeth never ceased to demand alterations to the palace Rastrelli was able to accept some private commissions. They had begun to pour in on him in 1746 from clients differing widely in their requirements, some wanting quite small houses, others churches, pavilions or theatres. Often Rastrelli supplied them with drawings and plans only, but in the case of patrons such as Kiril Razumovsky,† Mikhail Vorontzov, Baron Stroganov, the Naryshkins and the like he also supervised the work. St Petersburg is thus indebted to him for such magnificent edifices as the Stroganov and Vorontzov palaces. To begin with Rastrelli treated his town houses like country ones, setting them back from the street in the middle of large gardens. The grounds in front of the Vorontzov mansion ran down to the river Fontanka and failed to meet with Catherine's approval. Of Ivan Shuvalov's house, built by Rastrelli's assistant, Chevakinsky, Catherine wrote that

* I am indebted to Sir John Dimsdale for permission to publish this extract from Catherine Dimsdale's unpublished diary.

† Notably Baturino, a residence which held few attractions for its owner. Razumovsky allowed it to fall into ruin. Its rebuilding at the end of the century is sometimes ascribed to Cameron.

the owner had lavished all his taste on it . . . the house lacked taste and was richly and badly furnished. It contained a great many pictures, for the most part poor copies, one room was panelled, but the wood lacked lustre and it was therefore varnished; as a result it turned yellow, a disagreeable yellow, so that the room was considered ugly, and to improve it it had been smothered in very heavy and ornate sculptures, which had been silvered. From the outside the house, already large in itself, has owing to the profusion of its decorations come to resemble cuffs of lace d'Alençon.[2]

The house which Rastrelli built for Count Stroganov between 1750 and 1764 is more sophisticated in that it abuts on to the street as a town house should instead of standing back from it to form the heart of its garden. It was built to take the place of an earlier house which stood on the same site, but had been burnt out, and finally filled the corner formed by the meeting of the Nevski Perspective and the Moika Canal. Rastrelli gave it three storeys, placing the main reception rooms on the piano nobile and giving them larger windows than the other rooms. The house is splendidly proportioned and the external sculptures stress rather than conceal the soberness of its structure.

While Rastrelli was rebuilding Tsarskoe Selo he was also working for the empress both in St Petersburg and in her other country palaces and undertaking private commissions; yet his main efforts were concentrated on the re-building of Peterhof. There, as at Tsarskoe Selo, a small palace had been built for Peter the Great, this time by Leblond; Elizabeth loved spaciousness and wanted Rastrelli to enlarge it. He set to work in 1746. Once again he was reluctant to destroy the original residence, even to conceal it behind a new frontage. He preferred to retain Leblond's structure and, as at Tsarskoe Selo, to use it as the central section of another immensely long, straight building terminating at one end in a church roofed with five domes and at the other in a domed pavilion. In its interior Rastrelli made great use of elaborate parquet flooring, and of gilt mirrors and fittings. In the Hall of Mirrors he consciously set out to vie with Versailles. It was fortunate that this beautiful room met with the approval of Catherine II for, in contrast to most of the work which Elizabeth had commissioned from her architects, she allowed it to survive unaltered.

The palaces of Tsarskoe Selo and Peterhof may be regarded in the nature of trial runs for Elizabeth's finest residence, the fourth and last Winter Palace, the building she longed to live in, but in fact never inhabited. Although the estimated cost of rebuilding it was immense Elizabeth obtained the Senate's consent for work to be put in hand in 1754, two years after the building of Peterhof. She spent two and a half million roubles on it, using for the purpose all the money raised by the taxes imposed on wines, spirits and salt; even so the palace was neither finished nor fully paid for in her lifetime. Although it was habitable in 1762 further vast sums had to be spent on it in the following years. As we now know it the Winter Palace covers 42,118 square feet of ground; its inner courtyard alone measures 17,208 square feet and its rooms number 1,054, yet its great size does not detract from its beauty and the building is one of the finest in the world. It is made up of great corner blocks or wings, each of which forms one of its main façades. These sections are connected by smaller blocks which form enclosed gardens and inner courts. The outer walls of all these sections are broken up, diversified and embellished by columns and sculptured motifs, some taking the form of architraves, others of caryatids, masks and the like, in the baroque style. Within, the magnificent Epiphany Hall alone survives in the form devised for it by Rastrelli. It was used annually on the day on which the sovereign attended the traditional ceremony of the blessing of the Neva's waters, an event which took place on 6 January and which gave the hall its name.

Rastrelli was a great master of the palatial, but he was also successful as a builder of churches. The earliest, the Cathedral of St Andrew at Kiev, is essentially urban in character whilst the churches in the palaces of Tsarskoe Selo and Peterhof are chapels of the regal type. The church of The New Jerusalem Convent was conceived to blend with a more austere setting than the latter and is far more restrained than the church of the Smolny Convent. Elizabeth was in the habit of staying up late – often, indeed, spending the entire night at a ball. Since she never missed attending morning service she was often obliged to hurry to church in her evening dress. At Smolny the church's ornate decorations and the empress's magnificent jewels and elegant clothes must have complemented each other.

Quite early in his career Rastrelli had found it necessary to establish an architectural school of his own in which to train his assistants, but he never had any difficulty in finding skilled carvers able to execute his elaborate designs for floors, cartouches, wall panels and furniture, for the Russians had always excelled at working in wood. His assistants and workmen helped to disseminate the Rastrelli style throughout Russia so that, from about 1750, wooden buildings possessing pediments and adorned with pilasters, columns and sculptures were springing up in such widely separated provincial towns as Tula, Kaluga or Vologda.

Many of the architects who worked for Rastrelli were of the first rank. Savva Chevakinsky was among the most gifted. He was a countryman by taste and upbringing; born in his father's estate in 1713 he did not leave it till 1729, when he became a pupil in St Petersburg's Naval Academy. Two years later he transferred to the Architectural Department of the Admiralty and in 1744/5 he worked with Korobov in re-building the Admiralty. He qualified as an architect in 1746 and six years later had taken charge of the work being done at Tsarskoe Selo, even providing some of the designs used there. In 1748 he became assistant to Rastrelli, but he also undertook private commissions of importance in and around the capital. These included the Shuvalov Mansion in Italy Street (1753–5), so much criticized by Catherine, and one for the Sheremetievs on the Fontanka. He eventually became architect-in-chief to the Admiralty and his assistants there included Bazhenov and Starov, architects who were to distinguish themselves in the reign of Catherine.

Andrei Vasilievich Kvassov was also an outstanding architect. He too was employed for a time at Tsarskoe Selo, but in 1744 Elizabeth sent him to the Ukraine to build a replica of that palace at Kozeltse for she intended making a fairly long stay in it during her state visit to Kiev. Evlashev and more especially G. D. Dmitriev also made their mark, the latter working with Rastrelli on St Petersburg's Anichkov Palace. Another architect, Vist, the son of Menshikov's wealthy secretary, built the boat house in the SS Peter and Paul Fortress where Peter I's boat was to be preserved and M. D. Rastorguev, the son of a carpenter, built the Archbishop's Palace at the Alexander Nevsky Lavra. It is impossible to refer to all the architects of ability who were working in Russia in Elizabeth's day for architecture flourished then as it had done in Novgorodian times, buildings in the Rastrelli style springing up on all sides to gladden the eye, and to remain as monuments to the reign of the Empress Elizabeth.

10

The Last Phase

Elizabeth gazed upon a Europe in turmoil with profound distress. Her sadness and concern increased with her realization that every new development brought Russia nearer to war. She did not doubt Russia's ability to acquit herself favourably on the battle front. Her armies had been re-formed and provided with new equipment. Much though she hated warfare Elizabeth had no intention of remaining neutral if the nation's honour, glory and prosperity required her to become a belligerent. She gradually came to feel that she had two tasks to perform; the first was to fulfil the conditions of her offensive alliance with Austria, the second to acquire France as an ally.

Elizabeth had recovered from her stroke early in September 1756. She then appointed Count Apraxin Commander-in-Chief of the army she had decided to despatch forthwith to assist Maria Theresa in her fight against Prussia. Apraxin was venial in character, lazy and faint-hearted; he loved his physical comforts, delighted in court life and was most reluctant to leave St Petersburg at a time when it was very likely that the empress would succumb to another heart attack. Were she to die her place would be filled by a sovereign who was heart and soul devoted to the king of Prussia. Elizabeth was unaware of Apraxin's shortcomings. He was one of her oldest and closest friends; he was on good terms with the Grand Duchess Catherine and was liked by people of such widely differing political opinions as Alexei Bestuzhev and the Shuvalovs; she trusted in his patriotism. Although Apraxin was loath to leave St Petersburg he could hardly ask for his appointment to be cancelled; however, he managed to delay his departure for the army's headquarters till 10 November. His slowness disturbed Elizabeth and she talked of taking the Grand Duke Peter and going herself to take charge of the army, leaving Catherine and Paul in St Petersburg.[1] Eventually, however, Apraxin reached Riga, but even then he did not lead his troops westward, asserting that the men needed further training and more arms. He insisted on postponing military operations till the spring, and sent the men to winter in the district of Pskov and on the banks of the river Dnieper. Nevertheless Frederick felt deeply worried. Although he scoffed at the Russians in public, referring to them as barbarians and their army as a horde of undisciplined hooligans, he feared them all, especially the cossacks.

Having taken the necessary measures to fulfil her obligations to Austria Elizabeth put all her efforts into making an alliance with France. She sent Bekhtiev to Versailles for the purpose of renewing diplomatic relations and summoned Mackenzie Douglas and the Chevalier d'Eon to discuss the matter. Though not empowered to do so, Douglas clearly defined the terms of such an alliance and led the empress to believe that he had been authorized to do so. He even included in the agreement a secret clause whereby, should Russia find herself at war with Turkey, France would provide Elizabeth with financial assistance. The condition ran counter to France's carefully fostered friendship with Turkey and was one which Versailles could never have agreed to. Douglas's memorandum containing the terms he had agreed to was read with indignation at Versailles. The king and his ministers were furious with their envoy and decided on his immediate recall. Louis wrote personally to the empress begging her to withdraw the unacceptable clause. Elizabeth concurred. The draft of the offending treaty was destroyed in Douglas's presence. New terms were drawn up and duly signed by both rulers. With this matter satisfactorily settled Louis found it impossible any longer to defer sending an ambassador to Russia. On 23 December he appointed the Marquis de l'Hôpital to the post, Elizabeth choosing Mikhail Bestuzhev as Russia's ambassador to France. He had always favoured a French alliance and had never supported the pro-British policy of his younger brother, the grand chancellor. Thus, as the year 1757 drew to a close Elizabeth saw her dearest wish come true at last; Russia and France were allies. Yet, by putting her signature to the treaty which made them so, she had consolidated the breach which divided Europe into two camps. Now Austria, France, Saxony and Russia were aligned against Prussia and Britain.

Louis took good care that Elizabeth should not know of his refusal to regard Russia as a full ally, but merely as one acting by proxy or through force of circumstance, having become so by way of Austria rather than direct. He had always been antagonistic to Russia but, in addition, feared her as an ally lest friendship with Russia impair France's position as a traditional ally of Poland and Sweden. Elizabeth would have been still more alarmed had she known that the Franco-Austrian treaty contained a secret clause excluding Russia from sharing in whatever territorial gains might result from the war. Nor did she realize that Douglas had been instructed to report all her words and actions to the king. Douglas, for his part, made no attempt to influence the king in favour of the empress and Louis' distrust of Elizabeth remained so strong that, in May 1757, on finding it advisable to re-affirm the conditions of his Austrian agreement, he again insisted on retaining the clause debarring Russia from benefiting territorially from the war, on the grounds that the Russian army was acting as an auxiliary force and not as a belligerent one.

At the time Russian troops had not been involved in the fighting, but the diplomatic war continued to be vigorously pursued in the imperial court and its precincts. There the contest was being conducted by Bestuzhev and Hanbury Williams for the purpose of destroying those who supported France. The personal relationships of those concerned helped to envenom an already difficult situation. Thus the empress believed that, even though she did not approve of Bestuzhev's pro-British policy, she could rely on his loyalty because of his hatred of Prussia. Bestuzhev encouraged her in this belief by presenting her with a memorandum listing the services which he had rendered to her and to Russia. Hanbury Williams, though working closely with Bestuzhev, found himself at first obliged, and later more than willing, to act as a loyal supporter of Frederick. The Grand Duke Peter was openly and wholeheartedly on Frederick's side but his wife made no secret of her preference for Britain. Bestuzhev's hopes centred on keeping Russia neutral with regard to Britain – an aim which Hanbury Williams encouraged while working for Prussia's victory. Frederick was anxious for the British Fleet to assemble in the Baltic, not so much in order to engage the Russian but rather to ensure that the latter took no part in the war, but the French wanted the two navies to engage in battle in order that the British Navy should find itself tied to the Baltic leaving other waters free for the French, thus enabling them to maintain troops and supplies in America.

Apraxin should have started to prepare for the spring offensive in February, but he showed no signs of doing so. Bestuzhev observed his dilatoriness with profound concern. He ascribed the delay to Apraxin's innate indolence aggravated by his reluctance to increase the distance separating him from the capital, and he refused to accept the field marshal's argument that the army was in no condition to fight a major war.

Although Apraxin was making the most of his difficulties, some of them were real enough, even though Bestuzhev made little of them. He begged Apraxin to take to the field. The tone of his letters grew terse and eventually angered the field marshal. Bestuzhev attempted to mollify him, but he remained so anxious for the chance to attack Frederick that he turned to Catherine, asking her to do all she could to persuade Apraxin to make contact with the enemy. In April Catherine accordingly wrote a personal letter to Apraxin urging him not to delay the offensive. She was unaware that her own friendship with Hanbury Williams was known to all the court, and that Apraxin and many others regarded it as a sign of her approval of the support which the British Ambassador was giving to Frederick's cause. Catherine was in such complete agreement with the empress's and Bestuzhev's stand against Frederick's aggressiveness that the possibility of being so much misunderstood never occurred to her.

Catherine's conduct and intentions at this period in her life are of importance, not so much in themselves but because of the way in which the foreign diplomats living in St Petersburg reacted to them. Some actually misunderstood her; others intentionally misconstrued her position. During Elizabeth's reign Catherine could play no part in state affairs, nor could she obtain definite information about the empress's intentions. But the empress's rapidly failing health encouraged foreign observers to believe that she had considerable influence. They therefore attached an exaggerated importance to Catherine's statements and opinions. Bestuzhev's evident anxiety about the future and his attitude to Catherine gave substance to these views. He had in fact begun to think of Catherine as standing on the threshold of power and even drew up a memorandum in which he advocated her recognition, at Elizabeth's death, as Peter's consort. He asked Poniatowski to submit the document to Catherine for her approval, but the Grand Duchess refrained from commenting on it. Her silence may have been due to her desire for greater powers than a consort's, but it may also have been caused by Bestuzhev's request for an immoderate number of rewards in return for his support, and finally from the realization that her position was far from secure and that Bestuzhev's proposals were of no immediate use to her.

It seems unlikely, yet it is just conceivable that Hanbury Williams genuinely overestimated Catherine's influence. His despatches leave the reader with the impression that the letters he received from Catherine were based on secret information and not, as was the case, on court rumours and her own personal deductions. His reports encouraged

Frederick to believe that Catherine's attitude to the war differed from that of the empress and to regard Catherine as no less devoted to him and his cause than her mother had once been. At the very time when Catherine was writing to Apraxin to persuade him to attack the Prussians Frederick was contemplating asking her to bribe the field marshal not to do so.[2] Like so many other courtiers Apraxin must often have considered the likelihood at Elizabeth's death of Catherine wielding considerable power, and this is probably why he fell in with her request.

The king of Sweden had recently appended his name to the Treaty of Versailles. Louis welcomed Sweden's participation as a means of weakening Britain – an aim which was nearer to his heart than the defeat of Frederick. King George was also less concerned with Frederick and his commitments to him than with preserving Britain's strength for fighting the French. Elizabeth was the only belligerent whose conduct was that of a loyal ally, for her chief aim was to keep her promise to restore Silesia to Austria. Nevertheless, it was only in May, when Frederick's capture of Prague was countered by a French advance into Hanover, that Apraxin at last left Russia to lead his army in pursuit of the enemy.

The Marquis de Châteauneuf et de l'Hôpital, to give the new French ambassador his full title, had been instructed to obtain a commercial treaty from Russia and, while negotiating it, to manoeuvre himself into a position which would prove favourable should the empress die unexpectedly. Elizabeth's health had become a cause of constant anxiety. Her strength was failing, her legs were so atrociously swollen that she could scarcely walk, her sleeplessness had become so acute that she often refused to go to bed at night, but on the following day she would drop off to sleep fully dressed and in public. She was spending more of her time in her private apartments and was so seldom seen that speculation about her health reached such proportions that eventually it was forbidden to refer to the subject in public. Nevertheless she insisted on entering into a secret, personal correspondence with the king of France. It was conducted in cipher, but the king was careful never to touch on any matters of real importance in it; he wrote in such general terms and made use of so many platitudes that even Elizabeth derived very little satisfaction from his letters.

Meanwhile de l'Hôpital was floundering between two courts and two political parties. In the Little or Grand Ducal court Peter was flaunting his love for the unattractive, almost deformed Elizabeth Vorontzova, letting his hearers know that he intended marrying the lady when he became tsar.

Catherine, on the other hand, was more deeply in love than ever with Poniatowski and was often to be seen in Hanbury William's company. Bestuzhev was drawing closer to the Saxon Minister, Count Brühl, and Poniatowski was obviously enjoying his position as Saxon ambassador. In his anxiety to be on good terms with both courts de l'Hôpital tried to win Catherine's favours by giving her news of her widowed mother. She had been evicted from Prussia for her pro-French sympathies and had settled in Paris. Although Elizabeth appealed to the French to refuse to admit her, her request was ignored and the Princess of Zerbst was able to remain in Paris till her death in 1758. De l'Hôpital made use of a French officer, the Marquis de Fraigne, to get news from the princess and to transmit Catherine's letters.

In July the Russians learnt with delight that Apraxin had at last crossed Poland and, acting in concert with his second in command, General Fermor, had captured Memel and Tilsit. Unintentionally misled by Hanbury Williams, Frederick concluded that the Russians would push on into Silesia instead of turning on Germany. Louis, however, was not satisfied with Apraxin's achievements and instructed de l'Hôpital and the Austrian ambassador to convince the empress that Hanbury Williams's activities were harming the conduct of the war. Deeply offended by their words the empress asked for Hanbury Williams's recall. He left Russia in August an ill and broken man. Catherine was sorry to see him go. She owed him the happiness she derived from Poniatowski's love. She had also enjoyed his companionship and his flattery. She wept when the date of his departure was announced and her letter of farewell expresses heartfelt regret.

On 8 September 1759 news of the victory which the Russians had won on 30 August at Gross-Jägerndorf reached the empress at Tsarskoe Selo. The jubilation was general. The Grand Duke Peter refused to share in the nation's happiness, and Catherine, once again pregnant, wept in secret because Poniatowski had been recalled to Poland. An Austrian victory at Kolin and the penetration of Austrian troops into Lusatia and Upper Silesia coincided with a French advance into Hanover and Hesse and the defeat of the Duke of Cumberland's force. These victories led Elizabeth to hope for a short war and her spirits rose.

The court stayed on at Tsarskoe Selo for the celebration on 19 September of the anniversary of the Virgin's birth. Elizabeth was in the habit of attending the service held annually on that day in the parish church of Tsarskoe Selo. It was situated close to the palace's main gates and Elizabeth set out for the service on foot. The church was full of peasants who had assembled from the outlying districts as well as of courtiers and local residents. Soon after the start of the service Elizabeth felt exceedingly unwell. She was anxious not to disturb the worshippers and managed to slip unnoticed from her place. She found her way to the door and tottered down the porch steps, but collapsed on the grass below them. She had had another stroke. Many peasants had been unable to find places in the crowded church and had collected near the porch in the hope of hearing something of the service. They now gathered round the unconscious empress without daring to touch her. Eventually one more enterprising than the rest raised the alarm. Elizabeth's ladies rushed out of the church and gathered round her not knowing what to do. One covered Elizabeth's face with her kerchief; another went for her French physician, Foussadieu; panic-stricken he attempted to bleed her, and was horrified when he failed to draw blood. Elizabeth's personal physician, the Greek Condoidis, was himself so ill at the time that he had only some eighteen months to live, but on hearing of the empress's condition he had himself carried to her. He too tried, but at first failed to revive her. All this had taken place in full view of the crowd but now, at last, servants appeared carrying screens and a couch. The empress was lifted onto it and screened off. After a further two hours of ceaseless efforts the doctors succeeded in reviving the empress, but she was still unable to speak, nor could she recognize any member of her household. She was carried back to her bedroom and by the following morning she was able to speak again, but so indistinctly that it was feared that she had damaged her tongue. Her mind continued to wander and she was still unable to recognize any of her ladies. It seemed that she must die.

The news of the empress's illness caused almost as much concern and speculation abroad as in Russia. Louis seemed to have realized at last how valuable her friendship was to France; he wrote to her offering to send Dr Poissonier, one of his leading specialists, to attend her. In Prussia hope soared at the news; in Russian court circles it caused perturbation and in the country at large regret and anxiety. Catherine and Peter were living at Oranienbaum at the time. Poniatowski sent Catherine a hastily scribbled note informing her of what had occurred, but the grand ducal pair were never officially told that Elizabeth was ill. They waited anxiously for the arrival of the messenger who would notify Peter that he had become tsar, but none came. The empress's illness was being kept so secret that although the neighbourhood was full of rumours neither Peter nor Catherine dared inquire after Elizabeth's health lest by doing so they should endanger those who had informed them of her illness. It was not until their return in September to St Petersburg that they learnt that Elizabeth was making a complete and rapid recovery. By then Catherine's pregnancy was so advanced that she could not fulfil any court duties and, despite his intense annoyance, it therefore fell to Peter to do so. He minded so much being separated from Elizabeth Vorontzova even for a short time that he was heard petulantly to remark that 'God alone knows how it is that my wife becomes pregnant'.

Apraxin's behaviour on learning of Elizabeth's illness was to have most serious results. There can be little doubt that he knew that Elizabeth had had a stroke. The information, coupled perhaps with the tiredness of the troops and a shortage in their food supplies, accounts for Apraxin's decision to withdraw from Tilsit even though he realized that, by doing so, he was providing Frederick with time in which to pull together his shattered army. As a result, soon after, Frederick attacked the Russians and drove them out of Memel in such disorder that they abandoned much precious equipment there. Bestuzhev was appalled. Like most Petersburgians he could not accept Apraxin's reasons for the withdrawal. He was still more horrified when he learnt that a rumour was current in the town that he had himself sent secret instructions to Apraxin to return to St Petersburg as soon as possible because the empress was about to die. It was a mischievous and untrue accusation. Bestuzhev had in fact sent orders to Apraxin to resume the offensive immediately. Elizabeth felt humiliated by her army's withdrawal from Memel. She was furious with Apraxin and sent him a sharply worded command to advance into eastern Prussia and to engage the enemy forthwith. Nevertheless, Apraxin, supported this time by his senior officers, replied that the army was in no condition to do so. Elizabeth was obliged to accept their decision but her allies refused to do so. They had all expected to benefit from the Russian victories. They felt even more aggrieved when, on 5 November, the French suffered a severe defeat at Rossbach. Ten days later, when the Austrians were in their turn beaten at Leuthen-Lissa, they convinced themselves that the Russians had acted in bad faith and they blamed Bestuzhev for it.

Elizabeth's stroke had affected her personality, changing it for the worse. She became extremely suspicious and ill-tempered. Mackenzie Douglas reported that, 'it is possible clearly to foresee that the rest of Elizabeth I's reign will prove exceedingly difficult for all those who surround her. Henceforth the prince will become increasingly suspect,

possibly even more detestable to the empress.'[3] He added that he thought
it possible that Peter's life was in danger, commenting that there was 'no
denying that the Grand Duke was neither liked nor respected by the bulk
of the nation', and referring to Tsar Ivan as an alternative ruler. Throughout November Elizabeth was ill again, but this time largely from profound
depression. She spent most of the time in bed, much of it crying, most of
it praying. She could no longer delude herself into thinking that Peter
would make a satisfactory ruler, and although her thoughts sometimes
turned to poor Tsar Ivan, they were mainly occupied with Paul. She felt
more inclined than ever to dispossess Peter in favour of Paul yet whenever
she was on the point of doing so the thought of his extreme youth, en-
tailing as it did the necessity of nominating a regent, held her back. The
birth of a daughter to Catherine on 9 December 1757 could not help to
solve her problem. Peter was quite prepared to accept the child as his
provided he were left free to spend his time with Elizabeth Vorontzova.
The empress also recognized the child. She arranged for her to be called
Anna after her dear sister and wrote to Louis asking him to act as godfather, but the king refused on religious grounds. Once again the baby
was removed from its mother and placed in the empress's charge.
Catherine had expected this to happen and no longer cared. She had
taken steps to ensure her comfort and independence during her confine-
ment by having a screen placed in her bedroom and arranging for
Poniatowski and her close friends to be admitted to her at all times, telling
them to hide behind the screen if the empress called on her. Catherine's
thoughts were centred on the efforts being made by the pro-French
faction to ensure that Poniatowski complied with the order recalling him
to Poland. Just as she had yearned for Saltykov's presence at the time of
Paul's birth so now she longed for Poniatowski's company. The French
and Austrian ambassadors were, however, firmly opposed to the presence
in St Petersburg of this friend of Hanbury Williams and Bestuzhev, and
induced their governments to insist on Poniatowski's departure. Bestuzhev
was able to delay it by some months and during the time when Catherine
was bedridden Poniatowski was able to divert her. Catherine minded
neither Louis' refusal to act as godfather to her daughter nor her own
inability to celebrate the baby's baptism on the sixth day of its life. Her
happiness was not to last.

In January 1758 the empress sent Alexander Shuvalov to Narva to
question Apraxin about the withdrawal from Tilsit, to relieve him of his
duties as Commander-in-Chief, to seize and examine all his papers and to

instruct him to hand over his duties to General Count Fermor. There was as yet no talk of replacing Bestuzhev and the chancellor thought himself safe, but the arrival in February of Sir Robert Keith as successor to Hanbury Williams turned the full anger of the French and Austrian ambassadors on the chancellor. It was unreasonable of them to have held him responsible for Keith's arrival since, at any rate technically, Britain and Russia were still allies, but they were so determined to deprive Keith of Bestuzhev's support that they, and more especially the Austrian ambassador, induced Elizabeth to believe that Bestuzhev had transferred his allegiance from her to that of Catherine's Little Court, and that he was in consequence pursuing a policy which ran counter to hers. They also accused Bestuzhev of corresponding with Apraxin for the purpose of delaying the start of military operations in order to please Peter, Russia's next ruler. They affirmed that Catherine knew and approved of Bestuzhev's activities.

Elizabeth's confidence in Bestuzhev had been badly shaken by the Treaty of Westminster. Her misgivings increased when Shuvalov reported from Narva that Apraxin had destroyed most of his papers before his own arrival and that the field marshal denied that Catherine had discussed the conduct of the war with him though he admitted having received letters from her. Those of Bestuzhev's letters which he had been able to seize did, however, bear out the chancellor's assertions that he had invariably implored Apraxin to carry out the empress's orders to engage the enemy in battle at the earliest possible moment. Fermor too had by now succeeded in convincing the empress that the troops had not been in a condition either to advance deeper into Prussia or to retain Tilsit, yet the very fact that Catherine had corresponded with the Commander-in-Chief inflamed Elizabeth's anger and suspicions. Convinced as she had been by Bestuzhev's enemies that incriminating documents would be found in his house, distracted by worry, dreading the thought of Peter becoming tsar, her distrust of Bestuzhev was aggravated by his sudden and unwarranted absence from court. Although he claimed to be too ill to leave his bed the empress decided to force the issue by calling a Conference of Ministers for 14 February. When Bestuzhev excused himself from attending, giving ill-health as the reason, she lost her temper and sent for him. The old statesman rose from his bed, dressed slowly, and sadly made his way to the palace. He was placed under arrest as he entered the conference hall.

Bestuzhev's innocence and reputation depend to a great extent on the despatches which Hanbury Williams sent home in 1756 describing his attempts to win the chancellor over to Frederick's side. He averred that although Bestuzhev was at first adamant in his refusal he then asked for a pension of £2,500,[4] then preferred to borrow £20,000, and finally accepted a bribe of 10,000 ducats and that, as a result, when Apraxin left for Riga on 11 November 1757 Bestuzhev had persuaded him to delay military operations for as long as possible in order to avoid engaging the Prussians. These statements are not confirmed even by Frederick, whose explanation of Bestuzhev's behaviour is still stranger. He recorded that after his capture of Dresden certain letters were discovered there which had been sent by Bestuzhev to Count Brühl asking the latter to poison the Russian Resident in Warsaw because his behaviour was likely to endanger their two countries. Frederick added that Bestuzhev was so afraid of the king of Prussia publishing these letters that he promised to persuade Apraxin to delay the start of military operations in return for Frederick's silence. There is no evidence to support either charge. Surviving documents in fact indicate that he urged Apraxin to speed military operations. Bestuzhev had always hated and distrusted Frederick; he had more than once refused his bribes and the documents that exist show him entreating Apraxin to lose no time in fighting the Prussians.

Poniatowski once again warned Catherine of the impending danger. He wrote on the morning after Bestuzhev's arrest, telling her that the chancellor, her former Russian tutor Adadurov, the Italian jeweller Bernardi, who had often acted as Catherine's messenger, and Adjutant Elagin, a friend of Bestuzhev, Catherine and Poniatowski, had all been arrested. Catherine was frightened but sensibly decided to attend the evening court when a double wedding was to be celebrated in the empress's presence. She dressed for it with particular care and appeared looking gay and trouble free. She was determined to speak to Prince Trubetskoy, Field Marshal Buturlin and Alexander Shuvalov; she had heard that they were to serve on the commission charged with the examination of Bestuzhev's case. She daringly asked Trubetskoy whether he had found 'more crimes than criminals or more criminals than crimes' and was grimly told in reply that 'we are merely carrying out our orders. As for crimes, as yet we haven't discovered any, but we are still searching.'[5] Buturlin sadly admitted that Bestuzhev was under arrest and that it only remained for them to find proof of his guilt. Yet with the exception of his personal enemies all were convinced of Bestuzhev's innocence and regretted his arrest. On the following day, though closely guarded,

Bestuzhev contrived to send Catherine a message telling her not to worry for he had destroyed everything.

Catherine must have been immensely relieved that no documents involving her would reach the Commissioners for shortly afterwards she asked Alexander Shuvalov to inform the empress that she desired an audience. When he refused Catherine wrote to the empress. Her letter opened with touching words of gratitude for the empress's innumerable acts of kindness. Catherine continued by saying that she knew that the Grand Duke had come to detest her, that she had unwittingly offended the empress and that she was never able to see her children. She therefore implored the empress to permit her to return to her old home at Zerbst. There she would continue to pray for the empress, the Grand Duke, her children, and all those who had been unkind as well as kind to her in Russia. She asked Ivan Shuvalov to give the empress her letter. Later he informed her that the empress had read it and would receive her. Three agonizing weeks of complete silence ensued. Catherine found herself once again living in total isolation. Poniatowski was seldom able to visit her, some of her dearest friends were under arrest, others were under suspicion; it was evident that the empress mistrusted her and had no desire to question her nor, indeed, to have anything to do with her. Catherine could not allow the situation to drag on. Though Ivan Shuvalov assured her that his two powerful uncles were not inimical to her and that the empress would surely react favourably to a display of contrition Catherine was not convinced. She kept to her apartments, crying a great deal, but when Alexander Shuvalov dismissed her favourite lady-in-waiting she became desperate. Taking to her bed she informed her household that 'her soul was in danger' and that it was necessary for her to see her confessor. He was summoned and saw Catherine in private. She gave him such a moving account of her misfortunes and showed such distress that the priest's heart overflowed with sympathy. On leaving her he hurried to the empress and told her of Catherine's condition. Quick to respond to unhappiness the empress sent Shuvalov to inquire whether Catherine could come to her on the following evening.

Catherine was lying on a sofa carefully dressed at ten o'clock on the evening of 13 April 1758 when Alexander Shuvalov came to conduct her to the empress. As they neared the imperial apartments Catherine noticed Peter hurrying ahead of her. She had not seen him for some months. Entering the empress's presence Catherine found him waiting for her. She sensed that Ivan Shuvalov was also in the room, though concealed behind a screen. With tears streaming down her cheeks Catherine flung herself on her knees, implored the empress to send her home to Zerbst, and vigorously asserted her innocence. She was not so distressed as not to notice that Elizabeth, though still beautiful, looked ill and exhausted, and that she also had tears in her eyes and seemed sad rather than angry. The empress's attitude was probably partly dictated by her concern for young Paul, possibly too by the fear of any developments leading to the recognition of his illegitimacy, since these would turn people's thoughts and sympathies to Tsar Ivan. 'How can I let you leave?' she protested; 'think of your children.' 'They are in your care, and nothing could be better for them,' Catherine countered. 'But what reasons could I give for your departure?' asked the empress. 'Your Majesty can give those which have brought me into disfavour and which have led the Grand Duke to hate me,' Catherine replied. Greatly affected Elizabeth raised Catherine from her knees and reminded her of all she had done for her since her arrival in Russia as a very young girl; of how she had loved, nursed and cherished her. Then she accused Catherine of thinking herself cleverer than anyone else and of meddling in affairs of state. 'In the reign of the Empress Anna,' Elizabeth said vehemently, 'I would never have dared to do as you did. How dared you send instructions to Field Marshal Apraxin?' Catherine maintained that she had written only three letters to Apraxin, that she was innocent. 'Bestuzhev says you sent more letters than that,' stormed the empress, trying to frighten her into confessing. 'In that case Bestuzhev lies,' retorted Catherine. 'If so I will have him tortured,' came the answer. 'It is in Your Majesty's power to do as you think fit, but I sent only three letters to Apraxin,'[6] Catherine insisted. The interview lasted for several hours with Elizabeth, pacing and staggering about the room in a heavy silk dressing gown. Finally the empress dismissed Catherine. She then immediately sent for Alexander Shuvalov and told him to inform the Grand Duchess that she was not to worry. In her anxiety to be scrupulously fair, in her ardent desire to do what was best both for Russia and for Catherine, in her longing to be generous, it was Elizabeth who, torn as she was by illness, worry and exhaustion, emerged from the interview as the nobler if not the cleverer of the two women.

A second meeting took place at the end of May between the empress and the Grand Duchess. No records survive of what occurred but it is thought that Elizabeth began by imploring Catherine to reply absolutely truthfully to the questions she intended putting to her. Catherine contrived to extricate herself from her predicament with her position at court unharmed, but although she had been forgiven, and although there was no more talk of her leaving Russia, she was not pronounced innocent. Catherine was to remark in her Reminiscences that the empress 'lacked the firmness to render justice to one who was innocent'. But although Catherine was not responsible for Apraxin's reluctance to engage the enemy her correspondence with Hanbury Williams was, at best, injudicious and can, in fact, fairly be regarded as something very much worse. Elizabeth had no way of knowing how Catherine had behaved. Throughout the two interviews Elizabeth had striven to be just and had of her own accord decided to give Catherine the benefit of the doubt.

The examination of both Apraxin and Bestuzhev lasted into March when Apraxin, who had never ceased to affirm his innocence, died suddenly of a stroke. The Commission was still sitting at the time and decided to drop the case against him. Bestuzhev also consistently claimed that he was innocent, but although the inquiry failed to produce any evidence of his guilt he was nevertheless sentenced to death on a number of charges, none of which had been proved. Elizabeth was not prepared to endorse the verdict and Bestuzhev was therefore pronounced guilty of lèse-majesté – an offence which was not punishable by death. Then, in her customary manner, Elizabeth refused to decide the nature of his punishment. Bestuzhev continued to live under house arrest till July, spending up to five roubles a day on his food and seeing his wife and family whenever he wished. Towards midsummer Elizabeth at last annulled the court's death sentence by commuting it to one of banishment to Goretovo, his Mozhaisk estate.* She also passed sentences of exile on Adadurov, Bernardi and Elagin, sending Catherine's former tutor to Orenburg and the other two prisoners to the district of Kazan. In August Poniatowski was in his turn expelled from Russia. Catherine was deeply grieved. She had found him a considerate, charming and devoted lover. The final blow struck her five weeks later when their baby daughter died. Once again Catherine withdrew from court life to spend her days in her own apartments, either reading or plunged in thought.

During that anxious and distressing summer Elizabeth never faltered in her determination to continue the war against Prussia to the end. Things had taken a turn for the better on the Russian front. General Fermor, though old and not very clever, had advanced into eastern Prussia in

---

* The order was put into effect in January 1759. When she became empress Catherine hastened to pronounce Bestuzhev pardoned and to bring him back to the capital, where he died in 1766.

1758, captured Königsberg in January and entered Bradenburg by the early summer. Elizabeth was living in Monplaisir at Peterhof at the time. The news reached her there at seven o'clock on the night of 20 July. She arranged for his battle trophies to be put on display there and held a court to enable them to be seen. Then she hurried to St Petersburg to attend a *Te Deum*. The Russian victories warmed Marie Theresa's heart quite as much as Elizabeth's for Fermor intended using the conquered area as a springboard for an advance on Frankfort am Oder, where he planned to link up with an Austrian force. Supply difficulties similar to those which had faced Apraxin at Tilsit, however, forced him to abandon that idea. Instead he determined to lay siege to Küstrin, which, if captured, would give him control of the Oder and open the road to Pomerania. On discovering that Frederick with all the troops he could command was rushing to intercept him and prevent his army from linking up with another Russian force, Fermor concluded that it would be better to fight the enemy at once and so avoid the risk of being attacked in the rear later. He therefore decided to engage the enemy near the village of Zorndorf since his troops held strong positions there. The battle was fought on 25 August with intense ferocity and bitterness. Russian losses amounted to eleven thousand killed and thirteen thousand wounded; Prussia's dead numbered ten thousand. Both armies stood their ground and the outcome of the contest was so confused that both claimed to have won it. In retrospect it is clear that the Russians had the advantage, but Fermor's losses were so immense that he could not make use of his victory to pursue and harass the enemy. Though Zorndorf was proclaimed a Russian victory and enthusiastically celebrated as such, Fermor's failure to destroy the enemy was compared in St Petersburg to Apraxin's failure to follow up his capture of Tilsit by another attack, and was similarly criticized both at home and abroad.* Only the empress remained silent. With bitterness in her heart she realized that Austria had held back from the battle, sparing her troops at the expense of the Russians and proving as unreliable an ally as she had been some three decades earlier, when both countries were at war with Turkey. She taxed Marie Theresa with disloyalty, but the Austrian empress did not instruct her Commander-in-Chief to abandon his winter quarters in Pomerania to link up with the Russians. Instead she blamed the French. Elizabeth did not accept the

---

* Affaires Etrangères de l'Hôpital, despatches such as that of 10 August or 14 October 1758. Nevertheless it is thought that Elizabeth gave orders for a medal to be struck in honour of the victory (Waliszewski, *op. cit.*, p. 460).

excuse as valid and when, in October, the French suffered a serious defeat at Krefeld she behaved with great tact and courage. Though her legs were so swollen that she could scarcely use them she appeared firm and serene when receiving de l'Hôpital in audience. She spoke to him of better times ahead, and assured him of her constancy. Keith reported that she had told the Austrian ambassador that although 'she was very slow in taking her resolutions, yet she was very steady in them';[7] now she was determined to continue the war to the very end 'even if she should be obliged to sell her clothes and jewels for it'. Yet Versailles instructed de l'Hôpital to persuade the Russians to send an army down the Oder to Stettin to join Soubise in marching on London from Edinburgh![8]

In St Petersburg the number of Frederick's spies had multiplied. They supplied the king with political information and – what was far more valuable – with military information. The Grand Duke Peter and the British Ambassador also helped to keep Frederick informed. Keith's courtiers travelled to England through Berlin carrying information which had often being obtained by Peter from Mikhail Vorontzov, who had succeeded Bestuzhev as grand chancellor. Elizabeth had never been able to bring herself to treat Vorontzov with the severity his conduct deserved and now that she was so obviously not far from death the Shuvalovs joined Vorontzov in currying Peter's favours. It is to Catherine's credit that she refused to have anything to do with them. Mackenzie Douglas was no longer in Russia, but Louis xv's physician, Dr Poissonier, arrived in St Petersburg a year after his sovereign had suggested that Elizabeth should place herself in his care. On meeting Condoidis, the empress's Greek physician, Poissonier so offended the Greek that the latter refused to discuss the empress's health with him. Fortunately, at the time Elizabeth did not seem to require the Frenchman's advice. However, Poissonier stayed on in St Petersburg and proceeded to act as a French spy. But although Elizabeth had taken to him and derived pleasure from his company, she refused to follow his medical advice or to use him for political purposes, continuing to entrust her letters to the king to the Chevalier d'Eon.

The year 1759 opened with Elizabeth as determined as ever to continue the war until Frederick had been defeated, but she now insisted on her allies joining the Russians in a joint offensive. She had no idea that, on 30 December 1758, Louis had for the third time reaffirmed the Treaty of Versailles, once more renewing the clause debarring Russia from bene-fiting from the allies' territorial gains. Fermor's army now numbered ninety thousand men, but he too could not forget the way in which Austria had broken faith with Russia in 1739 and he was determined not to move his men until the Austrian army stationed on the Bohemian border had made some effort to link up with his. When the Austrians showed no sign of moving, Fermor displayed a similar obstinacy. The stalemate infuriated Elizabeth. She had pledged herself to action and was so anxious to take the initiative that she decided to replace Count Fermor by Petr Semeonovich Saltykov as Commander-in-Chief. Frederick dubbed Saltykov 'the stupidest of all Russia's fools', and may well have been right in his judgement, but Elizabeth had chosen the young, energetic and brilliant General Rumyantsev to act as Saltykov's second-in-command. They made a good team. Under their joint leadership the Russians pressed forward. To Frederick's horror they quickly reached Frankfort am Oder. There they were joined by a token force of Austrians who had hurried to meet them at Marie Theresa's express orders. In August, as the French suffered a major defeat at Minden, the Russians crossed Lusatia and won a brilliant victory at Künersdorf. Frederick was lucky to escape from the battlefield with his life. Of the 48,000 men who had fought for him there only 3,000 survived. Some 16,000 Russians died that day, but their valour had destroyed Frederick's army. He knew that he had received a mortal blow and thought that all was lost. Elizabeth was again living at Peterhof when the news reached her. It was with a glad heart that she hurried to St Petersburg to attend a *Te Deum* of Thanksgiving and to promote Saltykov to field marshal. Her satisfaction was soon spoilt by the news that the Austrians had once again refrained from joining the Russians in pursuing Frederick. Although a detachment under the Russian commander Totleben penetrated to Berlin in October 1760, occupying the Prussian capital for four days, Saltykov was obliged to withdraw his troops to the Vistula. Elizabeth's promise to restore Silesia to Austria had still not been fulfilled and it therefore remained necessary for her to continue the war even though the withdrawal would furnish Frederick with an opportunity to assemble fresh forces. Elizabeth was furious, but recognized that Saltykov could not have acted otherwise.

The French had been defeated by the British at Quebec and longed for peace in Europe, but Louis could not bring himself to be the first to propose a truce. He wanted Elizabeth to do this, but was reluctant personally to ask her to act. De l'Hôpital, by now ill and exhausted, did not discourage the empress from claiming eastern Prussia, yet he dared not broach the subject of entering into peace talks with the enemy. However,

Frederick also desired peace and on 12 December Keith was therefore instructed to ask the empress to act as mediator. Elizabeth replied to the suggestion with dignity and frankness. Expressing her sorrow at being at war she emphasized that peace depended on something more tangible then mere words, that she would remain loyal to her allies and never act without their full knowledge and agreement. She expressed a keen desire for an honourable, permanent and advantageous peace, but stated that she would never agree to a *status quo* with regard to Prussia's frontiers.

Elizabeth's relations with Austria steadily grew worse. Saltykov voiced Russian public opinion when he said that the Austrians expected 'others to extinguish their fire'. The Austrian refusal to take part in any major operation led Saltykov to reject all suggestions that the Russians should pursue the enemy alone. The Austrians reacted to his stand by launching the rumour that Saltykov had been bribed by the British. Elizabeth was deeply offended and indignantly insisted on a denial and an apology. Marie Theresa was obliged to retract. Nevertheless, Elizabeth found that she was the only one among her allies who was as determined as ever to continue the war until Frederick had been completely defeated. Undeterred by the entreaties of the francophile Mikhail Vorontzov and Ivan Shuvalov she again proclaimed her intention of fighting on.

By January 1760 Frederick was in such a desperate plight that he asked Keith to offer Peter a bribe of two hundred thousand roubles to obtain Russia's withdrawal from the war. Nothing came of the suggestion. Elizabeth now felt certain of victory and sounded Poland on the possibility of exchanging certain Polish territories in return for those which would fall to Russia in eastern Prussia at the peace. She informed Marie Theresa that she desired an immediate and clear-cut undertaking from Austria that the proposal would not be opposed at the peace conference and, in return for it, she renewed her promise to continue the war until Silesia and certain adjoining territories were restored to Austria. Count Esterhazy, Austria's ambassador to Russia, considered Elizabeth's demands reasonable and legitimate. On 23 March he accordingly put his name beside that of Vorontzov on an agreement which had been drawn up on these lines. When the document reached Marie Theresa she felt acutely embarrassed. Its terms were in direct contradiction to those embodied in the secret clause of the Treaty of Versailles. She decided to ignore the clause in the Austro-French treaty and, in May, both empresses ratified the Esterhazy agreement. Soon after, Vorontzov informed the French ambassador of what had taken place without, however, letting him realize the full extent of the territorial losses Prussia was to sustain. Since de l'Hôpital had been kept in ignorance of the secret clause in the Treaty of Versailles he saw no reason for objecting to the Austro-Russian agreement, but when Marie Theresa notified Louis the king hotly refused to accept the Esterhazy agreement. Indeed, he showed himself so determined to prevent Russia from benefiting territorially from the war that the Austrian empress felt unable to inform Elizabeth of his objections. Hoping for the best she remained the only guarantor of Russia's claims. Although the autumn was well advanced she at last agreed to Saltykov's demand that the Austrians should engage the enemy. Satisfied that their allies would take their share of the fighting, the Russians launched a fresh offensive.

Towards the end of 1759 Elizabeth had decided that the time had come for young Paul to have a tutor. Her choice rested on Nikita Ivanovich Panin, until recently ambassador to Sweden. He was of liberal outlook and favoured some form of modified monarchy for Russia. He belonged to the group of courtiers who, like Elizabeth herself, dreaded the prospect of Peter becoming sovereign and would prefer to see Paul declared the empress's heir. He was, however, too experienced a statesman to compromise his position by a careless word even to Catherine and the Shuvalovs, all of whom had come to fear Peter's accession.

Elizabeth's health was steadily deteriorating and her court was becoming increasingly oppressive. All were depressed and troubled by the thought that a change in rulership was at hand. Peter's frequent references to Frederick as 'the king, my master', pointed to the approach of another pro-German reign and his plan to invade Denmark for the purpose of regaining Schleswig heralded a pointless and costly war. Catherine became pregnant again late in 1760, this time by Grigory Orlov, and had nothing to hope for from Peter's accession and much to fear. Elizabeth's attacks of melancholia became more frequent. Nevertheless, in 1760 Christmas was celebrated as elaborately as ever. In April the little Grand Duke attended a drawing room for the first time. Keith described Paul as 'a very handsome child who dances wonderfully well for his age'.[9] The firework display included a set piece of a figure impersonating peace, holding a laurel leaf. It was evident that Elizabeth was very unwell. She appeared to be dying, yet she remained as determined as ever to continue the war. She knew that her troops were penetrating deep into Prussia and that they were on the point of delivering the final blow. To ensure that they should not relax their efforts she appointed Count Buturlin, her lover of long ago, Commander-in-Chief in place of Saltykov. Frederick realized that he stood no chance of beating the Russians in the field and in a last desperate effort to avoid complete destruction he attempted to bribe the Turks and the Crimean Tartars to attack Russia from the south, but they refused to become involved. Louis continued to long for peace.

Feeling desperately ill, longing for peace and quiet, Elizabeth had herself transported to Peterhof on 23 July. She was suffering from frequent nose bleeds and racked by violent fevers; her legs had become useless, her heart so weak that she could scarcely move. However, her mind remained clear and her thoughts seldom moved from the western front where, to her astonishment and mortification, Buturlin had still not launched an attack on the fortress of Kolberg. Deeply displeased, unable to control her impatience to see Frederick routed, she dictated an order to Buturlin commanding him to attack the enemy forthwith. He did not do so. It was not until October, when Elizabeth was being transported back to St Petersburg in a seemingly dying condition that he launched an offensive in conjunction with the Austrians and Swedes. Although a subsidy provided by Pitt's successor, Lord Bute, had enabled Frederick to raise fresh troops he met with reverses on all fronts. In 1761 Buturlin's capture of the fortress of Schweidnitz and Rumiantzev's of the key port and fortress of Kolberg spelt the end of his last hopes. He knew that he was doomed.

In St Petersburg, to everyone's surprise, Elizabeth's health had improved with the onset of winter. Louis' and Frederick's spies kept on the alert, reporting every change in her condition to their masters. On 20 December the empress was declared to be out of danger by her doctors. She marked the occasion by attending a play produced in her private theatre. She took the Grand Duke Paul with her, seating him on her lap so that the spectators could obtain a good view of Russia's future ruler. She may have been hoping for some definite sign or demonstration in the child's favour; if so, she must have been disappointed for the audience gave her no hint of their feelings. Nevertheless, she looked happy and all who saw her were deluded into thinking that she had many years of life ahead of her. But on the night of 23 December she had another stroke followed by a serious relapse. The news spread rapidly through the town, plunging the inhabitants in gloom. Elizabeth still possessed the love of the vast majority of her subjects. All dreaded Peter becoming tsar.

News of the Russian victories at Schweidnitz and Kolberg reached St Petersburg on 24 December, but Elizabeth was too ill to understand it. Frederick was on the point of capitulating when his agents' reports informed him that the empress was dying. He decided to hold his hand,

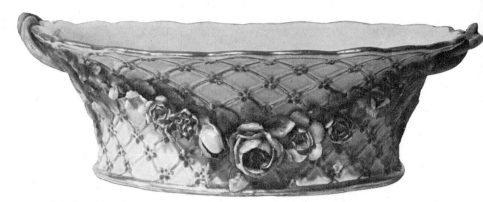

32. A bread basket from the empress's favourite 'personal' china service made for her in the Imperial Porcelain Factory, St Petersburg.

33. A lidded goblet with a vine design and a statuette of a young coachman. Both are early works by D. I. Vinogradov, founder of the Imperial Porcelain Factory.

34. A china plate with a chinoiserie design made for the empress Elizabeth in the Imperial Porcelain Factory.

35. A lidded goblet which the empress gave to Lord Hyndford. (Overall height 14½ inches.) It was engraved specially for Lord Hyndford and bears his initial and escutcheon (*right*). The decorations include the flowers and scrolls loved by the empress and features her fondness for hunting. One scene shows her wearing a long skirt and jacket in the act of shooting a stag, with her huntsmen coming in for the kill (*left*); another the killing of a bear. The events take place in the grounds of a palace, the domestic buildings of which are of late seventeenth century date (*right*). It is fortified by a wall with battlemented towers resembling those built in the 1680s round the Novodevichy Convent in Moscow.

36. This figurine of the empress Elizabeth was modelled for the Meissen porcelain works in 1742 by Johan Kandler. As in the famous portrait painted by Grooth ln 1763, she wears the uniform of the Preobrazhensky Guards and holds a field marshal's baton. (Length 8¾ inches.)

and was correct to do so. Her death would save him from disaster. She rallied what strength was left to her and sent for Vorontzov to inform him of her last wishes, but he venially pleaded ill-health and did not come, nor did Elizabeth's lucidity last. The brothers Razumovsky and Ivan Shuvalov had hurried to her bedside when she was taken ill and had not left it. Catherine joined them there and so did Peter. It was obvious that he was in terror of being deprived of the throne by a last word from the empress. Her ante-room was thronged with people devoted to her. Later in the day the empress regained consciousness. It was evident that she was much troubled by the thought of who was to succeed her. She sent for her confessor and asked him to perform the last rites. At her request he read the Otkhodnaya, the solemn and magnificent prayer for the dying, twice; then she took leave of her friends, entreating Peter not to treat any member of her household harshly. For once he seemed genuinely affected and willingly gave her the promise she desired. The courtiers who had gathered in the ante-room were overwhelmed by a sense of loss – a sentiment which the nation was soon to share. At four o'clock on Christmas afternoon in the year 1761 Prince Nikita Trubetskoy entered the ante-room with tears streaming down his cheeks and gravely informed the waiting courtiers that the empress had died and that her nephew had succeeded her as Tsar Peter III. Her death saved Frederick from a disaster so catastrophic that Prussia might well have never recovered from it.

Elizabeth had longed for Rastrelli to complete the new Winter Palace he was building for her in time for her to live in it. That wish was not to be granted. She died in a wing of the third Winter Palace, just as Peter the Great had died in one belonging to the second structure. Her body remained there for a fortnight after her death. Wearing deep mourning Catherine spent many long hours on her knees beside the open bier and was astonished by the beauty and serenity of the dead woman's face. Elizabeth's ladies and officers from the Guards regiments took turn in mounting guard over her body while priests prayed ceaselessly for her soul. Courtiers and members of the nobility came in tears to bid her a last farewell. Then Elizabeth's body was clothed in a silver robe with sleeves heavy with gold lace, a gold crown was placed on her head and the open bier set under a canopy in one of the palace's largest halls. It lay exposed there for another fortnight for mourners to come in their hundreds to pay her a final tribute. They filed past the coffin in silence in an unending line. She had served them loyally and to the best of her abilities; she had given them a peaceful decade and she had made Russia's voice resound in the palaces and ministries of Europe. Only Peter, the new tsar, was seldom seen in the death chamber, though his harsh voice and strident laugh all too often disturbed its peace.

Elizabeth's funeral was to take place on 25 January 1762. Peter had rightly decided that three branches of the Naryshkins, the family to which Peter the Great's mother belonged, and also the Skavronskys, Efimovskys and the Hendrikovs, all of whom were related to Elizabeth's mother, should be allotted places in the funeral procession befitting those ranking 'as persons who have the honour to belong to the Imperial family'.[10] Having given this proof of consideration Peter felt that he had done all that was necessary. As the funeral made its way from the palace to the Cathedral of SS Peter and Paul, situated in the fortress which Peter the Great had built and dedicated to them, the new tsar shocked the nation by his behaviour. As the procession advanced along a route lined by guardsmen, its progress punctuated by the sound of guns discharging at minute intervals, each regiment firing three rounds in memory of the late empress, Peter amused himself by varying the speed of his steps, walking either very slowly or racing forward so that the elderly courtiers who were carrying his train had to struggle to keep pace with him. In their efforts to do so many tripped and fell, as the tsar had hoped that they would. On reaching the cathedral the closed coffin was to stand exposed to the people for another fortnight with guardsmen mounting guard over it whilst priests succeeded each other in intoning uninterrupted prayers. During the fortnight workers from the towns and peasants from the provinces filed past in great numbers to pay their respects to a sovereign who had served her country well. Although Elizabeth had come to her task untrained she had succeeded in greatly developing her country's resources and in providing her people with new outlets and new areas of habitation. She had done much to raise living and cultural standards and, by signing Russia's first treaty of alliance with France, she had opened the road along which French ideas were to reach Russia. While she had herself freed the country from a German hold her armies had set a limit to Prussia's expansion. Her generals had defeated the west's foremost commanders yet she had given her people ten peaceful years.

Six weeks after her death a hundred guns fired a salute as her body was finally laid to rest beside those of her parents and sister in the cathedral's crypt. On the floor above it a sumptuous, empty coffin covered with a magnificent purple velvet and gold embroidered pall marked the position of the grave of Elizabeth, Empress of Russia.

Biographical Notes

The Tsarevitch Alexei Petrovich, 1690–1718. Following his mother's banishment to the Pokrovsky Convent (1698) he was brought up by his aunt, the Grand Duchess Natalia, at Preobrazhenskoe. He missed his mother's love and attention and grew up fearing his father. That fear led him to conspire against the tsar. He was charged with treason and died under examination, having probably been subjected to physical ill-treatment.

Apraxin, Field Marshal Count Stepan Feodorovich, 1702–58. A member of the ancient nobility, he served under General Münnich in the Turkish war of 1737–9, distinguishing himself at the siege of Ochakov. As Commander of the Astrakhan army stationed near the Persian frontier it fell to him to meet Tokmas Kuli Khan, envoy of Nadir Shah. His appointment as ambassador to Persia followed in 1742. Appointed to command the army chosen to fight in the Seven Years' War he was promoted to field marshal in 1756; two years later he was suspected of treason.

Argunov, Mikhail Petrovich, 1681–1752. The first director of the Printing Press of St Petersburg.

Beketov, Nikita Afanasievich, 1729–94. He came of a noble family having strong military traditions and fought in the Seven Years' War, taking part in the capture of Königsberg and the siege of Kustin. He was, however, taken prisoner at Zorndorf, but on his release two years later was promoted brigadier.

Bestuzhev, Mikhail, c. 1691–1760, elder brother of Alexei, started life as a soldier, but he was appointed Resident in London in 1720 and the rest of his life was spent in the diplomatic service. His career was not harmed by his wife's implication in the Botta Affair and her subsequent banishment to Siberia. After service in Warsaw and Vienna he was appointed to Versailles in 1755, dying there whilst in office in 1760.

Brevern, Carl von, 1704–44. An experienced diplomat who served both Anna Ivanovna and Ostermann loyally. He became involved in Biron's disgrace, but was reinstated by the Empress Elizabeth. As assistant to Alexei Bestuzhev he was concerned with the seizure, in 1743, of de la Chétardie's despatches.

Buturlin, Count Field Marshal Alexei Borisovich, 1694–1767. Came from an old military family brought into prominence by Peter the Great. Following the death of Peter II he was transferred to the Ukrainian army and then appointed Governor of Smolensk, but in 1735 he insisted on taking part in the Turkish war, serving under Münnich. On returning to St Petersburg in 1742 he was appointed commander of the western army and was promoted field marshal in 1756.

Chernyshev, Count Zakhari Grigorievich, 1722–84. A rather better general than many of his contemporaries had supposed.

Choglokov, Nikita. A member of the old nobility who married the empress's cousin, Maria Simonovna Hendrikova, and had eight children.

Dashkova, Princess Ekaterina Romanovna, 1744–1810. A daughter of Count Roman Illarionovich Vorontzov and a sister of Elizabeth, mistress of Peter III. She was a goddaughter both of the Empress Elizabeth and of Peter III. Orphaned in 1745 she went to live with her uncle; he took as much care over her education as that of his own children, all of whom learned to speak several foreign languages fluently. Ivan Shuvalov did much to encourage Catherine's interests in learning and the arts. She helped to bring Catherine II to the throne and became President of the Academy of Sciences.

The Dolgorukys trace their descent to the house of Ryurik. Prince Vassily Lukich was an accomplished diplomat who served under Peter the Great; in 1722 he attended the coronation of Louis XV, and at the Peace of Nystad he became Russian ambassador to Sweden. On returning to Russia he became extremely influential. Prince Alexei Grigorievich, the son of a diplomat, was educated in the west and learnt to speak a number of foreign languages, including Latin, fluently. Between 1700 and 1706 he visited Rome and Malta. His daughter Catherine (born 1712 at Gorenki) became engaged to Peter II after having been engaged to Count Millesimo and, according to some historians, also to Yuri Yurievich Dolgoruky (not a close relative). His son Ivan exercised a bad influence over young Peter II.

Dubiansky, Feodor Yakovlevich, died 1772. Father-confessor to the Empress Elizabeth. Considered the most learned member of the White Clergy he retained his influence over Catherine II.

Golovkin, Count Gavriil Ivanovich, 1666–1734. Chancellor of Russia, his son, Mikhail Gavrilovich, 1669–1755, Vice-Chancellor of Russia.

Galitzine, Dmitri Mikhailovich, 1665–1738. A member of the old nobility serving in the Secret Chancery.

Kantemir, Prince Antioch, 1708–1744. Poet and diplomat, son of the Hospodar of Moldavia. Though born in Constantinople he was educated in St Petersburg and died whilst serving as ambassador in Paris.

Kurakin, Prince Alexander Borisovich, 1697–49. Son of a diplomat. Whilst serving as a diplomat in Paris he came to Trediakovsky's assistance, bringing the poet back to St Petersburg with him in 1728. He became powerful at court, where he opposed Menshikov, though supporting Biron. He was appointed a senator by the Empress Elizabeth.

Lefort, Franz Johann, born in Geneva in 1656, died in Moscow in 1699. Was one of Peter the Great's boon companions. Baron Peter Johann Lefort was for a time Master of Ceremonies to the Empress Elizabeth.

Loewenwolde, Count Carl Gustavus, d. 1735. A courtier, brother of Count Rheinhold Gustavus, 1693–1758. The latter served with distinction under Peter the Great to become a chamberlain under Catherine I and to exercise considerable influence under Anna Leopoldovna.

Lopukhina, Natalia Feodorovna, née Baer, 1699–1763. Wife of a Vice-Admiral.

Naryshkin, Count Alexander Ivanovich, died in either 1773 or 1782, a court chamberlain.

Naryshkin, Count Lev Alexandrovich, 1733–59. A courtier.

Naryshkin, Count Semeon, born 1710. A diplomat, he lived abroad during Anna Ivanovna's reign. He was appointed ambassador to London by the Empress Elizabeth in 1741. He had his own private theatre and was the first Russian nobleman to possess his own orchèstra.

Mengden, Baroness Julie, 1716–86. Anna Leopoldovna's favourite lady-in-waiting.

Mengden, Karl Ludwig, Baron, 1706–61. President of the College of Commerce; he was banished to Siberia.

Münnich, Count Burkhard-Christophe, 1687–1767. Born in Oldenburg he came to Russia after a varied life to build a canal for Peter the Great. He re-organized the Russian army for Anna Ivanovna and commanded it in the Turkish war. Appointed First Minister in 1740 he was dismissed five months later and banished by Elizabeth in 1741. However, he was pardoned by Catherine and returned to St Petersburg.

Razumovsky, Alexei, 1709–71. At Elizabeth's death he destroyed all the letters she had sent him and all documents relating to her in the presence of Mikhail Vorontzov and withdrew to his house on the Pokrovka in Moscow. He died in St Petersburg and was buried in the Alexandro-Nevsky Lavra.

Razumovsky, Kyril, 1724–1803. Younger brother of Alexei, he came to Moscow with his mother in 1741 and stayed on after her departure in order to pursue his education. In 1743 he was sent to complete it at Königsberg and Strassburg. Appointed a count in 1744, President of the Academy of Sciences in 1746, Hetman of the Ukraine in 1750. He married Natalya Naryshkina, a relative of the empress, and planned to establish his capital at Glukovo. He intended founding a university in the Ukraine and began building a country house for himself at Baturino, but soon tired of life in the Ukraine. He returned to St Petersburg and wielded great influence over the empress even after Ivan Shuvalov had become her favourite. He was always popular for he was kind, friendly and generous.

Repnin, Prince Vassili Nikitysh, 1696–1748. Though Peter the Great sent him to Paris in the hope of turning him into a scholar he begged to be allowed to return home and to serve in the army. In 1746 he was appointed head of the Grand Duke Peter's household, but his marked sympathy for the Grand Duke probably accounts for his appointment in 1747 as Commander of the Western Army. He was struck by paralysis in 1748 and died soon after.

Rinaldi, Antonio, c. 1730–c. 1790. An Italian architect who, in St Petersburg, built among other things Gatchina, the Marble Palace and St Isaac's Cathedral.

Saltykov, Field Marshal Nicolai Ivanovich, b. 1736. A kinsman of the Romanovs. In 1748 his regiment, the Semeonovsky Guards, formed part of the army of 37,000 men sent to assist Marie Theresa, and notwithstanding his youth he went with it. In 1759 he personally brought the news of the Russian victory of Künersdorf to the empress.

Shafirov, Baron Petr Pavlovich, 1669–1739. Vice-Chancellor of Russia under Peter the Great, who, under Anna Ivanovna, lost his influence to Ostermann.

Sheremetiev, Count Peter Borisovich, friend and companion of Peter II.

The Shuvalovs, members of the ancient nobility who rose to prominence in the sixteenth century. Count Alexander, 1710–70, head of Elizabeth's Secret Chancery; Count Peter, 1711–62, became a page to Catherine I in 1723. He abolished internal tolls and invented a howitzer; Ivan, 1729–97, born and educated in Moscow he was brought to St Petersburg by his cousins, Alexander and Peter, in 1749, to become the empress's favourite. He did so in *c.* 1751 and wielded great influence during the remainder of her reign. Though to some extent a tool of his cousins, his love of France and interest in the arts were genuine. He sponsored Lomonosov, corresponded with Helvetius, Diderot, Dalembert, Voltaire and others, and was responsible for the use of the French language in court circles. He founded Moscow University, opening it on his mother's nameday, 13 January 1755, to become its first curator. He was also President of the Academy of Arts founded in 1758, but his career ended with the death of the Empress Elizabeth.

Trubetskoy, Prince Nikita Yurievich, 1699–1767. Procurator General to the Senate, Field Marshal, and President of the College of Military Affairs.

Vorontzov, Mikhail, 1714–67. Raised the family to prominence by assisting Elizabeth to win the throne; he married the empress's cousin Anna Skavron-skaya; became Grand-Chancellor of Russia at Alexei Bestuzhev's fall. The house which Rastrelli built for him in St Petersburg became, under Tsar Paul, the headquarters of the Knights of Malta, then the Corps des Pages and is now a Museum.

Vorontzova, Countess Elizaveta Romanovna, 1745–82. Sister of the Princess Dashkova, favourite of Peter III, she later married a Mr Poliansky.

Bibliography

Archives des Affaires Étrangères, Paris. Russie. Mémoires et documents, vol. I, no. 12, folio 192. Correspondances, vols. XXX; XXXI, folios 4, 10, 58, 62–83, 106; XXXII, folio 279; XXXIV, folio 79; XXXVIII; XL, folio 247; LII; LV; LXV

ARNETH, A. RITTER VON. *Maria Theresia's erste Regierungsjahre*, Vienna, 1864, vol. 2, 1741–4

BAIN, ROBERT NISBETT. *The Daughter of Peter the Great*, London, 1899
Pupils of Peter the Great; a history of the Russian Court and Empire, 1697–1740, London, 1897

BEAUMONT, C. W. *History of the Ballet in Russia*, London, 1930

BELL, J. *A Journey from St Petersburg to Peking*, ed. J. L. Stevenson, Edinburgh, 1965

BENOIS, A. *Tsarskoe Selo v tsarstvovanie Imperatritzy Elizavety Petrovny*, St Petersburg, 1913

BROGLIE, J. V. A. Duc de. *Frédéric II et Marie Thérèse*, Paris, 1883
Frédéric II et Louis XV, Paris, 1885
Marie Thérèse, impératrice, 1744–6, Paris, 1888
Le secret du roi, correspondence secrète avec ses agents, Paris, 1888

BLUM, J. *Lord and Peasant in Russia from the ninth to the nineteenth century*, Princeton, 1961

CATHERINE II. *Zapisky kasatel'no russkoy istorii*, St Petersburg, n.d.
Zapiski Ekateriny II, imperatritzy Rossii, St Petersburg, 1876

DASHKOVA, PRINCESS E. R. *Memoirs*, transl. by K. Fitzlyon, London, 1958

FLORINSKY, A. *Russia – A History and Interpretation*, 2 vols., London, 1952

FREDERICK II. *Politische Correspondentz*, ed. J. G. Droysen and others, Berlin, 1879–1925
Mémoires de Frédéric II, Roi de Prusse, ed. R. Boutaric and N. Campandon, Paris, 1866

GERHARDI, W. *The Romanovs – Evocation of the Past and a Mirror for the Present*. London, 1940.

GREY, I. *Catherine the Great*, London, 1961
Peter the Great, Emperor of all Russia, London, 1962

GORYANOV, S. *Correspondence de Catherine Alexeevna, Grande Duchesse de Russie et de Sir Charles Hanbury Williams, ambassadeur d'Angleterre, 1756–8*. Moscow, 1909, English edition, 1928

GRUNWALD, C. DE. *Les alliances Franco-Russe* (sixteenth to twentieth centuries), Paris, 1965

HAUMONT, R. *La Russie au 18me siècle*, Paris, n.d.

HERZEN, A. *Mémoires de l'Impératrice Catherine II de Russia*, London, 1859; English edition, transl. M. Budberg, London, 1955

ILCHESTER, LORD and MRS LANGFORD BROOK. *The life of Sir Charles Hanbury Williams, poet, wit, diplomat*, London, 1928

Correspondence of Catherine, Grand Duchess of Russia with Sir Charles Hanbury Williams and letters from Count Poniatowski, London, 1925

KAGANOVA, A. *Voprozy Istorii*, 1947, no. 7, Moscow

KLUCHEVSKY, V. G. *Sochinenia*, vol. 4, Moscow, 1958, p. 325-42

Sbornik Statey, St Petersburg, 1913

KOVALÉVSKY, P. *Manuel d'histoire russe*, Paris, 1948

LAUTON, L. *Études sur quelques instituts de Russie*, 1462-1796, Paris, n.d.

La cour de Russie il y a cent ans. Extraits des dépêches des ambassadeurs anglais et francais. Paris, n.d.

MANSTEIN, C. H. Baron von. *Memoirs of Russia*, foreword by D. Hume, London, 1790

MARSDEN, CH. *Palmyra of the North, the first days of St Petersburg*, London, 1942

MATVEEV, A. *Rastrelli* (in Russian), Moscow, 1939

Mémoires de la cour de Russie (Anon.), Paris, 1754

MILYUKOV, P. *Les premiers Romanovs*, Paris, 1930

(with C. Seignebos and others) *Histoire de la Russie*, vols. 1 and 2, Paris, 1932

MÜNNICH, B. CH. Count von. *Zapiski Feldmarshala Grafa Minikha in Zapisky inostrantzev v Rossii v 190m stoletii*, St Petersburg, 1874

OLIVIER, DARA. *Elizabeth de Russie*, Paris, 1962

OLDENBURG, ZOE. *Catherine the Great*, London, 1963

Peter the Great. Letters and Papers, St Petersburg-Leningrad, 1887-1952

Proshloe baletnogo otdelenia Peterburgskogo teatra l'nogo uchilishcha. Materialy po istorii russkogo baleta, vol. 1, Leningrad, 1938

Public Record Office, London. *Despatches of the Hon. Edward Finch*, vols. 85-91

Despatches of Cyril Wich, Lord Hyndford, Lord Tyrawley, Guy Dickens and Sir Charles Hanbury Williams in State Papers, Russia, 1742-59, 12 ms. vols. 24-68, quoted in footnotes according to dates

RAMBAUD, A. N. *Russes et Prussiens, Guerre de Sept Ans*, Paris, 1895

History of Russia, transl. L. Lang, London, 1879

RONDEAU, LADY. *Letters from a Lady who resided for some years in Russia to her Friend in England*, London, 1775

Ruuskiy biograficheskiy slovar', USSR Academy of Sciences, 1962

Saint Simon. *Mémoires*, ed. Chénal.

Saint René Taillardin, *Maurice de Saxe*, Paris, 1870

Sbornik Imperatorskogo Istoricheskogo Obshzhestva, St Petersburg, 1867-1917, vols. 3, 15, 40, 42, 49, 52, 58, 64, 65, 80, 85, 91-5, 100, 102, 103, 110

SOLOVIEV, S. M. *Istoria Rossii s dreknikh vremen*, Moscow, 1851-79, vols. 21-24 and 102

TIKHOMIROVA, T. N. 'Ustyuzhskie emali 170go veka s serebriannymi nadkladkami' in *Trudy Gosudarstvennogo Istoricheskogo Muzea*, vol. XIII, 1941, pp, 191-217

USSR Academy of Sciences History of Russia (in Russian) Moscow, 1947-9, vols. 1, 2

History of Russian Art (in Russian), Moscow, 1961, vols. 6, 7

VASSILSHCHIKOV, A. A. *Semeistvo Razumovskich in Gosudarstvenny Arkhiv*, 1868, 77, 80

VANDAL, A. *Louis XV et Elizabeth de Russie*, Paris, 1887

VOLTAIRE. *Correspondence*, ed. by T. Besterman

Histoire de l'Empire Russe sous Pierre le Grand

WALISZEWSKI, K. *La dernière des Romanovs*, Paris, 1912

YAZHEVSKY, V. *Ocherki tsarstvovania Elizavety Petrovny*, Moscow, 1870

References

1. A DIFFICULT START

1. Catherine II. *Occasions Perdues*, section 2 in A. Herzen, *Mémoires de l'imperatrice Catherine II de Russie*, London, 1895.
2. Saint Simon, *Mémoires*, ed. Chénal, vol. 14, p. 438.
3. A. Vandal, *Louis XV et Elizabeth de Russie*, Paris, 1887, p. 99.
4. Affaires Étrangères; de Campredon, diplomatic document dated 13 April 1725.
5. Affaires Étrangères; de Campredon, 9 June 1725.
6. R. Nisbett Bain, *The Pupils of Peter the Great*, London, 1897, pp. 82 and 123.
7. Dara Olivier, *Elizabeth de Russie*, Paris, 1962, p. 99.
8. Olivier, *op. cit.*, p. 69.
9. Bain, *The Daughter of Peter the Great*, London, 1899, p. 108.

2. A DISRUPTED LIFE

1. Soloviev, *History of Russia* (in Russian), vol. XI, p. 162.
2. A. Herzen, *Mémoires de l'impératrice Catherine II de Russia*, London, 1859, p. 115.
3. R. Nisbett Bain, *Pupils of Peter the Great*, p. 105.
4. Dara Olivier, *op. cit.*, p. 106.
5. Public Records Office, Russian State Papers, C. Rondeau's despatch 30 Dec. 1730; Lady Rondeau, *Letters from a Lady*, letter of 30 Dec. 1730.
6. Soloviev, *op. cit.*, vol. XI, p. 122.
7. Bain, *op. cit.*, p. 160.
8. Affaires Étrangères, Magnan's papers, 3 April 1730.
9. Public Record Office, London, Russian State Papers, Finch, June 1741.
10. C. H. Manstein, *Memoirs of Russia*, 1790, pp. 27-9.
11. *Mémoires de la cour de Russie* (anon.), Paris, 1754, p. 8.
12. Soloviev, *op. cit.*, vol. XI, p. 100.
13. Vassilshchikov, *The Razumovskys* (in Russian), St Petersburg, 1880.
14. Manstein, *op. cit.*, p. 62.

15. *Mémoires de la cour de Russie*, p. 395.
16. Manstein, *op. cit.*, p. 62.

3. THE GREAT DECISION

1. *Mémoires de la Cour de Russie*, p. 72.
2. Manstein, *op. cit.*, pp. 267 and 268.
3. *Ibid.*
4. Manstein, *op. cit.*, pp. 181 (footnote), 118–25, 315.
5. *Ibid.*
6. Public Records Office, Russian State Papers.
7. Frederick II, *Mémoires*, vol. I, pp. 199–232.
8. Manstein, *op. cit.*, p. 316.
9. Manstein, *op. cit.*, pp. 27–9 and 38–9.
10. *Ibid.*
11. Russian State Papers.
12. Affaires Étrangères, de la Chétardie documents, 14 April 1741.
13. *Ibid.*, 14 June 1741.
14. Manstein, *op. cit.*, p. 309.
15. Public Records Office, Russian State Papers.
16. Soloviev, *op. cit.*, vol. XI, p. 305.
17. Russian State Papers, 3 October 1741.
18. *Ibid.*, 13 October 1741.
19. Soloviev, *op. cit.*, vol. XI, pp. 119–20.
20. Manstein, *op. cit.*, p. 310.
21. Russian State Papers, June 1741.
22. *Ibid.*
23. *Mémoires de la cour de Russie*, p. 163.
24. Soloviev, *op. cit.*, vol. XI, pp. 104, 110–13.
25. Russian State Papers, 22 August 1741.
26. Archives des Affaires Étrangères, 2 September 1741.
27. Russian State Papers, 14 November 1741.
28. Manstein, *op. cit.*, p. 315.
29. Manstein, *op. cit.*, p. 317.
30. Manstein, *op. cit.*, pp. 308–10.
31. *Zapiski inostrantsev v Rossii v 18 stoletii*, vol. 2, pp. 82–5 (Zapiski Feldmar-shala Minikha), St Petersburg, 1874.
32. V. Yashevsky, *Ocherkii tsarstvovaniya Elizavety Petrovny*, Moscow, 1870, p. 38.
33. The empress's manifesto, written on 25 November and published on 28 November, is referred to by Manstein, *op. cit.*, p. 315, and Soloviev, *op. cit.*, vol. XI, pp. 129–30.

34. A. Vandal, *Louis XV et Elizabeth de Russie*, Paris, 1887, p. 161.
35. Archives des Affaires Étrangères, 28 November 1741.

4. THE START OF A REIGN

1. Rambaud, *op. cit.*, vol. 2, p. 94.
2. J. Blum, *Lord and Peasant in Russia*, Princeton, 1961, p. 357.
3. K. Waliszewski, *La dernière des Romanovs*, Paris, 1912, pp. 4-5.
4. Soloviev, *op. cit.*, vol. XI, p. 145.
5. *Mémoires de Frédéric II, Roi de Prusse*, Paris, 1866, vol. I, pp. 129-32.
6. Russian State Papers.
7. Catherine, *Mémoires* (ed. Herzen), *Occasions perdues*, section 2.
8. *Ibid.*
9. Archives des Affaires Étrangères, 12 January 1741.
10. Frederick of Prussia, *Mémoires*, p. 171.
11. R. Nisbett Bain, *The Daughter of Peter the Great*, London, 1899, p. 52.
12. A. A. Vassilshibikov, *op. cit.*, vol. I, p. 104. Semeistvo Razumovskich, Russky Arkhiv 1865, 1867.
13. Russian State Papers, 26 July 1742.
14. Soloviev, *op. cit.*, vol. XI, pp. 233-40.
15. Waliszewski, *op. cit.*, pp. 117-18.
16. Waliszewski, *op. cit.*, p. 8.

5. YEARS OF HOPE AND DISILLUSION (1743-7)

1. Catherine, *Mémoires*, p. 13.
2. Affaires Étrangères, de la Chétardie papers.
3. Rambaud, *History of Russia*, London, 1879, vol. 2, p. 193.
4. Catherine, *Mémoires* (ed. Herzen), p. 19.
5. Catherine, *op. cit.*, p. 270.
6. Rambaud, *op. cit.*, vol. 2, p. 97.
7. Rambaud, *op. cit.*, vol. 2, p. 349.

6. AN UNEASY INTERLUDE (1748-56)

1. Soloviev, *op. cit.*, vol. XII, p. 169.
2. Catherine, *Mémoires* (ed. Herzen), pp. 122-3.
3. Catherine, *op. cit.*, p. 200.
4. Catherine, *op. cit.*, p. 202.
5. Catherine, *op. cit.*, pp. 205, 208.
6. Russian State Papers, 27 September 1754.
7. Princess Dashkova, *Memoirs*, London, 1958, pp. 59-60.

8. Newcastle Papers, British Museum MS 32863, folio 25. Williams to Holderness (marked 'most secret') 21 Sept. 1755; Williams to Newcastle, 19 Feb. 1756.

9. A. Vandal, *Louis XV et Elizabeth de Russie*, p. 250.

7. LIVING CONDITIONS IN ELIZABETH'S RUSSIA

1. Catherine, *Mémoires, occasions perdues*, section 2.
2. Catherine, *op. cit.*, p. 188.
3. Münnich, *op. cit.*, p. 87; and Sbornik, vol. CII, p. 330.
4. Russian supplement, vol. 8, folio 290, Affaires Étrangères, Despatches of de l'Hôpital and Douglas; vol. 5, those of d'Eon.
5. Catherine, *op. cit.*, p. 292.
6. Catherine, *op. cit.*, p. 531–2. *Occasions perdues*, p. 2.
7. State Papers, 30 November 1745, Hyndford to Mannington.
8. Russian State Papers, 1–13 November 1753.
9. Waliszewski, *op. cit.*, p. 94.
10. J. Blum, *op. cit.*, p. 277.
11. Dashkova, *op. cit.*, p. 65.
12. For living conditions generally, see Soloviev, *op. cit.*, vol. XI, pp. 162, 344–7, 466–7, 503–7, 529–30.
13. Russian State Papers, 31 December 1737.
14. John Bell, *A journey from St Petersburg to Peking*, Edinburgh, 1965, pp. 84–5, footnote.
15. K. Waliszewski, *La derniére des Romanovs*, Paris, 1912, pp. 181–2.
16. Kluchevsky, *Sochinenia*, vol. 4, p. 331.
17. Waliszewski, *op. cit.*, p. 150.
18. R. Nisbett Bain, *The Daughter of Peter the Great*, London, 1899, p. 49.
19. Kluchevsky, *op. cit.*, vol. 4, pp. 337–9.

8. LEARNING, LITERATURE AND THE MINOR ARTS

1. Catherine, *Mémoires* (ed. Herzen), p. 341.
2. *Ibid.*
3. *Ibid.*
4. Bain, *The Daughter of Peter the Great*, p. 315.
5. Rambaud, *op. cit.*, vol. 2, p. 103; also Turgenev's address of 6 March 1879.
6. Affaires Étrangères, *Mémoires et Documents Russie*, vol. v.
7. T. N. Tikhonova. *Ustuizhskie emali 17ogo veka s serebriannymi nadkladkami, in Trudy Gosudarstvennogo Istoricheskogo Muzeia*, vol. 13, pp. 191 and 216.
8. Public Record Office, Dickens Despatch, 19 January 1753.

9. THE FINE ARTS

1. *History of Russian Art* (in Russian), USSR Academy of Sciences, ed. E. Grabar and others, Moscow, 1960, vol. v, pp. 177, 178.
2. Catherine (Herzen), *op. cit.*, p. 290.

10. THE LAST PHASE

1. Catherine, Correspondence, 13 September 1756.
2. H. Kaganova in *Voprozy Istori*, 1947, no. 7.
3. Affaires Étrangères, Mackenzie Douglas papers.
4. The two despatches, one marked secret, dated 9 July and others sent during that summer.
5. Catherine, *Mémoires*, p. 288 (Budberg translation). Soloviev, *op. cit.* xxiv, iii, p. 1035.
6. Catherine, *Mémoires*, p. 298–309 (Budberg translation).
7. Russian State Papers, Keith, 21 December 1758.
8. Waliszewski, *op. cit.*, p. 475.
9. Russian State Papers, April 1760.
10. W. Gerhardi, *The Romanovs – Evocation of the Past and a Mirror for the Present*, London 1940, p. 119.

Index

Duchy of Schleswi[g]

Frederick III
1597–1659
Duke of Schleswig-Holstein-Gottor[p]

Christian Alber[t]
1641–94
Duke of Schleswig-Holstein-Gottor[p]

Frederick IV = **Hedwig Sophia of Swed[en]**
1671–1702
Duke of Schleswig-Holstein-Gottorp

Charles Frederick = **Anna Petrovna**
d·1739
loses Schleswig

Charles Peter Ulrich
Duke of Holstein (Peter III of Russia)

Charles Augustus
d· 1727
Engaged to Elizabeth

Adolphus Frederick
elected King of Sweden 1743
King of Sweden 1751–71

Frederick Augustu[s]
Bishop of Lube[ck]
1st Duke of Olden[burg]